Free Enterprise Moves East

Free Enterprise Moves East

Doing Business from Prague to Vladivostok

Carter Henderson

A Publication of the
International Center for Economic Growth

ICS PRESS
San Francisco, California

© 1996 Carter Henderson

Publication signifies that the International Center for Economic Growth believes a work to be a competent treatment worthy of public consideration. The findings, interpretations, and conclusions of a work are entirely those of the authors and should not be attributed to ICEG, its affiliated organizations, its Board of Overseers, or organizations that support ICEG.

Inquiries, book orders, and catalog requests should be addressed to ICS Press, 720 Market Street, San Francisco, California 94102 USA. Telephone: (415) 981-5353; fax: (415) 986-4878. Book orders within the contiguous United States: (800) 326-0263.

Cover design by Kent Lytle

0 9 8 7 6 5 4 3 2 1

Library of Congress Cataloging-in-Publication Data
Henderson, Carter F.
    Free enterprise moves east: doing business from Prague to Vladivostok / Carter Henderson
      p.   cm.
    "A publication of the International Center for Economic Growth."
    Includes bibliographical references (p.   ) and index.
    ISBN 1-55815-325-X (cloth : acid-free paper).—ISBN 1-55815-482-5 (pbk. : acid-free paper)
      1. Europe, Eastern—Economic conditions—1989-   2. Former Soviet republics—Economic conditions. 3. Free Enterprise— Europe, Eastern—Case studies. 4. Free Enterprise—Former Soviet republics—Case Studies. I. International Center for Economic Growth.
II. title
   HC244.H45 1996
   330.947'086—dc20   95-18015 CIP

To Deborah Cornell Yarbrough

"No other single factor will have a greater political impact on the world in the century to come than whether political and economic freedom take root and thrive in Russia and the other former communist nations. Today's generation of American leaders will be judged primarily by whether they did everything possible to bring about this outcome. If they fail, the cost that their successors will have to pay will be unimaginably high."

Richard M. Nixon,
in his last book, *Beyond Peace*
(Random House, 1994)

Contents

Preface

The transition of the Central European and former Soviet Union countries to market economies presents them with enormous challenges and difficulties. There are few areas of economic and social life that are not undergoing radical transformation as those countries reform the underlying mechanism that allocates their resources.

Much of the debate on this transition has focused on institutional and policy issues: how to change both the "rules of the game" and the specific macro- and microeconomic policies that would encourage strong private economies to develop. Most of these countries—as well as the Marxist economies in Asia—are in the middle of difficult transitions. Some countries, such as the Czech Republic and Poland, are relatively advanced in their reforms. Others, such as Belarus and several of the Central Asian republics, have reformed very little.

One issue that has received little attention because it is not well suited to policy intervention is entrepreneurship: whether reform will bring forth entrepreneurs in these countries, seizing market opportunities and providing the creative spark that will produce economic progress. When the reform process began, this question loomed very large as people wondered whether a culture of entrepreneurship would or could emerge from the rigid and failed systems that had been so long in force.

To explore the issue of entrepreneurship in Central Europe and the former Soviet Union, ICEG commissioned Carter Henderson, a journalist and businessman who has spent much of his life studying entrepreneurs, to travel to these countries and report his findings. The result is this book, which is largely a journalistic account of the veritable explosion of entrepreneurial activity that is transforming these countries. It is a collection of extraordinary stories about what people are doing to start businesses and to create functioning market economies.

In telling his stories, some of his most interesting analysis focuses on the problems that businesspeople in these countries have in adapting to their new environments. In many countries, for example, middlemen are reviled as parasites, performing no useful function. The bias against middlemen was certainly strong in the former Marxist countries, and Henderson shows how entrepreneurs in these countries are discovering the important economic functions that middlemen perform. Similarly, their view of marketing, which the Marxist countries also considered to be parasitic, is changing.

The author explores common management problems, and he gives some attention to the efforts of Western profit and nonprofit ventures aimed at transferring information about Western business techniques to the former Eastern Bloc countries.

This book represents something of a departure for ICEG. Most of our publications present economic analyses and policy recommendations for economic and social reform. Although there is some analysis in this book and some recommendations, our main purpose here was to show how entrepreneurs perform the crucial role they play in market economies—here in this extraordinarily interesting and important part of the world.

We hope that the book will be useful for policymakers seeking to improve their understanding of the role of entrepreneurs and of the enabling environment that is important to encourage them. We also hope it will be useful for business leaders, who may be considering investments in these huge, potential markets. Finally, we hope the book will appeal to general readers who like good stories. For the transformation of these countries in such a short time is certainly one of the remarkable stories of our time.

Santiago, Chile

March 1996

Rolf Lüders

General Director

International Center

for Economic Growth

The Triumph of Capitalism

The sudden and unexpected breakup of the Soviet empire is giving birth to millions of privately owned businesses in nearly two dozen newly independent nations stretching from Prague east to Vladivostok, which have emerged from the wreckage of communism into the promise of capitalism.

This great transition to free enterprise is most advanced in the Czech Republic, Poland, and Hungary; begins to lose momentum in the Slovak Republic on through the Balkans and into Russia; and finally picks up steam again in Kazakhstan. It then rolls on toward resource-rich Siberia and the Russian far east, whose inhabitants are increasingly dazzled by the prosperity surrounding them in South Korea, Hong Kong, Singapore, Taiwan, Malaysia, Thailand, Indonesia, mighty Japan, and now in explosively growing China, whose Gross Domestic Product will—by *Business Week* projections—rocket past $2 trillion "by early next century."

Entrepreneurs struggling to build new businesses in the former Soviet empire, along with others destined to follow in their footsteps, represent the best hope—perhaps the only real hope—these nations have of surviving and prospering in the years ahead.

"Capitalism seems well on the way to dominating the entire world," says Robert Eisner, professor of economics at Northwestern University and one-time president of the American Economics Association. Should proof be needed, it can be seen behind the old Iron Curtain, where communist bureaucrats dedicated to fulfilling quotas are being replaced by entrepreneurs determined to meet hungry consumers' almost limitless needs.

These nations are being transformed with the help of billions in capital from the highly industrialized Western democracies, plus the best management know-how the world has to offer supplied by global corporations bedazzled by this emerging market of close to 450 million consumers.

Volkswagen, Royal Dutch/Shell, Hitachi, Phillips, Exxon, and hundreds of other Western firms are investing hard currency fortunes to develop the former Soviet bloc's rich natural resources, modernize its industry, improve its crumbling infrastructure, and raise its output of consumer goods.

Wealthy Westerners are also moving into this market in search of moneymaking investment opportunities, as are successful businesspeople ready to devote weeks working on a pro bono basis with inexperienced new companies requesting their help.

The main engine in the transition from communism to capitalism, however, is the homegrown entrepreneur this book celebrates and who in thousands of cases is burning up the track—like the thirty-seven-year-old owner of a Moscow company employing some 3,000 people that is growing so fast, and making so much money, that his wife says it is like being on a "runaway train."

Doing business in these former Soviet empire nations struggling to rebuild their tattered economies is a daunting experience since there is little in the way of the institutional backup that Western businesses take for granted—from property rights and working telephones to mechanisms for repatriating profits in hard currency. It took the Canadian owners of a McDonald's franchise seven years to open their first restaurant on Moscow's Pushkin Square, and when they realized they could not get their ruble profits out in dollars, they used them to put up a new office building nearby.

This coming of political freedom has brought with it the predictable efflorescence of opportunists. Newly rich wheeler-dealers trade in precious metals, oil, timber, radioactive materials, and other resources and deposit their winnings in numbered Swiss bank accounts. Old Communist party bosses are milking huge state-owned enterprises while there is still something left to grab. And an army of Mafioso types hold businesses to ransom at knife or gunpoint as undermanned police forces look on. Crime is so widespread in Russia today that it was one of the first things noticed by its greatest living writer and winner of the 1970 Nobel Prize for Literature, Aleksandr Solzhenitsyn, seventy-seven, upon his recent return home following nearly twenty years of self-imposed exile in Cavendish, Vermont. He called it " . . . the onslaught, really the epidemic of incredibly fast, quick, rampant capitalism in which some people grow incredibly rich very soon; an enrichment of a few, not by production, but rather really by stealing from others."

The International Finance Corporation (IFC), which serves as the West's fiduciary agent in this vast part of the world, commented in its 1993 *Annual Report,* "Most of the economies in the region are beset by severe problems including the collapse of trade and payment arrangements with traditional trading partners, diminishing government revenues, a decline in living standards, soaring inflation, underdeveloped financial systems burdened by non-performing loans, insolvent large state enterprises, and stiffening political resistance to reform."

The IFC is absolutely right. And yet the entrepreneurial energy that has been unleashed in the countries of the former Soviet empire is enthusiastically building countless new businesses every day of the week: A dental and medical electronics company in the Slovak Republic. A meat factory in Ukraine. A publishing house in Bulgaria. A specialty retailer in Hungary. A regional bank in Russia. All of them are battling to survive in a region of the world where starting and running a successful privately owned business was virtually a lost art.

This book tells that story.

It begins with insights into the remarkable economic revival taking place in the Czech Republic, Poland, and Hungary, where privately owned business is booming, shops are bulging with goods of every description from Mercedes cars to Yves Saint Laurent perfume, and companies as different as Sony and Gerber baby food are setting up shop and sending key executives to turn them into capitalist powerhouses.

The story next travels east through the Balkans, where privatization is moving less rapidly but making steady and highly visible progress.

It then moves on to the fifteen new nations that have emerged from the disintegration of the Soviet Union, starting with Russia whose 148 million people are grappling with a beleaguered economy, decaying infrastructure, horribly polluted environment, collapsing health care system, and an often lethargic bureaucratic attitude toward the conversion to a market economy after seventy years of being spoon-fed on the gruel of communism.

The transition to free enterprise is also encountering turbulence in the newly independent countries further east, beginning with near-bankrupt Ukraine being drowned in a tidal wave of crises from severe power shortages to lengthening breadlines. Georgia on Ukraine's southern border is in even worse shape—a basket case obliged to ask for Russia's military protection from its aggressive neighbors in return for agreeing to become what amounts to a satellite of Moscow. Uzbekistan's agrarian economy is flirting with collapse. Tajikistan is in ruins. Only oil-rich Kazakhstan under its entrepreneurial president Nursultan Nazarbayev seems headed for the uplands of prosperity.

Yet Western firms are fascinated by the moneymaking possibilities they see in the former Soviet Union and are hard at work establishing plants, selling products, concluding joint venture agreements, hiring key scientists, and exploiting the countries' often incredibly rich deposits of oil, coal, natural gas, gold, diamonds, and other valuable natural resources.

All this is happening in Russia even though it is seriously troubled by a limping economy mired in mistakes of the past, a fractious military, a falling birthrate, and the sudden appearance of the popularly elected rabble-rouser Vladimir Zhirinovsky, who is rattling Russia's nuclear arsenal and promising bread and borscht for all.

Russia's current troubles could further strengthen the military that supported Zhirinovsky, tempt Russia to resume its historical role as an imperial power, increase its isolation from the West, and even reignite the Cold War that cost the United States and the Soviet Union trillions of dollars wasted on weapons, which could have instead dramatically raised living standards in both countries.

The most optimistic prediction I have seen is that it will take a minimum of two generations—fifty years—to bring Russia's economy to where America's was in the 1950s. And as it is going forward, there is the constant threat of its backsliding toward a state-directed monolith.

The magnitude of the problem was dramatized at a mid-1994 forum held in Warsaw by officials from the Group of Seven industrialized nations and ten former communist states. In a declaration written by knowledgeable business executives attending the meeting, it was estimated that the countries of Eastern Europe alone would need $200 billion of direct foreign investment by the year 2000 to ensure the success of economic changes already underway. Add to that the far larger and infinitely more urgent needs of Russia, Ukraine, Kazakhstan, etc., and the financial dimensions of the crisis approach the kind of money the West spent on winning the Cold War.

Russia and the other members of its Commonwealth of Independent States are not going to get this kind of help, or anything remotely like it. Their economic salvation lies in their own hands. But as we have seen in post–World War II Germany, Japan, and South Korea, among others, and are seeing with astonishment in China today, even the most war-ravaged and resource-poor nations can become economic heavyweights during the productive life of a single worker.

While Russia and its neighbors will need decades to reach the standard of living the West's Group of Seven countries currently enjoy, these already highly industrialized nations are moving headlong into an advanced technology era of mind-boggling complexity and excitement.

This raises the question of whether Russia and the other victims of communist ideology can ever catch up, or whether they are forever doomed to be economic also-rans as the capitalist West further enriches itself on the bountiful high-tech harvest so obviously awaiting it in the onrushing twenty-first century.

A great deal will depend on the strategy Russia pursues in restructuring its economy, which is discussed in the final chapter of this book.

But no matter which one it chooses, it will be in the West's self-interest to support the country with investments of capital and know-how, along with the one-on-one transfer of hands-on experience from successful businesspeople to budding former Soviet bloc entrepreneurs. Only in this way can the unprecedented vote of confidence these recently communist countries are showing in the free enterprise system be encouraged for the benefit of us all.

Historic business opportunities await. Companies and individuals interested in pursuing them should find this book a useful primer.

1

Capitalism Returns to the Former Soviet Empire

"The most important international development of the second half of the 20th century is the collapse of communism in Europe and the effort to replace it with Western political and economic systems."

Michael Mandelbaum
director of the Project on East-West Relations
at the Council on Foreign Relations

C apitalism is running wild throughout the former Soviet empire, where several million private businesses have been launched in the past five years and households starved for everything from soap powder to videocassette recorders are getting their first taste of life in a consumer-driven culture.

Foreign investors have poured more than $15 billion into Hungarian, Polish, and Czech enterprises alone by launching their own businesses; going into partnership with both established and start-up companies in need of capital, management know-how, and access to Western markets; and investing in recently privatized state-owned companies. A few are even cutting deals with workers who have acquired the companies employing them.

The "three hopefuls" of Hungary, Poland, and the Czech Republic have made remarkable progress in creating vibrant, increasingly entrepreneurial economies. Countless small new ventures are being financed by family and friends, and well-heeled foreigners are recognizing these low-wage economies as ideal places to make products for sale both domestically and in the West while being offered tax holidays on their investments and the guaranteed repatriation of profits.

Great progress is also being made in creating the hundreds of new laws and institutions needed to run capitalist economies, and scores of expatriate business tycoons are coming home to help energize them. An example is Hungarian hotel operator Zoltan Palmai, Sr., who left for the United States in 1985 after the communists forced the sale of large hotels to the state. Now he is back, has opened Budapest's swish Victoria Hotel on the Danube with a spectacular view of the city, and is making plans with his son to build another hotel complete with spa in the center of town.

Hungary, Poland, and the Czech Republic have already taken important steps in converting their economies to free enterprise by lifting price controls, dismantling trade barriers, reining in their money supplies, and eliminating subsidies for bankrupt enterprises. But this hasn't come cheaply— many businesses have been forced to lay off workers and cut production. Some owners have even bankrupted their businesses so they could turn around and buy them back for a song.

"THE GREAT NEW FRONTIER FOR U.S. BUSINESS"

Dr. Richard Judy, of the Center for Central European and Eurasian Studies at the Hudson Institute think tank in Indianapolis, calls these three countries "the great new frontier for U.S. business with many, many opportunities for making money rapidly. But, " he adds, "you've got to be there, you've got to know the country, you've got to be sensitive to the way people do business, and you've got to be patient."

The real battle of ideas on how best to do all this, it is worth noting, is not between Marxists and capitalists, but among different views of how to transform a planned economy into a market economy. "The economies of our region must cope with the consequences of having been cut off by force from the technologies, the markets and the competition of the free world economy for more than forty years (and in the case of the former Soviet Union for more than seventy years)," said Hungary's first Prime Minister Jozsef Antall after the Berlin Wall was torn down in 1989 and the captive nations of Eastern Europe regained their independence. "Economic freedom and competition," Antall added, "are not without problems; they are not an easy road to follow. But it is the only one that can lead to sustained growth and general prosperity."

Prague, Budapest, and Warsaw were glittering centers of business, culture, and intellectual life far longer than they were under the dismal heel of Soviet-imposed communism. Today they are embracing the West and looking forward to full membership in the European Union and even the North Atlantic Treaty Organization (NATO), which they see as buffers against any aggressive moves Russia may decide to make in their direction sometime in the future.

The European Union, which grew from twelve to fifteen members on January 1, 1995, with the addition of Austria, Sweden, and Finland, has opened the possibility of Hungary, Poland, the Czech and Slovak republics, Romania, Bulgaria, and Russia joining as soon as they can demonstrate they are stable democracies, respect human rights including those of minorities, and have well-oiled market economies capable of withstanding competition from the West.

Leaders of the European Union elected Luxembourg's Prime Minister Jacques Santer, fifty-seven, as their chief executive as of January 1995, succeeding Jacques Delors. Santer is an energetic politician who has been a governor of the International Monetary Fund since 1989, and of the European Bank for Reconstruction and Development since 1990.

DOING BUSINESS IN
THE FORMER SOVIET EMPIRE

Billions of dollars worth of Western capital and know-how started moving into the former Soviet empire even as it was disintegrating. Money and expertise in almost any configuration you can imagine immediately started searching for opportunities in this new megamarket, which looked immensely promising but was plagued with problems some of which Western moneymen had never seen before.

Their extent is described in a 1993 report the European Bank for Reconstruction and Development did on the difficulties French, German, British, and Italian companies encountered in this market from late 1990 to early 1991. Quite a few are still plaguing Westerners today, and a few new ones have even cropped up such as the potential for havoc represented by Russia's bullyboy politician Vladimir Zhirinovsky. But the outlook is unquestionably improving as free-wheeling Western entrepreneurs and their ex-communist partners learn to work together for their mutual profit.

The European Bank surveyed eighty-two European companies doing business in Hungary, Poland, Czechoslovakia (before it split into two countries), Yugoslavia (when it was still one country), Bulgaria, and Russia along with other members of its Commonwealth of Independent States. Half the companies questioned had 500 employees or less, more than 70 percent were in manufacturing, just over 85 percent had been in business for ten years or more, all but four had solid positions in world markets, and most were involved in joint ventures with their former Soviet empire partners.

The first question these Western companies were asked was why they were investing their hard-earned assets in the former communist bloc. Their replies, on a descending scale of importance, were to penetrate new markets, broaden the outlets for their products, gain hands-on experience serving unfamiliar new customers, establish a foothold in these markets, acquire a dominant competitive position, exploit cheap labor and technicians, earn fast profits, take advantage of financial incentives offered by these countries, import locally made products into their home markets, and exploit incentives by their own governments to enter markets in the East.

Having spelled out why they were doing business behind the former Iron Curtain, the companies were asked to describe the risks. Again in descending order they cited the lack of clearly defined laws covering the operations of foreign companies, lack of property rights, lack of a developed market economy, lack of a capital market, and the uncertainty of price trends because of inflation.

The absence of clearly drawn laws under which Western companies would have to do business was by far the most serious problem, and to find out why, the survey asked the respondents to go into more detail. Their replies, beginning with the most onerous, were complicated permit procedures, an inadequate credit system, lack of sufficient protection for their investment, excessive taxes on repatriated capital, rigidity of the labor market, and inordinate taxation on profits.

When asked to detail the complexity of the permit procedures, along with problems encountered in registering joint ventures, the Western companies led off with bureaucratic delays and problems in relations with local authorities, followed by lack of a managerial mentality, organizational problems, difficulties with the various countries' legal-legislative frameworks, insufficient offices and logistical facilities, lack of information on the local situation, and problems relating to their local partners.

In the end, the Western companies were asked the big question I am sure a lot were waiting for, namely: "Under what conditions would you be willing to manage an ex–state-owned company that was now wholly owned by you?" Their reactions to running a business they had taken over in a recently communist country were not surprising, starting with that managers must be left free to run the company, local currency must be fully convertible, adequate guarantees must be provided to protect the investment, the company must be a joint stock company, and there must be substantial tax incentives.

The study noted that while taking over an existing business would make it possible to economize on registering the company, obtaining work permits, building the premises and infrastructure, etc., it is still not as good as starting from scratch. "Many companies evidently feel that it is more convenient to create a brand-new company," the study said, "rather than run the risk of inheriting antiquated structures and production and organizational processes which would require substantial resources in order to get them to work and operate according to Western management standards."

The European Bank for Reconstruction and Development operates out of its ultramodern, high-rise headquarters in the heart of London's financial district at One Exchange Square. The bank's members include more than fifty countries, the European Economic Union, and the European Investment Bank, and its mission—backed by billions—is to foster "the transition towards market-oriented economies" and "to promote private and entrepreneurial initiative" in countries of the former Soviet empire, "thereby helping their economies to become integrated into the international economy."

The European Bank is making a major effort to get recently communist state-owned businesses into private hands, although it admits, "Foreign investment, however important in terms of bringing in new finance, skills and market access, has and will remain marginal in relation to the overall portfolio of enterprises to be privatized." But having said that, the bank immediately goes on to caution that many state-owned companies eager to go private really don't stand a chance.

It notes how many "enterprises remaining in state ownership are unprofitable" and how liquidating them "would increase unemployment," which is why so many—particularly "energy-intensive heavy industry and much of the military industrial complex"—are among the high-priority targets for restructuring despite the almost insurmountable problem that presents to national leaders. In the meantime, the bank adds, precious resources desperately needed to rebuild the economy are wasted on make-work jobs for which there is no future.

A HUNDRED MILLION CAPITALISTS OVERNIGHT

Capitalism has been sweeping through Eastern Europe and the former Soviet Union with the distribution of privatization vouchers, making investors out of close to 100 million individuals who until recently probably didn't know the meaning of the word. Thousands of small and medium-sized businesses recently owned by the state are already in private hands. A slowly growing number of the biggest state-owned firms are also being acquired by their managers and workers, and by private citizens whose vouchers entitle them to buy a piece of the companies. Shares of these companies are increasingly being traded on fledgling stock exchanges such as the tiny one overlooking a cemetery in the Slovak capital of Bratislava.

The transition to private enterprise is not coming easily because for decades business in the old Soviet empire was conducted from the top down. State-owned companies were told what to do by bureaucrats who rarely even visited them. Managers and workers were rewarded on the basis of how much they produced with little regard for quality. Product design and marketing weren't important since the state bought and distributed everything produced. This meant companies could largely ignore market research, advertising, selling, publicity, credit, going head-to-head with competitors, blasting their way into foreign markets, and virtually everything else capitalist companies take for granted. It comes with the territory.

Today this difficult, but clearly irreversible, transition to a market economy is being assisted throughout the region by enterprise funds heavily supported by the government of the United States and managed by some of the smartest investment managers east of Wall Street. Funds with combined assets in excess of $1 billion are already up and running in the Czech and Slovak Republics, Hungary, Poland, Bulgaria, and Russia, with others slated for Ukraine, Belarus, and Moldova, as well as Kazakhstan, Uzbekistan, Turkmenistan, Tajikistan, and Kyrgyzstan.

The loans and equity investments being made by these funds are not only helping to create badly needed new goods, services, and jobs—not to mention the occasional millionaire—but are educating emerging entrepreneurs about what one fund calls "the mechanics of a market economy." These include requiring entrepreneurs in search of money to compete with thousands of other promising businesses beating the bushes for the venture capital they need to grow and prosper.

TRANSFERRING BUSINESS
KNOW-HOW FROM WEST TO EAST

Most people who have been rushing into business in the former Soviet empire in recent years lack what successful Western entrepreneurs consider to be the keys to any profit-making enterprise, from a credible business plan and access to long-term credit to a working knowledge of marketing and a dependable source of raw materials.

Yet hundreds of thousands of would-be Krupps, Agnellis, and Rothschilds are risking everything in their determination to start a business of their own. This is true even though most are doomed to fail in even greater numbers than in the West, where capitalism has been around for centuries and everything needed to succeed in business is readily available at a price. I examine all this in *Winners: The Successful Strategies Entrepreneurs Use to Build New Businesses*, which Holt, Rinehart & Winston has published in a number of foreign languages including Korean.

A valuable look at the shortcomings of entrepreneurs throughout the former Soviet empire, and how they're struggling to overcome them, can be had in the reports of hundreds of Western business experts who voluntarily spend weeks on end advising the entrepreneurs on how to improve their operations. These former presidents of major U.S. corporations, top management consultants, and successful entrepreneurs are allied with organizations working to strengthen the free enterprise system behind the old Iron Curtain, such as the Peace Corps, the Service Corps of Retired Executives, the MBA Enterprise Corps at the University of North Carolina, and the Citizens Democracy Corps, Inc. (CDC). I was on the steering committee of the CDC's Business Entrepreneur Program, whose staffs in Prague, Bratislava, Warsaw, Bucharest, Moscow, and Kiev were ideal jumping-off points for me in gathering material for this book.

As you read through the detailed reports these advisers regularly send back to their parent organizations, you get a sweeping picture of the difficulties confronting would-be entrepreneurs in this vast part of the world. Everyday business strategies implemented routinely here in the West are often unknown—or, worse, dismissed as too much trouble—by those who have lived much of their lives under "be thankful for whatever we give you" communism.

I noticed this time and time again during my trip, from a little shop in Moscow where the clerks were oblivious to customers to the cashier at the upscale Europejski Hotel in Warsaw who kept me waiting for what seemed like an eternity while she finished filing a pile of old bills.

The exception to all this is on view throughout the region at McDonald's restaurants, where the young women and men greet customers with a smile, fill their orders with dispatch, and say "thank you" as they pay their checks. I was told these youngsters are in great demand by other employers because McDonald's has already trained them not only to treat people with care and courtesy but to work hard with an emphasis on cleanliness. I made a point of visiting McDonald's restaurants wherever I went and never failed to be impressed by the nonstop mopping of the floors, the instant clearing of tables, and the restaurants' spotless exteriors (I watched one fellow at Warsaw's two-story glass McDonald's spend fifteen minutes removing a single clump of old chewing gum from the railing around the outside of the place).

A mind-boggling number of other nonprofit and profit-making consultants are also working to strengthen the former Soviet empire's private sector with help from the U.S. Agency for International Development (USAID). Among the more interesting are the Aga Khan Foundation, American Cyanamid, Futures Group, KPMG Peat Marwick, National Governors Association, International Republican Institute, and the Experiment in International Living. Major contractors like these have then hired on equally fascinating subcontractors to travel behind the old Iron Curtain, such as the World Wildlife Fund, Children's Hospital of Philadelphia, Global Technology Strategies, Vermont Insurance, Sovconsult, and the National Association of Securities Dealers, Inc.

These organizations are intimately involved with virtually every aspect of their host countries' national lives: Training fifty property appraisers in the capital of Kazakhstan. Conducting in-depth diagnoses of Russia's top fifty banks. Providing $30 million worth of agricultural and dairy products plus support services to some 1.4 million infants, mothers, pregnant women, and families displaced by ethnic strife in Armenia, Georgia, Azerbaijan, and Tajikistan. Improving unsafe nuclear reactors in Russia and Ukraine. And upgrading water supplies in Georgia.

While many of these projects have gotten high marks from the recipient countries, a recent front-page article in the *Wall Street Journal* drew attention to the fact that "U.S. Aid to Russia Is Quite a Windfall—for U.S. Consultants." The paper noted that while this country had "pledged $5.8 billion in aid to the former Soviet Union. . . . hordes of U.S. companies are gobbling up much of the U.S. aid pie" and in too many cases producing things the Russians say are a waste of money, such as a $7 million television campaign extolling the virtues of privatization.

THE OVERSEAS PRIVATE INVESTMENT CORPORATION

A major player in the great sea change from state-owned to investor-owned businesses in Eastern Europe and the former Soviet Union is the giant Overseas Private Investment Corporation (OPIC) founded in 1971 to "complement and supplement the lending and investing facilities of commercial banks; local, regional and international development banks and investment funds, and other agencies of the U.S. Government such as the Export-Import Bank of the United States and the Agency for International Development."

OPIC supports American businesses currently operating in more than 140 emerging economies worldwide, and in the last twenty-two years it has invested in projects worth nearly $60 billion, of which some $2 billion backed projects behind the old Iron Curtain with a further $3 billion targeted for these countries through the end of 1995.

"We've been much more active in scouting deals than in the past," says Daniel Riordan, OPIC's deputy vice president of investment development, "including some emerging from Russian scientific institutes which have recently been privatized and are seeking to work with U.S. companies. While Russia has some sophisticated entrepreneurs, its business climate is not good. Business codes are not well established, laws affecting business are constantly changing, and tax laws are egregious and not consistently applied.

"An issue we've been dealing with quite extensively is alternative ways available to U.S. companies for getting profits out of Russia in hard currency. There are some options, but they cannot satisfy anywhere near the demand that's out there. Most of the projects we're supporting have a major hard currency component such as crude oil that can be exported to hard currency markets. That's really how people are doing things now.

"There are some deals like Johnson Wax's $5 million investment in the Ukraine," says Riordan, "that are only attempting to satisfy the local market. They've made a long-term commitment since they're not going to get their Ukrainian coupons converted to dollars or any other hard currency in the near term. They're simply reinvesting their profits in the business. It's similar to the McDonald's model in Russia where earnings are reinvested in the local economy including real estate."

Amazing as it may seem for a federal government agency, the Overseas Private Investment Corporation has actually made money, with total revenues from operations in 1993 in excess of $160 million earned by supplying U.S. companies with medium- and long-term project financing through:

♦ *Direct loans*: for U.S. business overseas investment projects, typically ranging from $500,000 to $6 million.

♦ *Loan guarantees:* to U.S. lending institutions, usually running anywhere from $6 million to $50 million.

♦ *Equity*: medium- and long-term funding and permanent capital for overseas ventures wholly owned by U.S. companies, and for joint ventures between locally owned and American firms involving significant equity and management participation by the U.S. side. OPIC provides the permanent capital through capital stock investments and by purchasing the project's debentures convertible into stock, generally ranging from $200,000 to $2 million.

This financing is provided to projects that are commercially and financially sound, often in countries where conventional financial institutions are frequently reluctant or unable to lend, and where the form of the "project financing" is based primarily on the economic, technical, marketing, and financial soundness of the project. OPIC is also developing a number of venture capital funds in cooperation with the private sector to provide high-risk money for agency-eligible projects.

OPIC insures financing advanced to American companies against loss from currency inconvertibility, expropriation, political violence (war, revolution, insurrection, and civil strife), or disputes. All of its insurance and guaranty obligations are backed by the full faith and credit of the U.S. government.

The aid package passed by Congress in 1993 gives OPIC the authority to provide up to $1 billion of loan guarantees to support American investment in the Commonwealth of Independent States. OPIC also offered investors in the CIS $1.5 billion of political risk insurance. The total adds up to $2.5 billion or seven times more than it made available in 1992. OPIC figures this could generate $2 billion in American exports to Russia and the other CIS nations, create and maintain 38,000 U.S. jobs, and leverage several billion dollars of investment for the Russian economy. To encourage American business to invest in larger ventures in Russia and her CIS neighbors, OPIC doubled the maximum amount it will commit to financing and insuring individual projects to $200 million in each case.

OPIC is also guaranteeing 75 percent of the $100 million to be raised from private institutional investors to capitalize the Russian Partners Company L.P., a new U.S. and Russian–backed equity fund to support American investment in Russia and the other CIS states. When fully capitalized, the fund could generate several hundred million dollars of investment capital that these countries sorely need.

On January 13, 1995, OPIC announced its latest loan guarantees to two private equity funds totaling $340 million that could finance more than $3 billion worth of business ventures in Eastern and Central Europe. A $240 million guarantee will go to the Auburndale Central and Eastern European Property Fund L.P., and another $100 million to the Bancroft Eastern Europe Fund L.P.

A typical OPIC project is insuring an Ingersoll-Rand investment in a Russian company with 300 workers that makes power tools used in speeding the modernization of the country's heavy industry. Another OPIC venture is underwriting International Paper's $150 million acquisition of a privatized pulp and paper mill in Kwidzyn, Poland. The company is helping upgrade the mill's facilities—including the installation of state-of-the-art pollution control equipment—to better serve key sectors of the Polish economy such as the construction and packaging industries, while generating substantial export-related hard currency revenues.

THE REGION'S LEADING BENEFACTOR

While the U.S. is a major contributor to the revival of the former Soviet Union, the Federal Republic of Germany is doing far more. Recently, German Chancellor Helmut Kohl noted that his country's support for the reform process in these nations "over the past few years is unrivalled by any other country."

"German aid to Russia and the remaining successor states to the Soviet Union alone since 1989 totals 87.55 billion Deutschemarks (about $51 billion), or more than the combined total of aid provided by all other Western industrialized nations," said an official German statement issued in late 1993. "This is also true when all the payments made by the European communities, the International Monetary Fund, the World Bank, and the European Bank for Reconstruction and Development are taken into account. Germany is the most important contributor or shareholder in all these international organizations. German expenditures, existing financial obligations together with planned obligations for the reform process in central and eastern European—excluding the Commonwealth of Independent States—have totalled 37.5 billion Deutschemarks (about $22 billion) since 1989."

Chancellor Kohl said examples of Germany's financial assistance to Russia are $78 million, to be used in "improving the safety of Soviet-design nuclear power stations which is a major concern for us all," plus another $10 billion or so to support the "withdrawal and social reintegration of the Russian troops stationed in East Germany. The main focus of the program," notes Chancellor Kohl, "is the construction of over 36,000 dwellings for the soldiers and their families. A portion of the funds will be used to retrain the soldiers for civilian professions."

There were nearly 550,000 Russian troops in Germany before the collapse of the Soviet empire, and by August 1994 all were scheduled to have left. Hundreds of Russian officers have received several hundred hours of German instruction in product development, marketing, data processing, and other skills that should prove useful in finding work back home. What thousands of military families will not find is housing, and they will be forced to live in tents until the homes promised to them by the Germans as an incentive to leave their country are ready for occupancy within the next year or two.

A PARTNERSHIP FOR PEACE

Hungary and Poland, along with the Czech and Slovak republics, were occupied by Soviet troops for some forty years and remain wary of the shrunken, but still menacing, Russian Bear with its estimated 4,000 combat aircraft, more than 25,000 nuclear weapons, and still formidable army far too close and unpredictable for comfort. This is why these countries are so desperate to join the Western nations belonging to NATO in which an attack against one is considered an attack against all.

In the meantime, however, these nations are joining the American-designed "Partnership for Peace," which offers greater political and military cooperation with the West to all former Warsaw Pact members including Russia without promising early membership in NATO.

Hungary was the first to tell the Clinton administration it was ready to become a partner for peace, followed by the Czech Republic. But Romania was the first ex–Warsaw Pact nation to enroll formally when its foreign minister signed the agreement at NATO headquarters in Brussels on January 26, 1994. Two weeks later, Ukraine's foreign minister traveled to Brussels, making it the first former Soviet republic aside from the Baltic states to join the West's military alliance.

Western Europeans have long viewed a NATO backed by America's military might as a shield against the Soviet Union. This feeling is shared by recently liberated Lithuania, along with neighboring Estonia and Latvia, which have had Russian troops billeted on their soil because of their large Russian-speaking populations of nearly 40 percent in Estonia and 50 percent in Latvia.

Talks have been concluded to withdraw all 13,000 or so Russian troops from Latvia, with some 600 remaining behind to guard a Russian early warning radar station on the Baltic Sea under a multiyear lease. While the Russian enlisted men and retired military officers have been virtually eliminated from Estonian soil, the two countries have yet to sign an agreement liberating Estonia from Russian occupation. Russia's defense minister recently warned Estonia that if it did not behave itself, his troops would march back in.

NATO has recognized Russia's status as a nuclear superpower but has rejected the idea of giving it any kind of voice in NATO decision making despite Russia's concern about NATO moving its military power closer to its borders.

"A RUINED UTOPIA"

Environmental neglect and destruction was a hallmark of the former Soviet empire, and only now are the nations of this vast region beginning to spend the billions needed to clean up the deadly cesspool they have created—which is no respecter of national borders. As a result, countries throughout the region are working together to nurse their common life-sustaining environment back to health.

It is estimated, to mention just a few examples, that most of the trees in recently communist East Germany are sick, dead, or dying; that life expectancy in the Czech

Republic's heavily industrialized area of northern Bohemia is ten years shorter than elsewhere in the country; and that a large proportion of Poland's water is unsafe to drink.

The region's pollution crises have led the nations involved to attack these problems both domestically and internationally. The Delta of the Danube in Romania and Ukraine, for example, is one of Europe's last and largest wetlands still in a near-natural state. The Romanian government has declared most of the Delta under its jurisdiction to be a Biosphere Reserve, has established the Danube Delta Biosphere Reserve Authority to manage the area, and is working with the European Bank for Reconstruction and Development on a program to encourage investment, private sector activity, and the development of ecotourism, fishing, and the building of essential infrastructure.

The European Bank is working on a great many other individual country projects in what it calls "a ruined utopia," from the rehabilitation and upgrading of Budapest's public transit system on which residents depend for 80 percent of their urban transportation, to connecting the industrial and wastewater systems of six municipalities in and around the Polish city of Gdansk in such a way that it will cut 6 percent off Poland's organic pollution of the Baltic Sea.

Efforts to restore the Baltic Sea, its coastal waters, and the rivers draining into it are also being pursued by surrounding countries, as are numerous other international efforts to reverse decades of environmental neglect. One example nearly 800 miles to the south is the Black Sea Environmental Initiative to clean up this vast inland water body that is almost entirely devoid of life-giving oxygen because of the industrial pollution spewed into it from surrounding nations.

Another prime example is the effort five Central Asian countries are making to restore the Aral Sea a thousand miles to the east, which was once the fourth largest sea in the world, covering an area larger than France. Today the Aral Sea is heavily polluted and one-third its original size, virtually destroying a large fishing industry that once employed 60,000 people, devastating major plant and wildlife regions, and threatening the area's vital agricultural sector.

REGIONAL COOPERATION PAYS OFF

The same kind of regional cooperation being used to clean up the environment in Eastern Europe and the former Soviet Union is being pursued in other vital areas, including energy, transportation, telecommunication, and finance (again with help from well-funded global agencies including the European Bank).

Developing Energy Resources

The need to reduce reliance on the Middle East's vast petroleum reserves containing 60 percent of the world's oil, for example, has led to the creation of the European Energy Charter to integrate the oil and natural gas resources of the former Soviet Union with the West's growing energy needs. The ultimate goal of the nearly fifty nations signing the charter at the Hague in December 1991—admittedly still a long way from reality—is to reduce barriers to trade in energy while encouraging the foreign investments needed to replace used supplies with new reserves in Russia, Kazakhstan, Turkmenistan, and other oil-rich countries.

The International Council on Oil and Gas announced on March 2, 1993, is another step toward energy cooperation as it addresses the overreliance on cheap energy throughout the former Soviet empire. The empire had no sooner broken up than Russia and its oil and gas exporting neighbors tripled or quadrupled their prices to world levels, sending shock waves through Ukraine, Belarus, and the other energy-importing countries. They, however, were not completely defenseless since the oil and gas pipelines used to carry these supplies to rich West European markets pass through their territories, creating interdependence. How this will all end up is anybody's guess. But it will probably move in the general direction of equity until new pipelines can be built to transport energy from Russia's huge western Siberia fields, which produce 60 percent of its oil and gas, as well as from major fields in Kazakhstan, East Azerbaijan, and Turkmenistan.

All kinds of new oil and gas pipeline arrangements are under discussion since existing ones are both inadequate and now mismatched with major markets. One leading proposal, for example, would bring oil from Caspian Sea fields in Kazakhstan and East Azerbaijan through Turkey to the Mediterranean, by way of Iran to the Persian Gulf, or to the Black Sea and then on to the Mediterranean through Russia or Georgia. The oil could then be piped aboard tankers for delivery to its final destination in Western Europe.

Gas is another story, however, because of the expense of liquefying it before it can be transported by ship. Pipelines are the way to go, and a number of new ones are under discussion involving, among others, the Turkmenistan fields where a rich gas potential lies ready to be tapped. So far, three basic routes have been proposed to get Turkmenistan's gas to Europe, along with another one involving the construction of a gas pipeline from Turkmenistan to China's northeast coast through Uzbekistan and Kazakhstan, and then to Japan via a submarine pipeline, or by liquefaction and then ship.

The point is that there's no better resource in the former Soviet empire today than oil and gas. Supplies are abundant in the countries already mentioned, giant world oil companies have started moving in with their know-how and fat wallets, and there's a growing market in today's energy-hungry world with no end in sight.

The outlook is also promising for electricity, says the European Bank, even though the two giant systems serving the former Soviet Union and Europe are separate and technologically different. But linking the two systems is feasible and, says the bank, holds the promise of considerable benefits because "electricity can now be transmitted over long distances efficiently enough to capture savings possible through energy supply cooperation across different time zones simultaneously. With the various peak use times alternating and offsetting each other, significant cost reductions and improvements to the reliability of supply are possible."

The most incredible power-sharing plan of all is a proposal to link the Russian, North American, and Asian electricity grids into one globe-girdling system. This would entail building a 6,000-mile transmission line from Krasnoyarsk in central Russia, across the Bering Strait to Alaska, and on down to Chicago. Extensions to this line could reach China and/or Japan, or go from Alaska south to the Pacific Northwest. Engineers and government officials from Russia, the United States, and Japan have already met in Anchorage, Alaska, to discuss this proposal which, though admittedly grandiose, illustrates how the emergence of Russia and the other former Soviet bloc countries into the community of nations is creating exciting new opportunities of benefit to all.

Upgrading the Transportation System

This certainly applies to transportation with plans afoot to upgrade roads, rail, inland waterways, and aviation throughout Eastern Europe and the former Soviet Union.

Improving the region's roads, notes the European Bank, presents two immediate problems vis-à-vis the economic viability of various road projects. The first is the lack of accurate traffic data and the second is predicting how the changeover to a market economy and the growing use of roads compared to rail will orchestrate the need for more capital-intensive new highways.

This becomes even more complex when you consider the various projects being considered by Turkey, Iran, China, and the Central Asian and Transcaucasian states to build a southern route from Europe to Southeast Asia. The Soviet Union isolated its Muslim citizens in Central Asia and Transcaucasia from their coreligionists in Turkey, Iran, and Europe. But now they are independent and eager to build infrastructure ties to their Muslim neighbors in the south, further reducing their dependence on Moscow and the north.

This is planned through rail, rail and ferry, and a motorway along the ancient Silk Route serving the southern corridor between Europe and Asia. One rail line will connect Turkmenistan with Iran to the south, while the other is already providing service between Kazakhstan and China. The rail-ferry route will link Europe to Central Asia via Transcaucasia rather than going south through Iran. It will run from Krasnovodsk on the Caspian Sea in Turkmenistan, across to Baku in Azerbaijan, then to Georgia's capital of Tbilisi, and east to Poti on the Black Sea. From there it will cross over to the Black Sea ports of Varna or Burgas in Bulgaria, finally ending its journey in the heart of Europe. The old idea of a motorway connecting Kazakhstan with Beijing, skirting well south of Russia, has even been revived.

The most important single fact about air travel in Russia today is that its huge state-owned monopoly Aeroflot no longer controls commercial aviation. And a good thing too since its terrifying safety record, surly flight attendants, unappetizing meals, and poor on-time performance had reached the point where foreigners were being advised by their travel agents to avoid Aeroflot at all costs.

That this advice was sound was proven in March 1994, when an Aeroflot jet bound for Hong Kong crashed and burned, killing everyone aboard. When the flight recorder was recovered from the wreckage, it revealed that Captain Yaroslav Kudrinski had allowed his teenage son and daughter to play with the jet's controls. The youngsters had somehow managed to disengage the autopilot, which stalled the plane, sending it into a dive and seventy-five passengers to their deaths.

Aeroflot was the biggest airline in the world with more than 8,000 planes and possibly as many as 400,000 employees, according to reports in *Aviation Week and Space Technology*. Today's renamed Aeroflot Russian International Airlines is but a shadow of its former self, although it has managed to keep its basic route system intact while inaugurating commercial service to thirteen new destinations in 1993, stretching from Johannesburg to Panama City, and cargo service to places such as Beijing, China, and Dubai and Sharjah in the United Arab Emirates. Aeroflot is supporting this expansion by adding new planes, including five Airbus Industrie A310s on lease, and hopes to shortly lease two Boeing 767-300 ER widebody jets.

What is different is that Aeroflot is no longer alone, but until recently had to compete with an estimated 241 other operators—many of whose licenses are not being renewed because the government feels they are incapable of operating safely. Industry officials told *Aviation Week* that licensing renewal requests for about forty airlines were turned down in 1993, and that fifty or so additional rejections were expected in 1994.

One of Russia's most successful start-up carriers is Moscow-based Transaero, which began operations in November 1991 with charter flights, followed in 1993 by scheduled service throughout Russia, the Commonwealth of Independent States, and elsewhere. Transaero, which claims to have been profitable from the start, operates a core fleet of Boeing 737s and a 757 and plans to add 767s for long-range service, including flights beginning in 1995 to Washington, Chicago, Seattle, Dallas, Los Angeles, and Orlando.

While airline passenger traffic in Russia collapsed from roughly 60 million to 40 million during 1993, international air travel has fared much better. This is particularly true to places such as the United Arab Emirates where CIS visitors can buy electronics and other goods at knockdown prices for resale at a handsome markup when they arrive home in Moscow or Minsk.

The airline industry is also booming in sprawling Kazakhstan and in Turkmenistan, which are rich in oil and natural gas and have Boeing salespeople salivating. Kazakhstan Airlines has been buying Boeing 747SPs, plans to add one or two 767s a year, and is considering acquiring 737s. Kazakhstan's jets won't be troubled by the fuel shortages plaguing other CIS countries since its energy needs will be met by two national oil refineries. The country also has plans to add a new runway to the airport in its capital of Almaty while modernizing its air traffic control systems.

Turkmenistan has already received one new Boeing 737-300 for airline operations, a VIP-appointed 757-200ER for its president, and is expected to add more Boeings to its fleet in the next few years—possibly some of the 737-300s previously ordered by Delta Air Lines but never purchased.

Railroads are at the heart of the former Soviet Union's transportation network, and while work is underway to restructure the system, the European Bank says no major new regional rail projects are being planned. As with everything else in these newly independent states, responsibility for funding, ownership, and coordination must first be agreed upon before any intercountry rail improvements can be made. Once this is accomplished, however, the bank believes the most promising corridors for upgrading are Moscow-Warsaw-Berlin, Bratislava-Prague-Dresden-Berlin, Warsaw-Katowice-Bratislava, and Belgrade-Sofia-Istanbul.

One of the most extraordinary transportation projects, says the European Bank, is the just over 100 mile canal that begins in German Bavaria and links the Rhine and Main rivers to the Danube. This canal provides a waterway between the North Sea and the Black Sea exiting at the southern Romanian port of Constanta. The canal was completed in 1992 and cuts nearly 3,000 miles from the old North Sea–Mediterranean–Suez route. It has yet to prove itself economically when compared to rail, although projects to improve its viability such as creating a series of free trade zones along its route are under discussion.

2

The Czech Economy
Springs Back to Life

"For more than 40 years, there has been not one Europe, but at least two. One is the Europe of the West, the land of democracies and relative prosperity. The other is the Europe of the East, of totalitarianism until recently unchallenged, the Europe that has finally awakened."

Czech Republic President Vaclav Havel
U.S. News & World Report

I had been told that ancient Prague was a hotbed of entrepreneurship and that I would begin experiencing it within minutes after I left my hotel on the left bank of the Vltava River not far from the Gothic spires of Saint Vitus Cathedral and the assemblage of palaces, museums, gardens, and even cafes that make up Hradcany Castle.

One's eyes are constantly drawn upward in Prague by its intricate copper and red brick roofs, or downward to the swirling design of walkways made of what has to be billions of stone cubes two inches on a side that I was told were the work of prisoners. There was the usual lineup of glittering shops interrupted by a tiny cinema tucked away in a dark mews playing *Jurassic Park*. And then I walked right into what has been rightly called the most beautiful bridge in Europe, named after Charles IV who ordered it built in 1357. The medieval structure is lined with thirty Baroque statues of saints, long since blacked by smoke and soot, and crammed with tourists who stroll back and forth across its rough cobblestones all day long past an array of locals eager for their money. There's an old man playing the accordion, an artist ready to capture your likeness in charcoal, a blind couple singing a cappella, and a teenager selling Kodak film with postcards as a sideline.

A VENDOR'S PARADISE

You then leave the bridge, wait for Europe's ubiquitous little traffic light man to change from standing still red to legs stretched out green, and enter a maze of narrow streets and glittering shops, one of which will take you past the cream and green Tyl Theater where Mozart's *Don Giovanni* was first performed in 1787 and into Old Town Square, which is a vendor's paradise. Off to one side is the square's Astronomical Clock, placed in the tower of the old town hall in 1410, which draws crowds of delighted onlookers as it chimes the hour accompanied by twelve bowing apostles, a Turk shaking his turbaned head, a Jew clutching his moneybags, Vanity admiring herself in a mirror, and bony Death with his hourglass. In the square's center is a grieving assembly of monumental figures dominated by Jan Hus, the Czech priest and leader of a religious reform movement who was burned at the stake for heresy in 1415.

The square is alive with entrepreneurs displaying their wares, and to help me talk to them I hired an interpreter named Vera Burdova who was in her thirties, taught English in a Czech high school, was married to an engineer, had two young children, and felt things had probably been better under the communists when the basics of life were guaranteed by the state (a viewpoint I would hear more than once on my journey throughout the former Soviet empire). What worried Vera was the high rate of unemployment under capitalism (apparently unaware that it has been running at a mere 3.5 percent in the Czech Republic compared with 15.8 percent in neighboring Poland), the uncertainty over whether jobs would be available when her children reached working age, and what would become of retired people who she felt had a secure old age under communism but were being disregarded under capitalism, where making money is the name of the game.

The moment I walked into Old Town Square my eye was caught by a young woman selling puppets. Dozens of them dangled by their strings from her cart—puppet kings, queens, skeletons, ballerinas, and witches, along with Charlie Chaplin, Elvis Presley, Boris Yeltsin, and other famous figures. She said the puppets were made by her uncle, that kings and queens were her biggest sellers, and that on a good day she would sell half a dozen puppets, giving her a profit equivalent to about five dollars. I later passed two shops selling nothing but puppets and was told they are part of the Czech cultural heritage and may have actually been born there centuries ago.

We then walked over to an old lady displaying beautifully embroidered white, lacy table linens and napkins she made at home and sold from half a rented stall with a small roof. No one had taken the other half, but she meticulously confined her merchandise to the part that was hers. She said on a good day her sales would reach the equivalent of fifteen or twenty dollars, which was how she made her living after deducting the cost of a vendor's license and rent for the stall.

A short distance away was a little business the likes of which I had never seen before. It was a rolling open-air tavern drawn by a matched pair of horses. You climbed aboard, took a seat along either side of a table running down the center, were serenaded by an on-board accordion player, and served all the beer you could hold by a young waitress as you rolled along enjoying the sights.

My attention was then drawn to two young men hovering over an oven glowing with red hot coals who looked like they had just stepped out of the Middle Ages. They were wearing raggedy wool shirts, neck-to-knee leather aprons belted with rope, and grimy wool hats with earflaps tied tightly under their chins. They would take a pair of long iron pincers, grab a round brass blank out of a woven reed basket, heat it over the coals, and then stick it into a steel mold that they would bang with a sledgehammer, producing a commemorative medal with Charles IV's likeness on it.

The most successful vendor I met was an eighteen-year-old blonde woman in heavy woolen sweater and blue jeans selling famed Czech crystal from a long table beneath an alcove attached to one of the ornate pastel-colored gingerbread buildings surrounding the square. She had almost as wide an assortment of crystal dinnerware, vases, sculptures, and other pieces as the upscale shops on Old Town's fashionable Karlova Street, which she sold for a fraction of the price in the shops. She said her's was a family business and that she frequently made twenty-five or thirty dollars in commissions during a two-day weekend, and even more during the summer when the square is packed with well-heeled tourists.

The city's most common vendors are young people standing absolutely still with an open wooden case roughly four feet wide hanging around their necks. The cases are filled with rings, bracelets, decorative pins, and the like; and one college student told me he would sell an average of three pieces on a typical Saturday, which earned him three or four dollars. This fellow spoke English and was the only vendor I interviewed who asked me to buy something.

The most eye-catching entrepreneurs were the entertainers who amused the crowds and then passed the hat. One old man had three dogs who spent the day rolling over, doing back flips, and as an encore yapping what their owner insisted was the Czech national anthem. A young magician dressed in top hat and tails with green bow tie and cummerbund made rubber balls disappear with a flick of the wrist, pulled endless colored handkerchiefs out of his assistant's ear, and ended his sidewalk show by producing a dove out of thin air. The most ingenious entertainer was a young man who had built a flatbed trailer holding a grand piano, which he parked on the sidewalk and played with the panache and gusto of a Horowitz.

CZECHOSLOVAKIA SPLITS IN TWO

Until January 1, 1993, when they became two sovereign nations, the Czech Republic and the Slovak Republic were part of Czechoslovakia, founded in 1918 after the collapse of the Austro-Hungarian Empire. The Czech Republic has more than 10 million people and a relatively vibrant economy, a balanced budget, managed inflation, and growing foreign investment. The Czech Republic is in much better shape than Slovakia, which has just over 5 million people and an economy based on heavy industry, including the manufacture of armaments no longer being bought in quantity by Russia or hardly anyone else.

The Czech Republic is clawing its way out from under Czechoslovakia's old command economy, which—unlike in Hungary and Poland—was nearly 100 percent nationalized by the communists. Owners of private businesses were only allowed to employ family members, were heavily taxed, and mainly limited to services such as shoe repair and food shops. This created the most highly developed industry and workforce in the old communist bloc with the exception of the former East Germany, which has already started receiving what will amount to hundreds of billions of dollars worth of Deutschemarks now that it is part of a reunited Germany.

The Soviet Union was once Czechoslovakia's main trading partner, but sales collapsed by more than 50 percent even before the breakup, are still small to members of the Commonwealth of Independent States, and have even fallen to neighboring Hungary and Poland, whose economies have also been hard-hit and who have started purchasing more from the West. Today, close to one-third of the Czech Republic's exports are shipped to Germany giving it a higher level of economic integration with its Western neighbor than any of Germany's major trading partners in the European Union.

The new Czech Republic's leaders were confronted with a monster job in converting the country's economy to the rigors of capitalism. Fortunately, it had its two Vaclavs—

President Vaclav Havel and Prime Minister Vaclav Klaus. Havel is an internationally respected playwright, the nation's leading dissident whom the communists jailed three times for subversion (the longest period from 1979 to 1983), and today in his mid-fifties is the Czech Republic's philosopher king. Hard-driving Vaclav Klaus, who is several years younger than Havel, has been the main engine behind the country's privatization program. The program has been criticized for allowing big, overstaffed, and unprofitable industries to continue operating, but applauded for encouraging small businesses—whose numbers soared by one-third to 890,000 in 1993 with most firms expected to be in private hands by 1995, according to Minister for Trade and Industry Vladimir Dlouhy.

Klaus pulled off his near miracle by ordering the managers of most government-owned companies to unload them at auctions, transfer them to private hands using books of vouchers purchased by Czechs eighteen and older for 1,000 crowns (equivalent to about thirty-five dollars) per book, or sell them directly to foreign investors who were given the right to repatriate 100 percent of whatever profits they made from owning them, which would be tax free for the first two years. Neighboring German industrialists were particularly intrigued by this offer since the companies had both skilled workers and low labor costs even though their technology was often outdated.

This, however, is about to change. The Germans who currently dominate Europe's steel-making minimill industry were surprised to learn recently that a Czech company, Nova Hut Steelworks, has just ordered a $250 million minimill from a U.S.–Japanese consortium that can produce flat-rolled steel simpler and cheaper than ever before. The mill should allow the Czechs to make serious inroads into Europe's high-cost steel market.

"THE FIRE SALE OF THE CENTURY"

State-owned Czech businesses privatized in what has been called "the fire sale of the century" had to publish a prospectus containing basic data such as their sales, profits, and debts. Any companies that had trouble finding buyers were all but given away through a complex bidding plan, while those failing to attract any investors were simply allowed to die.

Czechs who became "instant capitalists" on May 18, 1992, could sell their vouchers to others, exchange them for shares in attractive companies such as Prague Breweries, or invest them in their favorites among more than 400 mutual funds. A dozen or so of these funds, such as Creditanstalt affiliated with an Austrian bank of the same name or the well-known Harvard Funds run by American-educated Czech promoter Viktor Kozeny, have thousands of stockholders and control roughly one-third of all the shares in public hands.

On June 22, 1993, some 6 million Czech and 2.5 million Slovak investors began experiencing the joys and sorrows involved in trading shares in dozens of corporations listed on the new Prague Stock Exchange. Among them were chocolate maker Cokoladovny Modrany, partially owned by Switzerland's Nestle; and the cigarette manufacturer Tabak, in which Philip Morris acquired a 30 percent interest in 1992 and has since risen to an absolute majority at a cost of close to $400 million (making it the largest foreign investment in the Czech Republic after Volkswagen's affiliation with Skoda, the big automobile manufacturer).

Limited trading on the Prague Stock Exchange began two months before its official opening so its computers could be phased in and any logistical bugs worked out. One of the exchange's greatest fears is that big cash-short investment funds that hold more than 70 percent of all the shares traded may be forced to dump large blocks of stock on the still-fragile market to improve their liquidity. What is more, many poorly run companies with large debts to juggle could fail within months after their shares begin trading, souring a lot of investors on the whole idea of free market capitalism from day one. This seems a virtual certainty since both the Czech and Slovak economies are far from robust and prone to setbacks.

A vivid reminder of what a heavy debt load can do in a soft economy is the Czech brewer Plzenske Pivovary, which makes the famed Pilsner Urquell beer. The company has invested millions to modernize its plants to deal with rough-and-tumble Western competition, and two-thirds of its shares are owned by private investors. Yet there have been rumors, which the brewery has denied, that its debt may force it into bankruptcy. Plzenske Pivovary could use a white knight and may have found one in the big Dutch brewer Heineken.

CEZ, the Czech Republic's biggest power company, has been one of the hottest stocks on the Prague exchange, and investors got a chance to buy more when the Ministry of Privatization sold another $5.2 billion worth of stock in state companies to eager buyers.

Foreign Investors Search for Bargains

Investors from Western Europe and the United States are aggressively searching for bargains and paying for any they find with welcome hard currency. A good example is the 31 percent stake Germany's huge Volkswagen company bought in Czechoslovakia's giant Skoda Automobilova A.S. on March 28, 1991, followed by an announcement of plans to borrow $878 million from the European Bank for Reconstruction and Development, the World Bank's International Finance Corporation, and a consortium of commercial banks—with the money going to double Skoda's car-making capacity at its three plants. But on September 16, 1993, financially hard-pressed Volkswagen announced that while it intended to take over an additional 39 percent of Skoda from the Czech government, bringing its ownership up to a controlling 70 percent, it would finance the purchase itself by investing $248 million in 1993 and $218 million in both 1994 and 1995.

Skoda officials, according to a Reuters dispatch, said the company had produced nearly 220,000 cars in 1993, an increase of 9.7 percent over 1992, and expected modest profits. Skoda cars, such as its four-door Favorit, are selling well in Britain and other overseas markets, and it has announced plans to double production to an estimated 450,000 cars a year by 1997 and to continue introducing new models. It also intends to reduce its workforce to 15,000 people from 18,000 by moving employees from its main plant near Prague to new service and supply companies. Skoda's streetcar factory at Ostrov near the German border laid off some of its 2,000 workers when it lost orders from the Soviet Union, but this has been turned around by orders coming in from Mexico and Kazakhstan. As a bonus to the Czech economy, some 150 companies are now involved in servicing Skoda's growing needs.

THE WESTERN PRESENCE IN PRAGUE

If you're one of the 50,000 or so Westerners living in the Czech Republic these days, you'll feel right at home surrounded by Kmarts, Benettons, McDonald's (five in Prague alone at last count), White and Case lawyers, the *Prague Post* owned and run by a young American named Lisa Frankenberg, and the country's first commercial television channel. Two American moneymen who wasted no time jumping into this market are former U.S. ambassador to Hungary R. Mark Palmer and Estee Lauder cosmetics heir Ronald S. Lauder, who has built a $1 million pink and white salon just off Wenceslas Square to serve the beauty needs of the more affluent Czech women. Lauder and Palmer are major investors in Polish television whose Central European Development Corporation recently committed $47 million for 75 percent of Eastern Europe's first commercial television station, called TV Nova, which began broadcasting in the Czech Republic on February 4, 1994.

TV Nova expects to break even in four or five years and, according to its director general, will concentrate on local news, Czech-produced programming (which will begin at about 20 percent but is expected to eventually hit 40 percent), and entertainment supplied by the likes of Walt Disney, CNN, MTV, Fox, Sony, Columbia, and Touchstone.

Advertising will average about 10 percent of air time but could rise to double that in prime time, including commercials during movies such as the Czech-dubbed version of *Ghostbusters* aired on TV Nova's opening night.

TV Nova's director general told an NBC reporter that being bombarded by commercials will be an unsettling new experience for Czech viewers, especially when they interrupt programs. "It will be a certain kind of shock because they have never been exposed to this kind of experience. But I hope they will accept it, and we will try to explain to them that for this excellent type of programming we must pay and advertising is the only source of revenue so that's logical." Among the first ads to appear on Czech television will be, not surprisingly, those from soap giants Procter & Gamble and Unilever.

If TV Nova works in the Czech Republic, says its director general, "it will be a good example for all post-Communist countries around us, maybe Poland, maybe Slovakia, maybe Hungary, maybe Ukraine, and not only our successes will be important, but our mistakes will be very valuable to them." A few days before TV Nova went on the air, Poland awarded its first television license to a local company called Polsat, beating out such foreign moneybags as Time Warner, Capital Cities/ABC, and Germany's Bertelsmann.

The Central European Development Corporation was founded in 1990, and its first investment was a 50 percent interest in the General Banking and Trust Company of Hungary, purchased for $10 million. It has also won a regional television license in Berlin, where the company is based, and another one is under review in Slovakia. It is determined to get a solid foothold in this big new market before Westerners such as Australian-born media baron Rupert Murdoch and his News Corporation buy up everything in sight in Eastern Europe, which they see as one of the world's most attractive new markets.

The Czech Republic has proven unusually interesting to Western firms, attracting such well-known names as Procter & Gamble, which acquired the country's biggest detergent maker; the French state-owned automaker Renault, which is investing heavily in a major bus manufacturer; a

Japanese-controlled Belgian company, which has acquired a substantial interest in a Czech glass manufacturer called Sklo Union; and the Swiss-Swedish electrical engineering giant Asea Brown Boveri (ABB), which is sinking millions into a fast-growing number of joint ventures with thousands of employees.

Kmart Struggles to Modernize
Czech Merchandising

The Kmart Corporation, based in Troy, Michigan, whose main business is general discount stores, has been going hog wild here as it has watched its share of the huge U.S. market dwindle for a decade and was looking for new worlds to conquer. The company combed Eastern Europe for something to buy, found it in 1992 in the Czechoslovakia government–owned Prior chain, and bought its thirteen best stores with six ending up in cities throughout the Czech Republic and seven in Slovakia.

Don MacNeill, Kmart's managing director for Eastern Europe, says the company invested an initial $100 million in the thirteen stores, including the one in Prague, which get 80 percent of their merchandise from Czech and Slovak suppliers and the rest from U.S. companies such as Colgate, Stanley Tool, and Dirt Devil. This Prague store features the first Little Caesars Pizza restaurant to open in the Czech Republic, a state-of-the-art optical shop, and now hardware, furniture, home and beauty, and artificial flower departments.

Kmart's well-stocked stores catering to their recently communist customers fascinate the U.S. merchandising media, with New York's *Women's Wear Daily* running an article spotlighting what it says Kmart has learned about the buying habits of its newest customers. "Sleeveless blouses? Forget it," says the report. "Athletic shoes? They're hot. Paper plates? No way. Synthetic blends? Slow movers—natural fibers, please."

Kmart's stores in both the Czech and Slovak republics will have to completely unlearn their old communist ways before they can begin turning a sound profit. Local manufacturers are suddenly being asked to make things Kmart customers actually want to buy, shopping hours are being lengthened, and salespeople are being taught that the customer is #1, which doesn't come easy for people who have been living under socialism for forty years. This is one reason some Western companies doing business here refuse to hire older employees—such as the lady working for Kmart who reportedly refused to wear a badge on her uniform proclaiming "I'm Here for You."

Kmart has also had trouble getting local manufacturers to meet its liberated customers' changing needs, forcing it, for example, to import goods such as inexpensive summer shorts and tops from Asia. MacNeill is going flat out to make sure that America's $34 billion retailing leviathan prospers in Eastern Europe, including hiring the Ross Roy Group in nearby Bloomfield Hills, Michigan, to open an office in Prague so it can handle all of Kmart's marketing communications in the Czech Republic and Slovakia. But it is still a slow haul.

Aiding the Czech Entrepreneurial Spirit

Sometimes marketing errors are so gross they leave Western advisers' heads spinning. This happened when Martin Locke, former president of Atlanta's famous Gibson electric guitar and keyboard company, showed up at the Delicia company in the town of Horovice in the Czech Republic as a pro bono consultant working under the auspices of the nonprofit Citizens Democracy Corps of Washington, D.C.

Delicia makes electric guitars, accordions, and harmonicas, and has succeeded in remaining profitable despite downturns in both the Czech economy and the worldwide guitar industry. Delicia's problem, and it is a beaut, is that 95 percent of its guitars were being purchased by just one customer—a musical instrument company in Germany.

Martin Locke was delighted to learn that Delicia's management understood this problem and was taking steps to correct it by diversifying into the production of furniture and clock frames, while investigating the possibility of becoming a supplier to a company in Prague that sells coffins. As a further step toward hiking profits, he urged the company to sell the plastic, wood, and metal parts left over from its manufacturing process for scrap.

Locke realized that Delicia lacked name recognition in the music business and had neither the management nor the money to do much about it. Two things it could do, he suggested, were to identify rising young stars in the music industry and get them to use Delicia guitars exclusively (as Nike does with its sports shoes), and to investigate the possibility of manufacturing guitars for a U.S. company that would be branded and marketed using the American company's established name and reputation.

One of the most common mistakes made by newcomers to capitalism is rushing into far too many unrelated businesses. They spread themselves too thin, and before they know it, they are doing nothing but putting out fires. This happened to the husband and wife team of Pavel and Zdena Fadrny, owners of the Kazado manufacturing company in the Czech city of Pilsen whose eighty employees were producing everything from wood playground equipment to steel industrial dumpsters. The Fadrnys were wild about introducing new things to sell even though materials and components were tough to find, their employees did not know what they were going to make from one month to the next, and coming up with accurate cost estimates in order to set realistic prices was almost impossible.

All that started to change when Robert Kennedy, president of the Superior Chaircraft Company of Belton, Texas, sat down with the Fadrnys and began giving them some tough love–style advice that some experts close to the company are convinced saved its life. Staying in business somehow is absolutely vital in the Czech Republic, which does not permit companies to hold creditors at bay while they attempt to reorganize (which distressed U.S. companies routinely do using our bankruptcy laws).

One of the first things Kennedy did was to get Kazado to stop selling its products to German customers at lowball prices, which they promptly marked up and sold to others at a nice profit. Kennedy wasted no time in getting Kazado's top financial officer to join him on a trip to Nuremberg, Germany, where they had little difficulty in negotiating a 50 percent price hike.

"The people at Kazado," says Kennedy, "admitted they were not good negotiators, and that they knew the Germans were taking advantage of them. They also admitted they were used to being intimidated, first by the Russians and now by the Germans and others because they simply didn't like to negotiate. I think they're still surprised that with a little wheeling and dealing they can actually get higher prices for their products."

By focusing its attention on what is really important, like realistic pricing, Kazado has succeeded in increasing its exports to Germany by 20 percent, has identified several new export opportunities, and is now hiring extra workers from Slovakia to keep up with the rising demand for its products.

SURPRISING OPPORTUNITIES

Kazado's experience also points up the opportunities awaiting businesses that may not yet be looking at this part of the world as the vast new market it is. How soon will it be, for example, before experts in negotiating begin holding seminars in Bratislava or Saint Petersburg? Or multiplex cinema companies begin putting up ten-screen movie theaters in Sofia or Minsk?

Who would have thought that Baskin-Robbins could make money selling ice cream in Moscow, where its big pink sign covering the side of a building looks slightly incongruous during wintertime when temperatures drop below freezing for months on end? Or that the swish Yves Saint Laurent fashion house could make money selling pricy high fashion jewelry, cosmetics, perfumes, scarves, and other accessories in downtown Budapest?

When I visited this shop several months ago, its windows were filled with bottles of the company's new Champagne perfume, which promised to give the wearer "the image and the gustatory sensations of joy and celebration" associated with the bubbly itself. Since then champagne producers have successfully petitioned the courts to enjoin Yves Saint Laurent from using the name of its product in France, although the company says it will continue using it outside the country in places such as Budapest.

I was reminded of the lure of foreign markets during a meeting with Pavel Chvosta, thirty-eight, a handsome, go-getting Czech entrepreneur who owns a fast-growing construction company called koba-zlin in Brno, has spent time in the United States trying to line up some American partners, and among other things was intrigued by U.S. stores packed with merchandise selling for one dollar or less. "This is a good idea," he said. "We have nothing like this in Czech Republic." Then he grilled me about how these stores operate and how he could go about setting up one back home.

Chvosta says he worked for a big state-owned construction company with 5,000 employees but decided to strike out on his own account a year after the revolution in the Czech Republic. "We started with sixteen employees, we have 120 today, and we do civil construction work exclusively in Germany," says Chvosta, "where we build banks, department stores, hotels, and clinics. We began in Germany because I had very little capital, and Germany was the only place where we could earn quickly money. Nobody has the big money to build things in Czech Republic, but we hope this will change.

"The competition is very stiff in Germany," Chvosta says, "and the only way to succeed is to do extraordinary things. We weren't able to start one job until late in the year and knew we couldn't work much after December 1st because it gets too cold to do concrete work. So I had three crews working around the clock, and we met the deadline.

"I used to work right along with my men," says Chvosta, "but today I spend most of my time bidding on new business, and we've been doing very good. The first year we did five million crowns or $200,000 worth of business and made a profit of about $40,000. The second year we grossed $400,000, and in 1993 we did $1.2 million with profits continuing at about 20 percent of sales.

"The secret of our success is that we do very high quality work. We keep to our time schedule in every weather situation. We stay close to our customers so we can give them exactly what they want. And we charge only 60 percent or 70 percent of what our German competitors charge. The reason we can charge this much less is that 90 percent of our costs are for labor, and since all our employees are Czech, they are happy to work for half of what German workers get.

"Our biggest problem is that the German government is very protective of the country's civil construction market, and only about 1,000 Czech people are allowed to work in it. At the very time America is opening its borders with Mexico and Canada, Germany is closing its border with Czech Republic. Another problem we had at the very beginning was with the discipline of our laborers. When someone is not on time for work, or uses alcohol in work, I send him immediately out. So people who want to earn good money in my company must be hard-working and disciplined.

"One of the big ways I hope to grow in the future," says Chvosta, "is to make joint ventures with some financially strong American entities and to interest them about building some hospitals, supermarkets, or a chain of cheap hotels in Czech Republic. I'm looking for someone to invest in these projects which my company will develop and build and have already started speaking with a good group of investors from Texas who are talking to me about building a gynecological and cardiovascular clinic in Prague. I would like also to make investment in this project because the Texas investors would like to see someone from Czech Republic also give money and be their partner.

"I'm hopeful about the future of my country," Chvosta said, "because we have a very stable government, and our Czech currency is almost convertible so that if someone from America invests dollars in a project he's pretty sure he can take his money back in dollars. The atmosphere in the Czech economy is finally very good for starting big construction projects. We need highways, bridges, hotels, and so on, and in the future I'd like to do all my business here at home because the competition is not so strong as in Germany.

"What I appreciate in American business life very much is that people there are very active, very aggressive, maybe in a little bit unpolite way aggressive, but it's very necessary. In Czech Republic all the people are waiting for somebody to come and give them something. This is a habit for forty years of living under a communist regime where everybody was very passive just waiting for the big boss to come. Now they must fight themselves to survive. It's not possible, " Chvosta concludes, "to change the minds of the older generation. It's up to the younger generation to make the new businesses our country needs very much right now."

One such entrepreneur is Ivo Kravacek, a short, bubbly, thirty-two-year-old businessman who lost his first company because of fraud on the part of his associates but started up another one in July 1993, with one Dutch and two Czech partners, in Brno located in the center of the Czech Republic. Three months later he was selling connectors and cables for use in telecommunications, computers and computer networks, audio and visual equipment, and industrial electronics imported from Taiwan, Japan, Holland, the United States, and other countries. Now he's looking for two additional U.S. suppliers of telecommunications and fiber-optic equipment.

"A small company like ours," says Kravacek, "can make nice sales and profits. In our first three months we had sales of 2.5 million crowns or roughly $100,000, and we're very optimistic about the future. Our biggest problem is money. We started the business with a little money we had saved, and our Dutch partner brought in more which we invested in a wide range of top quality items we could deliver fast and in quantity (some of the connections we sell cost only a few pennies apiece so we must sell thousands of them to make it profitable). Our competition is local and specialized, so we're doing everything we can to make our name instantly recognizable as the only supplier of quality components and connectors for telecommunications and computer systems.

"We've also invested quite heavily in promoting our products. We had 60,000 two-page color brochures printed describing our product line, and then we placed them in three major Czech trade magazines read by people in the industries we serve. We also participated in the recent big Invex telecommunications and computer trade show in Brno, which attracted 650 exhibitors.

"The market in Czech Republic is not yet established; it's still virgin, so you can enter it quite easily and be successful. But it's still about ten times more expensive to start up a business than it was several years ago. I could have launched my present company in 1990 for 50,000 crowns or so, but now I'd need 500,000 because there are so many more potential customers and the competition's a lot tougher. It simply costs more to get in business and stay in business today."

One of Ivo Kravacek's three partners is Martin Svozil, thirty-one, who heads the privately owned COMAR Svozil company founded in 1990, whose eight employees did some $600,000 worth of business in 1993 serving Czech and Slovak customers' needs for computer components imported from Germany, Holland, the United States, Hong Kong, and Taiwan.

"We started our business," says Svozil, "by rebuilding thousands of imported dot matrix computer printers so they could reproduce the Czech and Slovak languages with their various accent marks. Next we began importing computer accessories such as auto switches, printer buffers, and some parts which make easier communications possible between computers and peripherals. We're now planning to introduce some products of our own using parts imported from Taiwan. We'll begin with a bar code generator to create these groups of black vertical lines from text information using dot matrix or laser printers.

"Our business is very successful," says Svozil, "but we could grow a lot faster if we had more money and fewer problems with suppliers. In 1992 we did ten million crowns worth of business equal to $400,000 or so, in 1993 we did 18 million or more than $600,000, and we should keep up that pace."

The Importance of Raw Courage

One of the most impressive attributes of so many of these new enterprises is their raw courage in starting up businesses under frequently dismaying circumstances. A good example is a young Czech construction company called TAKO (short for Tazene Konstrukce Spolecnost) that had been part of a state-owned giant with thousands of employees before being taken over on June 14, 1991, by four of its ex-managers who had raised some $350,000 in working capital.

Most of TAKO's best employees had left, and it had no orders on hand for its high-rise, reinforced concrete silos, tanks, and towers used to store everything from water to wheat. So the partners went to work, hired a few key people, beat the bushes for business, and by the end of 1991 had booked orders worth some $500,000, which doubled to $1 million in 1992 and kept increasing.

TAKO quickly grew to more than 100 full-time employees, yet the founders knew they were missing a lot of business opportunities simply because they lacked the sophisticated management know-how that Western executives take for granted. So they called on the Citizens Democracy Corps, which introduced them to Tom Ryan.

Ryan had spent most of his adult life in the building business, joining M. W. Kellogg in 1964 as an accountant and retiring in late 1991 as Kellogg's vice president of venture operations after serving in various top management positions throughout the world.

Ryan flew into Prague, took an hour-and-a-half train ride to the industrial city of Pardubice, and began his two-month pro bono consulting assignment by looking over TAKO's financial records, along with the contract and bidding procedures it used to go after new business.

Ryan was quickly confronted by a pressing decision facing TAKO's management involving the Czech government's decision to sell the company's key fabrication and storage building, which it had been using under a long-term lease. All options were reviewed, and the decision was made to try to acquire the building using multiyear financing.

Czech banks were unwilling to lend companies money at a fixed rate of interest for more than one year. So Ryan advised TAKO to contact the Washington-based Czech and Slovak American Enterprise Fund (CSAEF) created by the U.S. government to loan money to small and medium-sized companies in these two countries.

Ryan next turned his attention to the office machines TAKO used to run its business, which consisted of circa 1930 typewriters, adding machines, and hand-held calculators. The company's bookkeeping, billing, payrolls, requisitions, purchase orders, and other back-office work was all laboriously done on these antique machines; and Ryan immediately began selling management on the idea that it should buy a small personal computer that could easily handle all this work, along with the time-consuming number crunching involved in bidding on new design and construction projects.

While Ryan felt he was making good progress in bringing TAKO up to speed on the basics, he was not doing nearly as well in areas the company considered less pressing, such as safety, quality control, diversification, joint ventures, and exporting (even though it was already doing business in the Middle East).

Worker safety is a must in the United States, but not yet in the developing world as Ryan soon discovered. Neither the Czech government nor TAKO management was ready to insist that workers doing dangerous jobs wear hard hats, safety glasses, steel-toed shoes, and the like. Ryan worked hard to sell TAKO on the importance of safety, but without noticeable success although he believes it may get on board eventually. TAKO, like most new companies, is more interested in getting product out the door than it is in the likes of worker safety and quality control. Ryan understood this, but still spent considerable time trying to impress TAKO management with its importance—particularly since Western European nations have recently established hundreds of quality standards that Czech and other companies must meet if they want to do business in this vast market.

No look at Czech free enterprise would be complete without mentioning a group of entrepreneurially minded

Franciscan nuns—some in their eighties—who capitalized on Prague's hotel shortage by renting out rooms in their nunnery.

The gloomy building they occupied on Bartolomejska Street in downtown Prague had been a nunnery since the 1850s but was seized by the communist secret police in 1948, who used its underground cells to interrogate and detain people they felt were enemies of the state—including Vaclav Havel.

The nuns got their home back in 1990 after Czechoslovakia's communist government was ousted. But the place desperately needed renovation, and to pay for it they decided to rent out 110 beds in basement and ground-floor rooms to tourists. One of the rooms is Cell #6 in the basement, whose steel door has an English language plaque on it that reads "President Havel was jailed here."

THE PAINFUL TRANSITION TO FREE ENTERPRISE

Vaclav Havel's government has unloaded most state-owned assets with the country's National Property Fund retaining 20 percent stakes in some 400 companies (although the Fund is expected to sell off all but sixty or so "strategic" holdings, mainly in banking and heavy industry).

The Czech Republic, Poland, and Hungary have long since cut state-owned enterprises off from the most egregious government subsidies, forcing them to sack workers, get rid of unprofitable product lines, and go after new markets. The Czechs, and to a lesser extent the Slovaks, are also determined to create Western-style capitalist economies in which entrepreneurs start and build businesses with capital supplied by profit-seeking investors. This rush to privatize in the Czech Republic has put companies valued at roughly $13 billion into shareholder hands. Some two-thirds of these shares, however, have ended up in the coffers of nearly 800 investment funds run by individuals with long-term management contracts but little if any experience in what it takes to grow a successful enterprise. This is the reason some of them trade at massive discounts of up to 80 percent.

In mid-1995, investors were given the chance to acquire what *The Economist* called "two of the most valuable privatizations in Eastern Europe: the Czech telecoms and oil-refining businesses." But when some of the West's top companies expressed serious interest, local officialdom threw up bureaucratic, legal, and financial roadblocks suggesting that free enterprise is not yet a *fait accompli* in the Czech Republic.

For nearly three years, a group of four Western petroleum giants operating as the International Oil Consortium have been trying to buy a 49 percent stake in the state-owned Czech Refiners, which runs the country's two oil refineries. These are valuable properties with plenty of room to grow since the Czech Republic currently boasts only 250 vehicles per 1,000 inhabitants or just over half that of most Western countries. More cars will also mean more oil consumption, which is expected to grow by a healthy 4 percent to 5 percent in the years immediately ahead.

Chemapol, the Czech Republic's monopoly importer of crude oil, also had its eye on the refineries, but its bid was topped by the International Oil Consortium's offer to pay the government $173 million for the equity together with a pledge to invest $520 million in upgrading the refineries. But the Czech government is dragging its feet, just as it has with SPT Telecom for which Western telecommunications companies appear ready to bid up to $1 billion for a 27 percent piece of the business.

3

Slovakia Learns the Price of Independence

"Slovakia is at a crossroads. Either it will strive toward a democracy or a dictatorship."
Slovak historian and former diplomat Rudolf Chmel
writing in the Polish newspaper *Gazeta Wyborcza*

I was able to travel by bus from Prague to the Slovak capital of Bratislava without so much as having my passport checked or luggage examined. The two countries had only been independent for a few months, and for all I know the Slovaks still considered Czechs family. They let our bus whiz across the border with little more than a wave.

When I got to Bratislava's Hotel Devin, which overlooks the Danube and is just a short stroll from an old square that is home to the U.S. Embassy on one end and the gleaming new Spaghetti & Company restaurant on the other, I was greeted at the entrance by two young guards packing big black revolvers. They said they were there to protect me and the other guests from Gypsies who, they said, will steal anything they can grab. There are an estimated 250,000 Gypsies in this struggling nation of 5.3 million people, although a recent census put the figure at only 80,000 (it seems Gypsies aren't all that eager to be counted). One reason advanced by the Slovak government is that some 40 percent of all crimes are attributed to Gypsies, and

40 percent to 50 percent of all youth crime to teenage Gypsies.

The Slovak Republic was born on January 1, 1993, when Czechoslovakia was broken in two. It had been independent once before when Hitler dismantled Czechoslovakia and it became a satellite of the Third Reich, fought against the Allies, and was reincorporated into Czechoslovakia in 1941.

Slovakia is the smaller, poorer, and more heavily industrialized part of the old Czech economy. Its GNP is about one-third that of the Czech Republic, which is its number-one trading partner although that's expected to contract by as much as 33 percent in the years to come. A handful of Western companies such as Nestle, Telefunken, Volkswagen, and Samsung have established operations in Slovakia, and Whirlpool has a joint venture going with washing machine maker Tatramat. But outside interest in the country so far has been modest with foreign investment estimated at a mere $130 million compared with more than $4 billion for the Czech Republic as of early 1995.

Retail, hotel, and restaurant businesses compose 60 percent of all private enterprise, with the manufacturing and extractive segment of Slovakia's economy dominated by mining, steel, aluminum production, petrochemicals, and munitions, which have all been suffering from worldwide overcapacity. Industrial production declined by an estimated 50 percent from 1991 through 1993, hitting machinery and appliance manufacturers particularly hard. Unemployment rose to a 15.1 percent in 1993, inflation grew to a worse 22 percent, and the country's hard currency reserves excluding gold were estimated at less than $700 million at the beginning of 1994. Then the economy showed signs of perking up with inflation falling, gross domestic product rising, and unemployment holding steady at 14 percent.

Slovakia's first prime minister was an erratic, middle-aged boxer and former Communist party functionary named Vladimir Meciar, who promised a new era of prosperity for all, but failed to deliver and was ousted following a parliamentary vote of no confidence on March 1, 1994.

Meciar, who was also in effect minister of privatization and head of the National Property Fund, apparently believed it was in his own best interest to keep control of Slovakia's biggest state-owned industries rather than selling them to private buyers. A mere 500 or so state-owned companies valued at around $5 billion had been sold as of the beginning of 1994, with many of the most attractive snapped up by government officials and Meciar supporters. Only about 5 percent of Slovakia's state-owned firms are in private hands, and many Western companies expressing an interest in investing in manufacturing plants have been discouraged. Thousands of enterprises have had their bank accounts frozen, and more than 100 of the better-known ones face bankruptcy.

Slovakia simply was not able to get its economic act together under the hapless leadership of Vladimir Meciar, who led a fragile two-party coalition, doggedly held on to power, and was never seriously challenged by a first-class leader like Czech Republic's Vaclav Havel. Meciar was replaced as prime minister by the former Czechoslovakian Foreign Minister Jozef Moravcik, who appeared to be moving the country in the right direction by speeding up its privatization program before he was ousted by the indomitable Meciar, fifty-two, who pledged at his swearing-in ceremony on December 13, 1994, to postpone further privatization for as far as the eye could see.

SMALL BUSINESS TAKES OFF

Yet despite this turmoil, it is difficult to ignore the way business is growing—often dramatically. I remember visiting a graphics arts studio of all things that is going flat out ten or twelve hours a day, seven days a week, producing everything from eye-catching covers for audiotape cassettes to posters for the latest Hollywood films. The studio is totally modern with young designers struggling to meet deadlines as they sit hunched over state-of-the-art computer terminals, while the firm's forty-five-year-old president in a wild

T-shirt and blue jeans confides to a visitor that if the pressure does not let up he will be a candidate for the old men's home.

I then took a cab across town to visit Slovakia's leading business newspaper called *Trend*, which is printed on pink paper like Britain's *Financial Times* and run by a slim, vivacious brunette in her mid-thirties. *Trend*, with a circulation of 40,000, is the *Wall Street Journal* of Slovakia with no-holds-barred coverage of business including the action on the Bratislava Stock Exchange.

I spent a delightful few hours one morning at the exchange, which revolves around a single room equipped with two dozen computer terminals. Several brokers usually wander in around 10 A.M., turn on a terminal to see if anyone is interested in buying or selling the few listed shares, and then leave by noon. "We have only several dozen companies," said an exchange official, "but expect to have hundreds in the next few years."

Capitalism is also alive and well in cities outside Bratislava—at a start-up company called Ameta that makes plastic hoses for washing machines, at another one producing sailboards used in windsurfing (not bad for a country that is landlocked), at a hydroponic greenhouse that is heated with effluent from a nearby electric generation plant and grows both vegetables and flowers, and at a small hydroelectric power generating plant with one employee that is expected to produce 3.5 million kilowatts of electricity per year.

WESTERN BUSINESS KNOW-HOW VISITS SLOVAKIA

Business experts from Germany, Britain, the United States, and other Western countries have started working closely with a small, but increasing, number of local firms requesting their help as volunteer consultants. This happened to Chirana Stara Tura, a mid-sized dental and medical electronics firm that got a helping hand from Ken Preston of

New York City, who spent forty years as the owner of a physical therapy and rehabilitation equipment business and is currently a professor of management at New York University.

Preston began by getting Chirana to write its first one-year marketing plan and to appoint a new sales agent in America, where it is now doing business. Then he helped Chirana get on the approved bidders list for the United Nations Children's Fund (UNICEF) Central Purchasing Center in Copenhagen, arranged for it to bid on the health sector needs of a Russian Rehabilitation Loan from the World Bank, and got the Seattle-based international health agency PATH to give it a list of potential buyers for its products in developing countries.

Manufacturing is less of a problem than marketing in former communist countries, but there are still widespread opportunities for improvements. This was instantly obvious to Carl Lavin, a retired executive from Canton, Ohio, with twenty-five years of experience in the meat processing industry, who was invited to share his hard-won know-how with the owners of the Vizop slaughterhouse and meat processing company in Presov, Slovakia, not far from the Ukrainian border.

Lavin is a hands-on guy who knows meat. He spent considerable time studying Vizop's business in detail and then held a lengthy meeting with its general director and manager, at the end of which it was decided Vizop should:

♦ cover its food containers with paper or plastic sheets to protect their contents

♦ stop piling boxes on top of each other since the bottom ones tend to collapse under the weight, damaging their contents

♦ have meat cutters wear safety gloves so they wouldn't waste valuable time protecting or repairing their hands instead of doing their work

♦ tell workers at the company's hog killing station how to

avoid creating blood spots on the animals, which reduces the quality of the meat and hence the value

♦ raise the temperature on the hog scalding machines so any hair left on the carcasses can be removed by hand (buyers had been complaining about unsightly hair on the company's smoked pork legs)

♦ stop thinking of the business as a supplier of hog meat— which limits sales and profits—and begin thinking of it as a specialty business offering a complete line of superior pork and related products, with better packaging, faster delivery, more valuable customer information, and so on

♦ hire three full-time salespeople to canvass for new business and develop customer loyalty

Lavin then stressed the critical importance of marketing by getting Vizop's management to:

♦ join him on visits to local stores to sample competing meat products, observe how Vizop's and its competitor's products were arranged in the stores' display cases, and talk about meat with the stores' managers and customers

♦ conduct marketing seminars for Vizop's eight top executives; beginning with the admonition, "We want to please our customers;" and then send out two-person teams to meet with customers and report back on what they think of the company's product line

♦ create a taste panel to track consumer reaction to Vizop's products including their flavor, color, aftertaste, and freshness

Lavin's advice has been taken to heart, and Vizop is racking up one new sales and profits record after another.

One problem mentioned time and time again by managers in Eastern Europe and the former Soviet Union is their employees' tendency to wait around for others to give them orders. This is even more pronounced among workers such as those at Vizop who have not yet learned to take pride in what they do or to think for themselves—which is undoubtedly why employee suggestion boxes are all but unknown behind the former Iron Curtain.

General Motors was confronted with thirty years of employee passivity when its Opel unit bought the assets of a defunct state-run automaker in East Germany. The first thing G.M. did was weed out people it felt could not work in teams; then it taught the survivors its "just-in-time" manufacturing methods, where parts aren't delivered to the assembly line until right before they're actually needed, and gave them the power to stop the line whenever they detected a quality problem. Today, Opel is one of the more profitable carmakers in Europe.

THE CZECH AND SLOVAK
AMERICAN ENTERPRISE FUND

The Czech and Slovak American Enterprise Fund (CSAEF) was established in March 1991, prior to the dissolution of Czechoslovakia into two countries. The CSAEF has since taken on the aspect of a holding company with operating funds headquartered in both Prague and Bratislava. CSAEF is chaired by John R. Petty, retired chairman and chief executive officer of the Marine Midland Bank, who says the fund will remain a single entity with representatives on its board from both countries, and he "does not believe this separation will have a material impact on the financial position or results of its operations."

The Czech and Slovak American Enterprise Fund, like those in Poland and Hungary, was formed pursuant to the 1989 Support for East European Democracy Act (known as the SEED Act), with a total grant of $60 million plus another $5 million for technical cooperation to bring in management consultants and training experts to work with companies in which the fund has an interest through loans or equity investments.

The CSAEF wasted no time jumping into the market, and as of September 30, 1993, its board had authorized investments totaling $22 million in forty-seven companies in both countries. In Slovakia, for example, it put money into a cattle breeder, dental instruments maker, and a helicopter company patrolling the transnational pipeline connecting Russia with Germany. It also backed a provider of real-time financial news and market data, a start-up bakery and candy shop located within a 5,000-unit apartment complex, and a cooperative for the disabled that started as a producer of decorative paper flowers but today has 375 employees making everything from kitchen products to toys and plastic components. Not all of these investments, needless to say, are successful. One example is the $103,000 loan and equity investment the fund made in a bakery that has since closed "due to difficulties penetrating the market."

Among CSAEF's first clients were two Czech mountaineers who had started up a little business making backpacks and rucksacks in their home after work. They needed money to expand, got a $69,000 loan from the fund, and now cannot keep up with demand. This presented them with a whole new set of problems, and to help solve them the fund provided an American with an MBA who lived with their business and is supported by one of the fund's technical cooperation grants.

In commenting on the CSAEF's mission before a U.S. Senate Foreign Relations Subcommittee, Chairman John Petty said, "In the communist world, enterprises thought in terms of production units and all data was gathered for that purpose. Management received commands from on high and they issued commands to those below involved in production. Prices were fixed and all economic relationships were static. In general, people were not aware of what they did not know."

Now things are different, Petty says. Three years ago, he notes in the fund's 1993 *Annual Report*, would-be entrepreneurs had only a limited understanding of the basics such as a business plan or equity capital. "Today," he adds, "we witness a different entrepreneur, one who presents more sophisticated issues, better-analyzed problems, and more thoughtful business plans. The intervening years have been well employed."

The fund's mission, Petty concludes, is to pick winning entrepreneurs in the Czech and Slovak republics "who have the likelihood of becoming commercially viable in a free market environment." Investments of priority importance to both the Czech and Slovak funds are those that help create good jobs, promote exports, improve the environment, develop energy efficiency, and strengthen agriculture.

PRIME MINISTER MECIAR CALLS A HALT TO PRIVATIZATION

In June 1995 just weeks before the scheduled date for Slovakia's second wave of mass coupon privatization, Prime Minister Meciar announced plans to suspend it in favor of distributing government bonds valued at 10,000 Slovak korunas ($339) to all 3.5 million citizens who had signed up for the privatization plan. The announcement, according to a report in the *Wall Street Journal,* stunned many people because the government had recently published a list of companies set to be partially sold through coupon privatization. The *Journal* went on to report that Mr. Meciar had never liked the coupon scheme used to privatize 500 or so companies in 1992 and that when he returned to power after his ouster from office in 1994 he immediately postponed plans to auction off shares in companies valued at more than $2.5 billion.

4

Prosperity
Comes to Poland

*'Many investors buying shares don't even know what the
company produces, and some even place orders for the
index thinking it's a listed company.'*

Polish stockbroker commenting on the runaway
Warsaw market, whose twenty-four issues
had soared 717 percent as of early 1994
New York Times

Even Poland's ex-President Lech Walesa, a former ship-
yard electrician from Gdansk, must do a doubletake
when he strolls through downtown Warsaw and spots
the Italian Snobissimo clothing palace featuring $300 shoes
and $600 cocktail dresses. Or sees, as I did, a group of
festive young people pile out of a white stretch limousine
clutching bouquets of flowers that they ran up and placed
on Poland's Tomb of the Unknown Soldier, patrolled by two
goose-stepping guards, before dashing back to their limo
and driving off. But it is all part of Poland's economic miracle
with more than half the workers among its 38 million people
employed in privately owned enterprises accounting for half
of its gross domestic product (GDP)—which surged more
than 4 percent in 1994, putting it among the fastest-
growing economies in Europe.

Polish consumers have been known to rub their eyes in disbelief as they stroll down Nowy Swiat (New World Street) in Warsaw and are dazzled by cafes, antique shops, and fashionable new boutiques selling the latest in Italian shoes, French perfume, and American lingerie. Mercedes, Porsches, and Cadillacs sparkle in auto showrooms, supermarkets rival those in Paris, and elegant restaurants such as the Belvedere on Gagarina Street with its delightful neoclassical eighteenth century dining room and orangerie overlooking Lazienki Park are waiting to be discovered.

The weekly English-language *Warsaw Voice* describes the rich variety of the city's theaters, films, musical groups, and museums, as well as the Royal Castle built in the fourteenth century and the Wilanow Palace that King Jan III Sobieski used as a summer retreat. It is just a short stroll from the center of Warsaw to picturesque Old Town Square, which looks like a Hollywood movie set since almost everything has been rebuilt following the devastation of the city during World War II when Poland was overrun by Hitler and Stalin and then partitioned for the fourth time since the eighteenth century.

The cobblestone square is alive with outdoor cafes, artists showing their wares, gift shops, and restaurants— including an unlikely Irish pub decorated with liberally captioned pictures of that country's legendary writers and poets (Synge, Wilde, Shaw, Eliot, Joyce, et al.). The place is packed with a rollicking group of young people who had parked their cars nearby after carefully removing their radios and carrying them inside since they are a favorite target of smash-and-grab thieves the world over.

An impressive 82 percent of Polish homes have color television sets. In early 1994 the government awarded the country's first license to operate a nationwide television network not to global media giants such as Time Warner and Capital Cities/ABC, but to a small Polish-owned broadcaster called PolSat that had a young Polish staff and was already legally beaming programs into the country from abroad. The Polish national channel is considered to be the jewel in the crown among several other television licenses available in Eastern Europe, so much so that it attracted the attention of media baron Rupert Murdoch, who has been holding talks with PolSat's owners. They will need an estimated $80 million or more to get the new station up and running.

In a move the Western publishing industry will be watching with interest, the *Wall Street Journal*'s European edition has begun publishing a weekly Polish language version of the paper that is inserted in Poland's biggest newspaper, *Gazeta Wyborcza*. The sixteen-page *Journal* supplement comes out every Monday, is the first version of the paper to appear in a foreign language, and is aimed squarely at the fast-growing number of turbocharged Polish businesspeople who want to stay in close touch with moneymaking opportunities throughout the world.

A handful of such opportunities are on display at the Warsaw Stock Exchange, which was founded in April 1991, does its trading in the library of Poland's old Communist party headquarters, and boasted a mere twenty-four listed company stocks as of early 1994. One reason is that the Polish Securities Commission makes tough disclosure demands on companies applying to list their shares on the exchange. The Warsaw exchange saw its stock index soar nearly 800 percent by early 1994 before collapsing by more than 50 percent as the speculative bubble burst and investors stopped snapping up pieces of companies they knew absolutely nothing about. They had been warned that the market was severely overheated, panicked the moment it ran out of steam, and headed south.

A Polish foundation recently signed an agreement with the Chicago Board of Trade—where contracts for the future delivery of wheat, corn, oats, and other commodities are constantly bought and sold—to create a similar futures exchange in Warsaw. The Chicago Board of Trade, which will own 15 percent of the exchange, has already helped establish commodity trading exchanges in Hungary, Russia, and China.

My first impression of today's Poland came when I boarded a LOT Polish Airlines Boeing jet in Moscow for the flight to Warsaw. The plane's interior was spotless, the hostesses attentive and attractive, and dinner with complimentary champagne a delight. Poland has gone all out to make its government-owned airline a world-class operation, from hiring KLM Royal Dutch Airlines to train its 1,400 people in the basics of Western-style customer service, to signing a deal with American Airlines, giving it greater exposure in the United States. All this was reflected in the airline's 1993 results when it posted its first profit of $2.8 million on $350 million earned from flying 1.4 million passengers—a 20 percent increase over the prior year.

The downside of life in Warsaw is the sharp increase in crime including an explosion in narcotics trafficking common throughout the newly independent countries of the former Soviet empire. Recently, Polish customs officials seized more than half a ton of cocaine with a wholesale value of $20 million on a Polish freighter from South America loaded with bananas and coffee beans. Warsaw's crime wave is partially blamed on Russians and Ukrainians who visit the city for several days at a time selling their wares at outdoor markets, and on the suspected arrival of the Italian Mafia.

THE POWER OF "SHOCK THERAPY"

Hanna Suchocka, who was Poland's first female prime minister at age forty-seven, gets much of the credit for the radical "shock therapy" that has given Poland a powerful entrepreneurially driven business sector, an emerging middle class, and on the community level well-entrenched local self-governing bodies that have been replacing old-line authoritarian decision makers.

This happened even though more than a third of Poland's adults still work the land (successfully, I might add, since as far back as 1991 the country's prime minister during a visit to Moscow offered to sell the Russians some 4 million metric tons of surplus potatoes, grain, sugar, meat, and vegetable oil). Unemployment continues to be a problem as recently all-powerful and now obsolete state-owned enterprises continue to fade away under the weight of their inefficiencies, leaving 2.5 million people, or some 15 percent of the nation's labor force, looking for work. This is partly responsible for the longing, visible throughout the former Soviet empire, for a return to communism when everyone at least had a job and a paycheck—even though it often amounted to little more than a handout and that ended when the system self-destructed in 1989.

RETURN OF THE COMMUNISTS

Anyone visiting Poland these days could be excused for believing that capitalism is triumphant since its economy is among the strongest in Europe, helped by just over $3 billion in foreign investment as of the beginning of 1994. But lurking beneath the surface is widespread discontent among unskilled young people who cannot find jobs, middle-aged workers whose jobs have been eliminated by privatization, older people who remember the days when the communists were in power and there was a paycheck waiting for anyone who wanted one, and Poles of every stripe who voted against the government because it had forced abortion restrictions and other teachings of the Catholic Church into the country's daily life.

All this came together on September 19, 1993, when former communists led by Aleksander Kwasniewski, head of the Democratic Left Alliance and a member of Poland's last communist government, received just over 20 percent of the vote; followed by the Polish Peasants Party, which is allied with the communists and received 15 percent; and Prime Minister Hanna Suchocka's Democratic Union, which got over 10 percent.

Waldemar Pawlak, leader of the Polish Peasants Party, was named prime minister to succeed Hanna Suchocka, who, before leaving office, said she hoped "the next government will continue our reforms; otherwise the economy will be in chaos." But the leaders of the Democratic Left Alliance obviously did not share her alarm. While they favored capitalism and integration with Western Europe, they believed their mandate was to advance reforms with a "human face" such as doubling pensions for the elderly, increasing government subsidies for state-owned enterprises employing thousands of workers and threatened by privatization, and upping spending on education and health. This caused the International Monetary Fund (IMF) to withdraw its promise of additional loans since it raised the likelihood that increased spending would bring back uncontrolled inflation. These fears were put to rest, however, when Poland's leftist-led Parliament actually reneged on its campaign promises and passed a budget in March 1994 that limits social spending and keeps Poland squarely on the road to free market capitalism.

There was a widespread feeling among Polish economists that, while privatization may have gone too far too fast, a return to a communist-style command economy was simply not feasible. They felt that Poland's new leftist regime was in for a short and bumpy ride even though its leaders had promised foreign investors they would neither turn back the clock by unleashing runaway inflation, which hit 29 percent in 1994 but is targeted for 17 percent in 1995, nor significantly increase the country's budget deficit.

Finally, the Polish government realized that if the economy was to grow in the foreseeable future, it would have to reach an agreement with Western commercial banks on settling a huge debt of more than $13 billion run up in the 1970s when hard-line communists were in power.

This was accomplished in early 1994 when a consortium of more than 450 banks—following four years of negotiations—agreed to reduce Poland's debt by about 45 percent, from over $13 billion to some $7 billion. This should make it possible for Poland to again tap Western financial markets, hastening its development toward a flourishing market economy.

In the meantime, Poland's new leaders had to cope with increasingly restless and militant workers. In February 1994, Solidarity, the labor union once headed by President Walesa that grew into a political movement and ousted the Communist party, organized a massive march protesting the government's failure to keep its campaign promises to increase wages and welfare outlays. The already-weak governing coalition that had vowed to continue a tight money policy and market reforms was caught between a rock and a hard place. The only certainty is growing political turmoil.

In commenting on the return of a communist-led government in Poland during a talk to the World Economic Development Congress, Henry Kissinger, secretary of state in the Nixon and Ford administrations, said using a "cold turkey treatment" to convert a communist economy into a capitalist one demands social and human costs that are unbearable in a democracy and can probably only be carried out in an authoritarian state. "So I suspect (Poland's) new government will try to create more of a social safety net and it may actually slow down economic progress a little bit. I don't think the communist government can go back to dictatorial ways, but it's not a good development," Kissinger said.

Polish-born Zbigniew Brzezinski, who was former president Jimmy Carter's national security adviser, is now a counselor at Washington's Center for Strategic and International Studies, and recently authored *Out of Control: Global Turmoil on the Edge of the 21st Century*. He sees difficult times ahead for Poland's Democratic Left Alliance, which he emphasizes was rejected by 80 percent of the country's voters.

During an interview on the MacNeil-Lehrer television program the day after the Poles' sweeping swing to the left, Brzezinski predicted—among other things—an increase in the government's intervention in the economy, the budget deficit, and inflation (including a rise in the price of food for the sake of peasants who grow most of it); and a slowdown in economic reform, privatization, foreign investment, and the entry of Poland into the Western economic community.

"I think most major corporations currently contemplating going into Poland will be taking another look," said Brzezinski, "and this will probably slow it down. I personally don't think such panicky reactions are justified. We're going through a kind of transitional phase in which people (in Poland who were) shocked by the cost of reforms pulled back and wanted to literally stick it to the government."

Polish heavy industry was hit by the collapse in trade with the Soviets, a runup in oil prices, and tight money. But it responded by trimming workers and cutting debt repayments, which kept it alive even though some companies went bankrupt waiting for the economy to turn around—which it has. State-owned businesses have been sold by the thousands, financial institutions from banks to securities markets have been rebuilt and are flourishing, and a promising high-tech sector has taken root. Nevertheless, in March 1995, Prime Minister Waldemer Pawlak was removed and replaced by former communist ideologist and parliament speaker Jozef Oleksy, who quickly flew to Brussels to urge Poland's admission to the NATO alliance in 1996.

U.S. GIANTS INVEST IN POLAND

Foreign capital has been attracted to Poland by mouth-watering investment opportunities, a large and increasingly affluent consumer sector, new laws allowing 100 percent repatriation of profits, and the economy's incredible growth.

General Motors, to mention one example, has announced plans to invest $25 million to build 10,000 Opel Astra cars in Poland. Opel car bodies produced in Western Europe will be painted and trucked into the Warsaw plant of Fabryka Samochodow Osobowych (F.S.O.) in boxed kits for final assembly by some 250 workers. Production was expected to start in the fall of 1994, and if the cars sell well, as G.M. believes they will, it is ready to triple output to 30,000 units a year. G.M. insisted on several tax breaks that the Polish government readily granted, including waiving charges on the parts contained in its kits so it can price its cars to meet the competition. G.M. also signed contracts with Polish suppliers for shock absorbers and wiring harnesses that it will ship to its other plants in Europe.

Italy's big Fiat automobile company has pledged $2 billion for 90 percent ownership of Poland's Tychy/F.S.M., which produced 200,000 low-cost Cinquecento subcompacts in 1993, most of which were exported to Western European buyers. And in mid-1995, Poland's Industry Ministry announced that South Korea's Daewoo Motor Company was about to sign a joint-venture agreement with Polish car maker Fabryka Samochodow w Lublinie to build 90,000 vehicles a year.

Poland's automobile industry had its spirits lifted in October 1994, when the government announced plans to build 1,550 miles of toll highways over the next fifteen years at a cost of $8 billion. This is expected to create some 150,000 badly needed jobs, while upgrading the country's roads, more than half of which are in serious disrepair.

Pepsi's $500 Million Stake

PepsiCo, Inc., plans to invest $500 million in Poland by 1998 to hype its snack chip, confectionery, beverage, and restaurant businesses. This massive injection of greenbacks—the largest yet in Poland's consumer products industry—follows the $25 million paid in 1991 to acquire 40 percent of a leading manufacturer of chocolate, confectionery products, and biscuits, which it planned to increase to nearly 70 percent by the end of 1994. These investments are expected to help raise Pepsi's sales in Poland from $100 million in 1993 to $600 million by the year 2,000 (and they come on top of the $115 million the company is planning to invest in the Czech and Slovak republics through 1998).

Some 9,000 new jobs will be created by Pepsi's huge investment in Poland, with 40 percent of the money going into soft drinks, another 40 percent into snack foods, and the remaining 20 percent into developing restaurants. New eateries will include a trailblazer in Warsaw that is Pepsi's first "three-in-one" outside the United States with a Pizza Hut, Taco Bell, and KFC (formerly Kentucky Fried Chicken) all under one roof.

Poles have been gobbling up the big restaurant chain's thick-crust pizza, its top-selling ham and exotic Hawaiian pineapple pizza, its cleanliness, and even the murals on the walls featuring views of Chicago—which is home to more Poles than anyplace outside of the mother country. Poles today have more disposable income than ever before and can afford to pay well over a dollar for a slice of pizza in a wedge-shaped container. Fast food restaurants are profiting from a sea change in Polish eating habits from the traditional big hot meal after work to our Western routine of breakfast, lunch, and dinner.

Few could have predicted that Poles would go hog wild over pizza, burritos, American-style fried chicken, or corn on the cob, which is a hot seller even though the corn has to be imported from Hungary (although three different varieties of corn have been given to Polish farmers in the hope that they can begin growing something that is just as good). French fries are imported from the Netherlands because Polish potatoes aren't good enough, although here too local farmers are struggling to grow spuds that can meet KFC's quality standards. Taco Bell's Mexican menu is also filled with ingredients that are foreign to Poland and must be flown in, with one big exception—iceberg lettuce.

PepsiCo, McDonald's, Burger King, and other chains have found that while the U.S. market for fast food is nearing saturation, Poland—like its neighbors—is practically virgin territory. PepsiCo has several restaurants in Warsaw and is opening new ones in other major cities including the university center in Cracow. McDonald's has half a dozen bustling restaurants in Warsaw and another one in Gdansk on the Baltic Sea. Burger King has opened four restaurants in Warsaw and plans to have a total of fifty throughout the country by 1998. DuPont's Conoco gasoline subsidiary plans to invest $300 million to build up to 150 gasoline stations on the outskirts of Poland's big cities and along its highways during the next six years. Finally, Hollywood dominates the movie business in Poland, accounting for all of 1993's top ten box office hits. Attendance has been declining in recent years, however, because of the popularity of videocassettes, ticket prices that have soared from twenty cents in 1990 to two dollars or more today, and the emergence of Poland's own movie industry that is starting to produce low-budget pictures dealing with local themes that Poles are flocking to see. A recent example is the thriller *Dogs 2* about Russian arms smugglers, which was written and directed by a young graduate of Poland's Lodz Film School and stars the country's top male heartthrob, Boguslaw Linda.

HOW NOT TO DO BUSINESS IN POLAND

Business literature is replete with often uproarious examples of ghastly mistakes American companies make when they begin doing business in a strange land, and Poland is no exception.

Mighty Procter & Gamble, for example, wanted to introduce its Wash & Go shampoo in Poland, so it mailed out thousands of free samples to consumers all over the country. People were delighted to find the samples in their mailboxes, one postal worker was so entranced with this gift that he sent the company flowers, and Procter & Gamble marketing mavens were patting themselves on the back. Then disaster struck when thieves started breaking into hundreds of mailboxes to grab the samples. To make matters worse, a television commercial Procter & Gamble had been running showing a woman emerging from a swimming pool and going into a shower was blasted by a Polish market research expert because "we don't have swimming pools, and most of us don't have showers. We have baths."

All this is in stark contrast to communist-built heavy industry, which turned Poland into one of the most polluted nations on earth. Black smoke from factories such as the big steelworks at Nowa Huta, a treeless satellite city not far from Cracow, routinely turns day into filthy night as it blocks out the sun.

Foreign investors want no part of these monsters while investing heavily in companies on the cutting edge of tomorrow. The big German electronics company Siemens A.G. did this when it bought two formerly state-owned Polish telecommunications companies in mid-1993, which it will use as springboards in upgrading Poland's antiquated telephone systems. Siemens purchased Zwut S.A. of Warsaw and Elwro S.A. of Wroclaw for $38.5 million, assumed $30.2 million in liabilities, and promised to invest an additional $35.3 million in capital in the next two years and $57 million in both money and training over six years.

PRIVATIZATION COMES TO POLAND

Poland began privatizing its state-owned enterprises in 1993 when it decided to give 27 million adults born after January 1, 1974, shares in 400 companies accounting for 25 percent of Poland's industrial production and employing 12 percent of its workforce, or 1.6 million people. Sixty percent of these initial shares went into "National Wealth Management Funds" run by Western investment experts, 30 percent were retained by the government, and 10 percent were given to workers. Poland's President Lech Walesa lost the leadership of his country on November 19, 1995, to forty-one-year-old Aleksander Kwasniewski, who immediately resigned from the Democratic Left Alliance that had evolved from the old Communist party and who is a firm believer in pursuing market reform, privatizing government property, and joining NATO and the European Union.

The first five Polish companies were put up for sale in late 1990, but only one attracted the interest of investors despite a television advertising blitz urging Poles to buy shares while explaining such unfamiliar terms as "assets," "liabilities," and "equity." Prospective investors wanted no part of Slaska Fabryka Kabli (wire cable), Tonsil (electronics), Krosno (glassware), or Prochnik (clothing), but they oversubscribed shares in the construction firm Exbud, whose stock was the highest priced at eleven dollars per share.

More than half of Poland's GDP is now generated by the private sector, and Poland is well on its way to privatizing in excess of 7,000 state-owned enterprises once responsible for most of its industrial production. When the conversion is finally finished, it should give Poland's economy a major shot in the arm since the managers of these companies will be able to do some things unthinkable under communism—get rid of lazy or unnecessary workers, take risks to increase profits, and unload products that are not pulling their weight.

On April 30, 1993, the Polish Parliament approved a privatization plan that calls for turning over a majority of the shares in 600 more state-owned companies to the National Wealth Management Funds, to be operated for the benefit of the country's new citizen investors with the help of loans from the World Bank.

The International Finance Corporation has been active in Poland by participating, among other things, in a joint venture between Poland's recently privatized leading steel producer and an Italian company planning to invest $299 million modernizing its facilities so it can produce 600,000 tons of alloy and specialty steel a year. The IFC has also advanced money for a $176 million joint venture between Britain's Pilkington Sandoglass and Poland's biggest sheet glass manufacturer to build the country's first float glass plant with a capacity of 140,000 tons a year.

Poland's biggest privatization was the $400 million an estimated 818,000 investors bid for a 30 percent stake in the state-owned Slaski Bank. This is the country's third largest bank with assets of $1.3 billion, and interest in it was so intense that the 80 percent of investors who bid for the minimum of ten shares were only awarded three apiece, and something like 19 percent were said to be either pensioners or unemployed.

A few days earlier, the big Dutch bank Internationale Nederlanden Groep N.V. had agreed to pay about $60 million for 25.9 percent of the Slaski Bank, making it the largest Western banking investment in Eastern Europe. The Polish government also gave the Dutch bank first refusal on purchasing another 25.9 percent of Slaski Bank, which it said it may sell after three years.

What is really interesting about the privatization of the Slaski Bank is that it was wildly undervalued by the Polish government. Within weeks after its stock was offered at about twenty-four dollars a share it was trading at $313, effectively robbing the Polish treasury of a fortune worth millions. What makes this deplorable situation even worse is the bonanza the government lost on the 25.9 percent of the Slaski Bank's shares sold to the financially savvy Dutch.

These companies and others like them are the jewels in the crown of privatization. For the remaining thousands of companies, it will be up to native sons and daughters to convert them to investor-owned enterprises able to survive in the new dog-eat-dog world of capitalism.

The Swarzedz Furniture Company: A Case Study

The government officials running Poland's privatization program undoubtedly got a Ph.D. education in the art of doing it successfully simply by watching how the country's first five state-owned businesses were put into private hands— including the Swarzedz Furniture Company.

Swarzedz Furniture owns and operates eight furniture making plants surrounding the town of Swarzedz, about 200 miles due west of Warsaw. Its more than 3,000 employees produce everything from inexpensive assemble-it-yourself chairs and tables to high-quality sofas, and for years it had been exporting about 80 percent of its output to Germany and Sweden under fixed price contracts denominated in Deutschemarks and Swedish krona.

But a massive rise in the value of the Polish zloty in 1991 clobbered Swarzedz's foreign business while increasing its indebtedness at an alarming rate. This caused it to turn its attention homeward where the soaring zloty had greatly increased its profit margins on furniture sold in Poland. The trouble was that while it knew how to get its output into the hands of foreigners, it was relatively unfamiliar with the attractive Polish market, where there was a considerable latent demand for its furniture, which has a strong brand name.

Swarzedz had been managed for fifteen years by Andzej Pawlak, an energetic hands-on executive who was caught unawares by the sudden need to run the business as a profit-making enterprise. Pawlak thought nothing of using high quality veneer for the undersides of Swarzedz's tables, which meant little if anything to customers, assuming they were aware of it. He also had a habit of making products whose materials and direct labor costs alone exceeded their price. He allowed margins to roam all over the place from -43 percent of the sales price for one brand of mattress to +65 percent for a television cabinet sold domestically (the same cabinet sold abroad yielded less than half that or +24 percent).

Poland's Ministry of Privatization realized this was the way businesses had been managed under communism, and it retained the International Finance Corporation, headquartered in Washington, D.C., and the Polish firm Doradca Consulting to help its newly liberated companies operate in the unfamiliar world of open markets. The story of Swarzedz, and what the IFC did to help, is told by Gavin Wilson, a senior investment officer in its Corporate Finance Services Department, writing in the Spring 1993 issue of *The Columbia Journal of World Business*.

Swarzedz's prospects were anything but rosy in late 1990 when it suffered a 10 percent loss for the year adjusted for inflation. "A vicious cycle of operating losses leading to more debt, higher interest charges, larger net losses and more debt had set in," says the IFC's Wilson, "fueled by a continuing deterioration in operating margins."

The Ministry of Privatization realized it could never find buyers for Swarzedz's business unless it could first reverse its negative cash flow and solve other longer-term structural problems. To do this, it focused on overcoming two conundrums facing many companies doing business in formerly socialist economies—that is, marketing know-how and pushing decision- and profit-making responsibilities down to where the rubber hits the road.

Pawlak was admittedly adrift when it came to marketing since Swarzedz's big export business had been left to a state-owned foreign trade bureaucracy, which handled the entire Polish furniture industry and had done absolutely nothing to promote the company's brand name outside the country.

This changed following the fall of communism in Poland when Pawlak realized he was now on his own and immediately set up a Sales and Marketing Department, including a product design unit run by a manager with marketing experience. Pawlak planned a sixteen-person sales force whose cost would be more than offset by savings generated by not having to pay the old foreign trade bureaucrats their usual cut off the top.

Pawlak had been accustomed to making all the business decisions at Swarzedz, and although he was an experienced executive, his one-man rule had turned his senior managers into factotums with little incentive to accept profit responsibility let alone think creatively. To make matters worse, he had no management information system in place to tell him what was going on inside the business.

Just how bad things were was quickly discovered by the consultants the Ministry of Privatization had hired to get a grip on the situation. The International Finance Corporation and Doradca Consulting found, for example, that the largest and most modern of Swarzedz's eight factories was in fact the worst performer in terms of the margins it was contributing to the business—this news came as a revelation to senior management.

The consultants decided that in order to decentralize decision making at Swarzedz, and give its second-tier management an incentive to work flat out, the company should regroup its eight factories into four profit centers based on their machinery, raw materials, customers, manufacturing methods, and the type and quality of their products. In addition, factory managers would be given control over their sources of supply, process design, production scheduling, labor logistics, and distribution.

The single most important change the consultants imposed on Swarzedz, however, was to shift the company's long-held business orientation away from export orders, which were producing generally negative margins, and toward Poland's far more attractive domestic market with special emphasis on its highest-margin products.

The Ministry of Privatization figured it could achieve the following four objectives by selling Swarzedz and four other attractive government-owned companies to the investing public:

1. Use this pilot privatization program to interest Polish people in all walks of life in investing in moneymaking companies, with the richer ones eventually becoming institutional investors.
2. Attract foreigners, including institutions, to acquire up to 40 percent of the shares in new public stock offerings, which could then be traded on the Warsaw Stock Exchange.
3. Interest government-owned Polish companies in going public by allowing them to keep some of the proceeds for investment in the business.
4. Develop Poland's capital market infrastructure as rapidly as possible so new stock issues could be efficiently distributed through the country's commercial banks.

The Ministry of Privatization felt Swarzedz was finally ready to be sold on the morning of May 20, 1991, following months of preparation. It valued the company at 125 billion Polish zlotys (equivalent to about $11 million) and launched a public offering of 1.9 million of the company's 2.5 million outstanding shares at a price of 50,000 zlotys per share, worth roughly $4.44 at the time.

Large investors were offered 1 million shares on a subscription-plus-allotment basis, which was oversubscribed by 12 percent eliminating the need to call on four Polish banks that had agreed to underwrite the issue. Just over half of these shares were purchased by foreign investors—the first time they were to play a significant role in the privatization of a Polish company.

Small investors were offered 900,000 shares through a network of 200 bank branches around the country on a first-come, first-served basis, and they were gone within hours.

The remaining 600,000 shares were divided up among the company's employee stock purchase plan, the Ministry of Privatization's financial advisers, the specialist brokers who handled the offering, the various bank branches that had sold the shares under an incentive plan, and Poland's State Treasury.

Poland's Ministry of Privatization was tickled to death by this result since Poles were unaccustomed to the idea of investing in stocks, the Warsaw Stock Exchange would not open for another month—casting a shadow over whether investors could unload their shares if they decided to cash out, and millions of potential investors were totally caught up in their country's first free presidential elections since the 1930s.

AN URGENT NEED
FOR MANAGEMENT CONSULTANTS

The withering away of communism as a kind of Big Daddy, asking little more from companies than constantly increasing output, has created an urgent need for management consultants knowledgeable about what it takes to survive and prosper under ferociously competitive capitalism. The three companies discussed next show these consultants in action. The work consultant William Kilponen did with the third company—a small pulp and paper mill—is described in some detail simply to show what managements in formerly communist countries have to go through to stay alive and hopefully prosper under capitalism.

Delecta Foods

Delecta Foods, founded in 1816, is at first glance a capitalist's dream. It turns out an up-to-the-minute line of eatables beloved by Polish consumers, has no debt and a positive cash flow, posted a small profit in 1992 on sales of $25 million, and did even better in 1993.

Yet if you visit Delecta's plants near Wloclawek about a hundred miles or so west of Warsaw and talk with Managing Director Dariusz Borysow, you'll soon learn that this producer of everything from coffee and pudding to canned meat and pretzels is aggressively searching for a foreign equity or joint venture partner to supply the capital it badly needs to finance a hard-hitting marketing plan and modernize its production facilities.

Delecta has a lot going for it. It is the leading producer of a money-saving coffee substitute made from chicory-flavored roasted rye and barley that is extremely popular with cash-strapped Polish consumers. It produces a pretzel stick called a Paluszki that is such a hit the company is running three shifts a day, seven days a week, in one factory and is getting ready to open another. Delecta is also Poland's leading producer of cake mixes and bakery supplies including frostings, coconut, spices, and raisins, and is number one in various types of dry cream mixes such as those used in coffee and in frozen desserts.

Delecta's quandary is that it is struggling to make the transition from being a state-owned to an investor-owned company while grappling with some very real problems enumerated by Richard Winger of Wheaton, Illinois, who was dispatched by the Citizens Democracy Corps to Poland to give it a hand. Delecta needs capital (and borrowing money at 40 percent is prohibitive), its key plant was last modernized in 1938, it badly lacks marketing skills, it has been hit by foreign competition, and its 750 holdover workers making between $150 and $300 a month have yet to be energized by the go-go demands of capitalism. If that wasn't enough, the management of this cornucopian business must make thousands of decisions a day on the basis of information that is far from computerized, while struggling to deal with an inadequate banking system.

Prioritizing these problems led Winger to conclude that what Delecta needed to do more than anything else was to put an end to its lousy maketing because that is where the money is. "They price wrong," he says, "package wrong, miss a new product trend, miss competitive action, don't understand their market share, don't promote, don't advertise, etc. The upshot is that they fail because they decide what to do *deductively* from their personal beliefs or past experience, rather than *inductively* by learning from the market place and testing each decision versus what competitors are doing."

Delecta is working to remedy this situation with the help of a volunteer marketing executive from a big international food company who is helping it with pricing, market segmentation, advertising, brand management, distributor contracts, taste paneling, comparison shopping, shelf-stocking strategy, and even labeling (it didn't matter if labels were put on upside down when Delecta was filling railroad boxcars to ship to government-owned warehouses for distribution to the people instead of fighting for every sale as it is doing today).

Margo Trading Company

Marketing also turned out to be a critical factor when Minneapolis food industry expert Robert Piker met with the management of the Margo Trading Company in Zielonka, Poland, which runs a big food warehousing and distribution business with operations throughout the country.

Bob Piker had forty years experience as president of U.S. companies in the food industry, had worked with other executives in the business from Jamaica to Japan, and jumped at the chance to help a company in Poland where his family had many of its roots. Piker was immediately impressed by Margo's extensive distribution system, its physical plant and equipment, its aggressive management, and its excellent reputation. He was worried, however, that it had "no economic control over its business, no specific economic goals, no budgets, and no plan to achieve economic success."

If Margo wanted to reach its full potential, Piker told the company's top management, it would have to take "a much more sophisticated approach to the needs of the marketplace." This meant using market research—which is practically unknown in Poland—to better understand its customers' requirements, and then give its sales force the training and back-up necessary to meet them. Piker urged Margo to establish monthly budgets designed to achieve specific sales and profit targets and recommended that its sales people receive bonuses when these targets are met. He also suggested Margo use local sales agents throughout Poland instead of concentrating them all in Warsaw, and begin promoting from within to encourage employees to give the company their all.

Piker believes the Margo Trading Company is at a cross-roads reached by very few businesses. It can continue its old unfocused ways and never reach its full potential, or it can exploit the opportunities ahead and achieve greatness.

Zaklady Papiernicze Wloclawek

The profusion of things a company must do right if it is to make money and grow can be seen in the specific ideas professional engineer Bill Kilponen gave the management of one of Poland's many small pulp and paper mills.

Zaklady Papiernicze Wloclawek, founded in 1899, produces students' copybooks, drawing paper, copying machine paper, and toilet paper. In 1992 it was split into four separate state-owned companies with 711 employees, down from 2,296 in 1989. After reviewing the company's operations in depth, Kilponen told management it needed to make serious changes in virtually every aspect of the business if it hoped to survive in the new world of private enterprise.

Zaklady Papiernicze Wloclawek must, among other things, upgrade its production facilities and products to Western standards, reduce air and water pollution, train its employees to work as teams, keep pushing decision-making responsibility down to lower and lower levels, and improve communications throughout its mills so that management can better handle its day-to-day responsibilities, long-term strategy, and planning for the future.

Zaklady Papiernicze's discharging of dirty water back into the Vistula River was so bad that the Polish government hit it with huge fines that become payable in 1996 and 1997, and ordered it to shut down its pulp mill until discharges were reduced, which they have been. Air pollution is also an ongoing problem, and Kilponen told management it might make sense to eliminate it by converting to natural gas.

To get Zaklady Papiernicze's problems under control, Kilponen recommended that the environmental manager report directly to its CEO and be given complete authority to act on his behalf. He also urged the company to maintain a continuous dialogue with state and federal agencies since the company's output of paper products and accompanying effluents are headed higher and thus it needs to know now what their reactions will be, and, finally, to become involved with the Polish Paper Mill Lobbying Group so it can positively influence legislation of importance to the industry.

Since the company's facilities for converting pulp to paper products are operating efficiently, Kilponen urged management to increase production in-house by installing more and better equipment that would add a lot of value to the product at a relatively low production cost. A marketing firm should also be hired to analyze the sales potential of different size papers, along with the company's ability to produce them if it installed a new pulp-to-paper machine.

Protecting the environment is important to today's schoolchildren, and Kilponen suggested the company capitalize on it by printing the universally recognized recyclable paper symbol on the front cover of its copybooks. Shipping labels should always be centered in exactly the right spot and completely glued down. They should be redesigned with the mill's name in larger, more prominent letters. Also, a new logo should be designed—one that does not show a smokestack emitting clouds of noxious pollution.

Zaklady Papiernicze Wloclawek's purchasing department must computerize as quickly as possible so that real-time information can be used in determining production levels for various products, and so there will always be sufficient materials on hand to keep the costly production machines running smoothly.

The company must also make sure that key details are agreed to in advance when negotiating with suppliers of big ticket assets. Among the most critical, said Kilponen, are:

♦ payment terms

♦ start-up services and technical information on new equipment to be provided at no cost

♦ penalties for late delivery

♦ product warranties, with suppliers responsible if a product does not perform as guaranteed and with payment withheld until it is satisfactory

♦   supplier to maintain ownership until equipment arrives at the mill site and to be liable right up until delivery occurs

The company's purchasing agents—long used to dealing exclusively with the state—should be educated in free market buying and selling procedures as soon as useful training becomes available.

Bill Kilponen then told the management that with half the output of its big new paper-making machine slated for export, its salespeople would have to quickly get up to speed on selling to foreign markets. He also suggested hiring a new financial manager with responsibility for collecting past-due receivables (or turning them over to a collection agency), finding a buyer to purchase its trucks and hire its drivers while continuing to make the company's deliveries, and closing or selling its factory retail stores if they were not solidly profitable. He further urged the company to sell its summer cottages—used as an employee benefit—along with apartments it owns.

After noting that Zaklady Papiernicze's maintenance department operates about the same as those at mills in North America, Kilponen said some changes are occurring there that might be of interest such as hiring outsiders to do routine maintenance work including elevator, computer, and communication system repairs; over-the-road vehicle maintenance; general construction (carpentry, bricklaying, concrete work, and painting); motor rewinding; and office cleaning.

Maintenance costs are also being reduced in the West, he said, by cross-training workers to do other jobs, such as teaching welders mechanical and pipefitting skills. Or requiring people whose normal job is, say, running a paper-making machine to assist maintenance workers when the machine goes down and needs repair. Repairs are being reduced in the West by using new computer software for maintenance planning, as well as predictive maintenance where the chance of a major equipment failure is being reduced by procedures such as vibration analysis, lubricating oil analysis, and temperature monitoring of high-voltage transformers and switch gear using infrared monitoring.

After telling the company's top executives that "in Western paper mills the tracking of all elements of the cost to produce any product is a very important function," Kilponen added, "it is the continuous analysis and control of these costs while maintaining high quality and productivity that will challenge this mill from now on." Specifically, he urged management to begin presenting department heads with the following operating data in high-impact graphical form each month:

♦ fixed versus variable costs

♦ lost production time versus total time in percentages for its two biggest paper-making machines

♦ production in tons per day for these machines, both planned and actual

♦ their energy cost in kilojoules per ton, total raw material cost per ton, and conversion costs per ton

♦ cost of discounts and replacement paper due to poor quality

Then Kilponen suggested management get a double whammy out of this data by setting up a "continuous improvement" team consisting of one person each from production, purchasing, accounting, sales, maintenance, planning and economic analysis, operators of the two big paper-making machines, and converting operators. The team would review each month's operating data to familiarize themselves with the costs of production and might go on to do an in-depth analysis of one of the high-cost elements and then brainstorm ways to bring it back into line.

Kilponen next turned to the vital importance of quality, which must be first class if Zaklady Papiernicze hopes to succeed in doing business in the West. He suggested that management launch a quality awareness program by demonstrating the difference between quality standards in Poland and the West. Workers must be taught how to increase quality, and every month charts must be put up showing the cost to the mill of providing discounts for poor-quality paper products and of running an order again if it is returned, along with letters of complaint received from dissatisfied customers. Employees must also become familiar with the international guidelines listing the exact specifications paper and other products must meet in order to be accepted in Western Europe and North America.

Kilponen's final suggestion to management had to do with its accounting department, which is gradually becoming computerized and can play a critical role in controlling costs. Once the computer is fully on-line, operating reports should be given to management a few days after the end of each month so it can get its operating strategy rolling for the following month. Accounting should also use the data to prepare a monthly operating report containing financial data along with consumption rates for raw materials and energy on a per-ton basis, plus all other facts usually shown in a cost report but on a consumption basis. A brief summary of the prior month's operation of each functional department in the mill should be included in the report, and managers should describe their major accomplishments, continuing concerns, opportunities, and so on.

Management should also start the annual preparation of a five-year business plan. The first year should contain details on production schedules, cost projections, sales, investments, possible changes in employment, and so on. The remaining four years would be described in only enough detail to provide a clear road map into the future.

In the not-too-distant future, Kilponen told Zaklady Papiernicze management, labor unions will begin pressuring you to improve safety conditions. "In American mills," he explained, "federal laws require hearing protection for employees in noisy areas, safety glasses for eye protection, shoes with steel toes to protect against foot injuries, plus a lot of others to safeguard workers against injuries. Hearing protection with simple ear plugs would be a good first step for you."

To provide employees with information on safety and other developments, said Kilponen, you should consider publishing a weekly employee bulletin. It could contain news about sales, market conditions, quality, employees and their families (births, deaths, marriages, promotions, etc.), government regulations, and new products that are being considered for the future.

If Zaklady Papiernicze Wloclawek puts Kilponen's suggestions into operation, and it appears it will in many cases, then it has an excellent chance of becoming a growing and profitable company along with many others helped by American management know-how—including that supplied by key executives running the Polish-American Enterprise Fund.

THE POLISH-AMERICAN ENTERPRISE FUND

The Polish-American Enterprise Fund, capitalized at $341 million, was formed in May 1990 and is headed by John Birkelund, former chairman of the distinguished Wall Street investment banking firm of Dillion, Reed; and Robert Faris, ex-president of hard-charging Alan Patricof Associates specializing in venture capital deals.

In a "Letter from Management" in the fund's 1992 Annual Report, the two men noted that Poland's "economy has stabilized and appears to have commenced the grinding process of recovery from the severe recession that has gripped it since stabilization was introduced. If so, Poland may be the first post-communist country in Central and Eastern Europe to resume sustainable growth. The process has been largely the function of a burgeoning private sector which now accounts for more than 50 percent of economic output." The fund's 1993 report added that the "private sector now accounts for some 60% of the Polish economy," and "while unemployment and industrial restructuring remain daunting problems, the worst of the wrenching adjustment to a free market economy should be behind us."

The Polish-American Enterprise Fund's biggest capital contribution is the $240 million it received from the U.S. government. A further $101 million quickly arrived from the European Bank for Reconstruction and Development, the Creditanstalt-Bankverein of Austria, and a group of seven leading American pension funds and other institutional investors. This $101 million, plus $50 million from the enterprise fund itself, was used to start the closed-end Polish Private Equity Fund to pump still more millions into Poland's independent sector.

The Polish-American Enterprise Fund also set up a wholly owned subsidiary in Warsaw called the Enterprise Credit Corporation (ECC). The ECC, it says, has become the major source of loan financing for small businesses in Poland, having approved more than 2,500 loans totaling nearly $60 million, of which in excess of $40 million has been disbursed and nearly $20 million repaid. While ECC loans were made throughout Poland's small business community, nearly half the money went to four industries: medical and health care, food production and processing, carpentry and construction, and miscellaneous services. Recent investments include:

- A $6 million working capital loan to ITI Holdings S.A. in Warsaw, whose diversified activities range from food production and distribution to advertising, entertainment, and consumer electronics distribution.

- A $1 million loan to W. Krug Ltd. in Poznan—Poland's oldest jeweler, founded in 1840—to be used in replenishing its working capital and expanding its retail network. An equity investment followed in 1994.

- A $214,053 loan to Lodgar in Nysa near the Czech border, which makes ice cream and distributes it to outlets across Poland. Lodgar used the loan to finance sandwich and stick ice cream production equipment that will enable it to reduce its direct costs of production and maintain its position in an increasingly competitive market.

The ECC makes its small business loans repayable in U.S. dollars at fixed rates through a network of ten regional Polish commercial banks with "loan windows" at thirteen locations throughout the country. These banks screen applicants and process and monitor loans, for which they receive fees based on a percentage of the interest income earned while sharing in any losses on loans originating in their branches.

The Polish-American Enterprise Fund, as you would expect, has its share of problem investments, including two early ones: Akita International Company Ltd. in Cracow and Secura B.C. Ltd. in Warsaw.

Akita designs and assembles custom electronic elements and printed circuit boards used in manufacturing subassemblies for the electronics industry in Poland and Western Europe. Akita needed money to improve its products and modernize its facility, so the enterprise fund lent it $725,000 and the equity fund invested $375,000 in return for 25 percent of its common stock.

Secura makes industrial protection gear, and air and fluid filtration products, and is the only supplier of breathing masks for Polish coal miners. It wanted to expand and received $2.5 million from the fund in the form of a $1.2 million loan and a $1.3 million investment in return for 49 percent of the business.

The Polish-American Enterprise Fund's next move was to create the country's first bank to finance private construction and mortgage financing. The Polish-American Mortgage Bank completed its first full year of operations in 1993, but it got off to a slow start because it "found that most proposals from Polish home developers were not suitable for financing. To address this issue, the bank has launched a training program which, as in the case of the ECC, is beginning to produce the disciplines and skills required for successful housing developments."

The mortgage bank makes residential construction loans to developers and individuals for up to one year. When construction is completed, it offers fifteen-year, fixed-rate mortgage loans, most of which are approved before construction begins. As of September 30, 1993, the bank had closed loans for the construction of twenty single-family homes and approved financing for twenty-two more.

The Polish-American Enterprise Fund provided $10 million of the mortgage bank's initial $16 million in capital, with Poland's Wielkopolski Bank Kredytowy S.A. and the international design and engineering firm of PHZ Polservice investing the rest. The bank was the first freestanding institution of its kind in Poland and is serving as a role model for local banks to emulate. One reason is that Poland needs financing to build an estimated 2 million new homes that would create hundreds of thousands of jobs while giving the country's economy a colossal shot in the arm.

The fund has invested in Poland's residential construction industry through a private engineering company in Gdynia on the Baltic Sea called the RB Polish-American Enterprise Company Ltd. The company sold its first housing development of seven homes for which it received an architectural design award from Poland's Ministry of Building Industry, and seventy more moderately priced "Bernadowo Hill" homes are under construction.

The Polish-American Enterprise Fund saw an opportunity to beef up the small First Polish-American Bank in Cracow, which had been started in 1989 but was in trouble because of poor credit controls. The fund brought in two experienced American bankers who introduced a whole new business strategy focusing on new products, tighter credit standards, and more aggressive marketing. They also established a workout group that recovered delinquent loans and brought accounts back up to a current basis. Of the 241 loans granted since June 1992, when the fund's management took charge of operations, only a few were nonperforming.

The fund has also made forty direct investments in private companies that it believes have good growth potential and can strengthen Poland's private sector. The most important created the Polish-American Printing Association, which immediately purchased two state-owned newspaper printing plants through liquidation. The association is completing an $18 million capital improvement plan that includes modernizing its presses and expanding its facilities at its Cracow and Gdansk plants. It is also upgrading the plants' production lines and energizing their marketing. It recently signed a long-term contract with Poland's highest-circulation newspaper, *Gazeta Wyborcza*, which joined with America's largest printer—RR Donnelley—and opened a $14 million printing plant to turn out high-quality magazines and newspaper inserts for the Polish market, which were largely imported in the past.

The fund is playing an interesting role in Poland's privatization process by locating attractive businesses, acquiring them with the help of their managers who agree to stay on, and then supplying the technical, managerial, and financial support needed to strengthen their competitive positions. These firms, says the fund, will be able to use their enhanced capabilities to forge lucrative partnerships with foreign companies. Two recently privatized firms in which the fund has made large investments are $3,184,506 for 70 percent of Hydrotrest (a top hydro-engineering construction company) and $1,122,677 for 60 percent of Energoaparatura (it installs control and automation systems in power and industrial plants in Poland).

The Polish-American Enterprise Fund and the Polish government have established and funded the Educational Enterprise Foundation to support business education by providing grants to schools, underwriting conferences, translating publications, and supporting promising business students and professors. Among the foundation's projects are an extensive bank training program, accounting and management information training, and direct technical assistance support to companies in which the fund has investments. The fund's Enterprise Assistance Corporation also provides "highly-focused grants to improve the institutional infrastructure needed for Polish private sector development. Such grants have supported the Polish-American Enterprise Clubs, the Polish Business Roundtable, the Women's Rural Lending Program, notary system reform, an economic educational television series, and assistance to Polish Government agencies restructuring domestic banks."

"The overall objective of the Polish-American Enterprise Fund," says President Robert Faris, "is to reach beyond economics to create vehicles which enable people to help themselves, to take control of their own lives, and to do so in a way that develops high standards of both financial discipline and ethical behavior."

THE BALTIC STATES
THROW OFF THE SOVIET YOKE

Directly to the north of Poland lie the three Baltic States of Lithuania, Latvia, and Estonia, which were annexed by the Soviet Union in 1940 following a secret pact between Hitler and Stalin, but took back their independence in 1990 a few months before the Soviet Union self-destructed.

These three tiny nations with a combined population of about 8 million (of which some 1.5 million are of Russian extraction) are enjoying comparatively low inflation, stable currencies freely convertible on Western exchange markets, few shortages of essentials, and continuing economic growth. Kellogg has opened a $22 million Corn Flakes factory in the Latvian capital of Riga even though it is aware potential customers have long breakfasted on heavy-duty sausage, cold cuts, potatoes, and eggs, and that it may take decades to begin Americanizing their palates. Estonia's almost completely privatized economy grew by more than 6 percent in 1994 as trade with the European Union roared past 60 percent and should easily top 80 percent in 1995 when Sweden and Finland join the union.

Lithuania has the Baltic States' largest population at 3.5 million, followed by Latvia with 2.7 million, and Estonia with 1.6 million. Lithuania's President Vytautas Landsbergis—who like the Czech Republic's Vaclav Havel is a man of the arts, highly regarded as a pianist and musicologist—was elected to his country's highest office on March 11, 1990, when it declared its independence from the Soviet Union.

Russian troops withdrew from Lithuania on August 31, 1993, and five months later the tiny country asked to join the West's North Atlantic Treaty Organization, angering Russia. Although the Russians removed their last two thousand troops from Estonia on August 31, 1994, they still have hundreds of retired Russian officers billeted on Latvia who Moscow says will be out of the country by the end of 1995. These two countries have large ethnic Russian populations including a great many retired military officers who have largely failed to assimilate by even learning a smattering of their involuntary hosts' languages. Most Latvians and

Estonians look upon the Russians in their midst as occupiers, and have not rushed to grant them citizenship or access to scarce housing.

The Richest Country in Eastern Europe

"In a region of Communist collapse, Budapest has out-paced all rivals to become Eastern Europe's unchallenged capital of capitalism."

Michael Meyer
in *Travel Holiday*

There is no better view of Budapest, Hungary, than from the picture windows of the Hotel Victoria on the promenade bordering the Danube. The city gleams across the water, and if you have the time a great way to explore it is to stroll across the Chain Bridge built in 1849 and up glittering Vaci Utca Street lined with exotic shops of every description. One of Budapest's pure joys is its rich array of spas, from the Art Noveau Geliert Baths with its elaborate mosaics and towering marble columns to the 400-year-old Rudas Baths guaranteed to cure whatever ails you—including hangovers from too much goulash, paprika chicken, and "Bulls Blood" wine topped off with mocha and caramel cake.

Hungary is the richest country in Eastern Europe; and with nearly 700,000 self-employed entrepreneurs, its market-driven economy is attracting the lion's share of international investment capital within the region, including a great deal from dozens of stellar American companies such as Alcoa, Ford, General Electric (GE), Lockheed, R. J. Reynolds, United Technologies, and IBM. IBM is opening a plant outside of Budapest in the fall of 1995, and is planning on producing more than one million computer disk drives per year beginning in 1996. An estimated $7 billion of direct foreign investment has streamed into Hungary during the past few years with $2.3 billion of that arriving in 1993 alone, thanks in part to the $875 million that Deutsche Bundespost Telekom and the Ameritech Corporation paid for a 30 percent interest in Hungary's state-owned telephone company, known as Matav.

Foreign investors, who much prefer putting their money into manufacturing rather than services, produced at least 10 percent of Hungary's GDP in 1993. Yet substantial structural changes must be made in Hungary's economy, suffering from a declining GDP, the collapse of trade with the former Soviet Union and its ex-satellites, stubborn inflation still hovering around 20 percent, high unemployment, and deteriorating exchange rates. Private enterprise continues to grow in this climate and now accounts for at least 50 percent of Hungary's GDP including unreported business activity. The sale of state-owned enterprises, incidentally, has put the bulk of the country's cement, sugar, cigarette, distilling, newspaper, confectionery, bread, paper, and glass industries in the hands of Westerners.

Hungary has a relatively homogeneous population of skilled, hard-working, and highly educated people (its literacy rate is close to 100 percent). The trouble is that this population has been both declining and growing older because the country has one of the lowest birthrates in the world and a high proportion of old folks, totaling 13.4 percent (of its 11 million people).

Hungary has largely enacted the legal infrastructure it needs to attract foreign private investment along with the policy incentives to encourage it, including tax holidays and the guaranteed repatriation of earnings and capital. This is one reason there were recently some 17,000 Hungarian joint ventures with foreign companies, plus another 2,500 companies that are completely foreign-owned. "If we look at the number of joint ventures and the amount of foreign capital invested in Hungary," says Dr. Ivan Toldy-Osz, executive president of Hungary's Joint Venture Association, "and especially if we look at the trend of development, we can estimate that by the end of 1995 the total amount of foreign capital invested in Hungary will have reached $9 billion to $10 billion." As 1994 drew to a close, however, Hungary's export earnings collapsed, its per capita foreign debt rose to the highest in Europe, and foreign investment continued to slow, making predictions of the country reaching upwards of $9 billion in capital investment by the end of 1995 very much of a question mark.

Western capital has been pouring into Hungary's automobile industry. Ford and General Motors are already in, followed by Japan's Suzuki with a $235 million joint venture to erect an automobile plant with 1,200 employees working two shifts to produce 50,000 Suzuki Swift passenger cars a year. Since the subassemblies going into these cars from the European Union and Hungary total 60 percent of their value added, they can be exported throughout the union. Suzuki also hopes to sell its Hungarian-built cars in Russia and Ukraine.

"Industrial output and construction activity is growing," noted officials of one leading Hungarian investment group. The government budget deficit is lower than expected; and the Budapest Stock Exchange, which reopened on June 21, 1990, recently traded the shares of twenty-eight companies.

Markets run by vendors selling precious foreign goods are doing a land-office business in Hungary while avoiding taxes. "We have no money and no energy to go after them," said Hungary's industry minister. "We're just happy they exist."

Government-owned firms, such as the Herend Porcelain Manufacturing Company located some sixty-five miles from Budapest, are being sold to their workers under an employee stock-ownership program voted into law in 1992. Herend Porcelain was founded in 1836 and is Hungary's oldest continuously operating factory, turning out beautiful plates, vases, and similar handpainted objects decorated with birds, flowers, and other adornments. The company has sold nearly 75 percent of its shares to its 1,500 or so employees, making it one of several dozen Hungarian companies to turn its workers into capitalists.

THE *READER'S DIGEST* COMES
TO HUNGARY (AND RUSSIA TOO)

Carole Howard is vice president of the Reader's Digest Association; and after it had launched the magazine in Hungary and Russia, she told the Westchester Advertising Club in Scarsdale, New York, about some lessons she learned.

"You've got to realize," she said, "that office space in Hungary is almost nonexistent. What is available is very expensive and usually needs extensive renovation." Even more scarce, she adds, "are phone lines with many companies choosing an office not for its location or amenities but because it has a phone line although there's no guarantee it will work, particularly during rainstorms."

In Hungary, she says, direct mail is virtually unknown and hence a hard-hitting new way of delivering your message. It can be a great marketing advantage, although she noticed that lists of names offered to her "seemed padded with names not even close to our target audience." A direct mail campaign that did work well, she noted, was a special one to 100,000 households with above-average demographics in Kharkov, an industrial city in Ukraine, that attracted attention because no company had ever done such a broad consumer mailing before.

"In Russia," Howard says, "it's best to send your material registered mail—and in a plain brown envelope. Attractive packages tend to get 'lost' in the postal system—like pretty postcards that never reach your family at home. Registered mail is very cheap—and payable in rubles—so cost is not an issue.

"It won't take you long after arriving in Budapest," she said, "to notice the traffic jams and think, 'Ah, drive time radio!' And it's true. Our research told us that generally speaking Hungarians listen to the radio more than people in Western Europe, and watch television less," adding that almost all Hungarian households have a television, about 300,000 homes have satellite dishes, one-fifth have a videocassette recorder, and one-quarter watch cable television—and that was in 1992. Radio is a weak advertising medium in Russia, she added, "because of the lack of car radios and the fact that in the evenings people prefer to read or watch television."

Point-of-sale displays on kiosks are used effectively in both Hungary and Russia (where they are called "spot-of-sale" displays). They are inexpensive, and a company's message can be easily updated every month as the *Reader's Digest* does whenever a new issue comes out.

There are problems, says Howard, but they can be handled although it takes time. In Budapest, she said, all the proposed sites for a press conference initially shown for the magazine's approval were "much too small and had no provision for translators or television." You also have to be ready for inflation "where prices seem to go up almost every day."

While office supplies are readily available in Hungary, she said, they are tough to find in Russia. "After one trip to Moscow," she notes, "we returned with a long list of supplies our editor-in-chief needed to do his job—supplies ranging from fairly sophisticated equipment like light tables and layout boards to basics like pads of paper, pens, pencils, pencil sharpeners, Scotch tape, Post-it notes, typewriter ribbons, a three-hole punch, and manila folders. He also asked us to send lots of staples. The only way to get staples is to buy another stapler—if you can find a store that has any for sale."

This problem of finding what you need has also impacted some foreign companies doing business in Hungary. Guardian Industries, based in Michigan, for example, bought a Hungarian glass company and had trouble getting everything from telephone lines installed to roads leading into the plant repaved.

Carole Howard said it was not easy launching *Reader's Digest* in Hungary and Russia. But, she concludes, "we want to be there now, encouraging the entrepreneurial spirit and being part of the rebuilding of a free market economy."

The *Reader's Digest* has a monthly circulation of 28 million and on May 24, 1995, published its first Polish-language edition with an initial print run of 160,000 copies.

WESTERN GIANTS BUY INTO HUNGARY

While thousands of Hungarians are working hard to build new businesses, and foreign companies are doing the same, some of the world's giant corporations are reaching into their treasuries and spending hundreds of millions to buy into several of the best-known companies in Hungary. This is despite the strong showing of Socialists—as the former communists have renamed themselves—in the country's May 1994 national elections, which is expected to have little impact on its market-oriented economy, dedication to democracy, or long-term integration with the West.

The biggest Hungarian deal was the $875 million Deutsche Bundespost Telekom and the Ameritech Corporation paid for a 30 percent stake in its state-owned telephone company. The two giants put up $437.5 million apiece and signed a twenty-five-year contract to operate and upgrade Hungary's 1.5 million telephone lines. They also promised to double that number by the year 2000, which should significantly reduce the current thirteen-year wait to get a phone installed. The Hungarian phone company later announced plans to sell another 25 percent of the company to the public as part of its privatization program. Hungary has also licensed a Dutch-Scandinavian consortium to build what it claims will be one of the most advanced cellular communications systems in the world.

The largest and most intriguing privatization deal concluded in Hungary so far is General Electric's 1990 stepped acquisition of Hungary's ailing, state-owned Tungstram Company, which makes lighting products and in which GE has invested close to $600 million.

Tungstram was an outrageously overstaffed manufacturer with an aging product line, an antique computer system, very little quality control, and a management that discouraged new ideas from employees—who had minimal initiative and even less team spirit. Part of the problem was that the Hungarian government had routinely confiscated most of Tungstram's profits, denying it the capital needed to improve the business. So before GE agreed to take over the company, it got Hungary to give it total control over running the business—including shrinking its army of 18,000 employees, whose wages averaged about forty dollars a week compared to ten times that much for GE's American employees.

The man GE chose to turn Tungstram into a winner was a fifty-four-year-old Hungarian executive named George Varga, who fled his homeland in 1956 when Soviet tanks crushed its bid for freedom and had risen to head a $500 million-a-year GE plastics plant in the Netherlands. Varga has since retired and been replaced by a savvy young executive named Charles Pieper, who is president and CEO of GE Lighting in Europe (and head of Tungstram), and who has built the company into a powerhouse. He has nearly doubled Tungstram's sales, he has hiked its market share from 2 percent to 18 percent in just four years in the face of Europe's worst recession since World War II, and in 1993 he posted a small profit after three years of heavy losses. And he has done it as Tungstram's sales to the former Soviet bloc and several third-world nations have been dropping like a stone from $140 million in 1990 to $60 million in early 1994.

Pieper has turned Tungstram around so that its business is now, according to him, "growing like crazy" by using every strategy in the London School of Economics playbook, beginning with speeding up the reduction of the company's workforce begun by Varga from 18,000 employees down to 9,000 through early retirement, assistance in finding other good jobs, and normal attrition. When queried about what he thinks of the company's workforce today, Pieper said, "We asked ourselves if people who come from a long legacy of working in a socialist environment can respond. And the answer is 'You bet!' and a whole lot faster than you think."

Hungary's lamp market, says Pieper, is only worth about $10 million, which is why almost all of Tungstram's production is exported into the big European market that spends some $3 billion a year on lighting. One of Pieper's first moves, after throwing away a lot of Tungstram's old inventory, was to invest a lot of money in new, advanced technology products such as high-pressure sodium mercury vapor lamps. "When you make one compact electronic fluorescent light and sell it for ten dollars," says Pieper, "it represents a whole lot more value and leverage on the organization than a lamp for use in the home selling for fifteen cents." That is why he has moved Tungstram heavily into Europe's commercial and industrial lighting market.

Another gauge of Tungstram's success apart from its rising sales and profits, says Pieper, is its progress in gaining on its two arch-rivals—the Netherlands' Phillips and Germany's Siemens subsidiary Osram. "Today we have pretax profit levels equal to Osram," says Pieper, "and next year (1994) they'll be equal to Phillips. And we're gaining at least one point in market share on them per year."

It is worth noting that six years ago when GE bought a majority interest in Tungstram it saw great potential in Eastern Europe. It still does, perhaps more than ever, but today this $60 billion-a-year megacompany, which investors value more highly than any other business in the United States, sees its biggest growth opportunities in China, India, and Mexico.

HELPING THREE VERY
DIFFERENT HUNGARIAN FIRMS

Hungarians have a reputation for being eternally depressed, pessimistic, and morosely introspective—confirmed by a high suicide rate. An international Gallup poll conducted soon after Hungary threw off the Soviet yoke found that its citizens were still the most gloomy in Eastern Europe. But attitudes are changing, and nowhere is it more evident than among Hungary's entrepreneurs, who are out to make their fortunes and calling for help when problems arise as they inevitably do. Three very different Hungarian firms that have directed their calls to the Citizens Democracy Corps are an automobile dealership, a big coal and bauxite mining company, and a security guard firm.

Stay Open on Weekends

Don Smith is a jolly giant from Dunwoody, Georgia, who recently retired as sales and service manager for the Chrysler Corporation and flew over to Pecs, Hungary, to see if he could juice up the sales of an automobile dealership named Autofit, which had been in business for thirty years.

Smith says he was dumbfounded to learn that Autofit did no advertising since it figured it has been around so long everyone knew where it was and what it did. To make matters worse, says Smith, they closed the dealership on the weekends because "they didn't think anybody would come. And when I explained that American car dealers advertise and stay open on the weekends, they said, 'That won't work here.' So I had to show them it would work here."

One Saturday Smith rounded up Autofit's managers along with several of their cars and took them to the grand opening of a new shopping center outside of Pecs featuring music, a hog butchering, and a large crowd of potential customers. By the end of the day, Smith had sold four cars, and Autofit decided to try staying open on Saturdays.

Then Smith dropped another bombshell. He suggested the company pay its salesmen a commission on every car they sold. "They had trouble understanding this idea," says Smith. "They felt selling cars was what salesmen did, just like sweeping floors was what janitors did. And they didn't see any reason why salesmen should get more money for selling more cars."

It looks like Autofit has taken Don Smith's advice to heart—it sold a record sixty cars the month after he left for home, it is now advertising in local department stores, and it is welcoming customers on both Saturday and Sunday.

Upgrade Marketing Skills

A very different kind of marketing problem faced mining industry consultant Hugh Evans of Boulder, Colorado, when he sat down with the management of a big coal and bauxite mining company called Volan in Budapest. Volan was going through the agony of transforming itself from a state-owned to a privately-owned company at the very time the industry's efforts to reduce pollution and conserve resources had cut Hungary's coal output by more than one-third in less than a decade.

Hugh Evans had spent some thirty years in coal project development and management as vice president of coal operations for ARCO, a major U.S. producer, and as president of Old Ben Coal, and felt Volan was doing a good job of moving toward privatization and would benefit from the pressing need to rebuild Hungary's infrastructure. Volan had, among other things, slashed its payroll from the bloated 2,000 employees it had under socialism down to a mere 400 and divided its sprawling operations in half to better serve the eastern and western parts of Hungary.

"Volan had managed to stay profitable at the outset," says Evans, "through careful and dynamic management and the sale of unneeded resources." But he felt it had to make some major changes in marketing, beginning with its dependence on "short-term, break-even type contracts won through a highly competitive bidding process."

Evans suggested Volan upgrade its marketing skills in order to diversify its operations by going after infrastructure, environmental, and waste management contracts. He advised its management to do this within the context of a five-year plan that would examine every aspect of the company's business, including working with government agencies such as the Hungarian Geological Survey to gather information on the location and quality of existing coal and bauxite reserves it would need to ensure its future growth.

An expanding Hungary, Evans believes, "will need newer, more efficient power plants and energy equipment," and this, together with a more aggressive marketing effort, should improve Volan's long-term growth prospects in what he admits is currently a "very depressed industry."

Resist Doing Too Much Too Fast

Hungarian companies are rapidly learning what it takes to build a profitable business—from the importance of good design and worker incentives to an emphasis on quality and not letting the moneymaking opportunities inherent in capitalism go to their heads. This last point is critical as I experienced firsthand after meeting with Dr. Tamas Matrai, a former practicing attorney and go-getting forty-seven-year-old Budapest entrepreneur who recognized the need for security services in Hungary and pulled out all the stops.

His company is called Bross Security, and to reach him I had to pass through a guard station, identify myself, and wait until Matrai himself confirmed that I had an appointment. A guard then accompanied me across the inner courtyard and up to his office, where I was greeted by two secretaries, asked to wait, and finally ushered into a huge office and directed toward a large overstuffed sofa where I was served coffee and cakes.

Dr. Matrai began our conversation by showing me a booklet listing all the security businesses he was in, from operating an armored car he said was among the first in Budapest to providing security guards to the surging number of Hungarian companies wanting protection. It was instantly obvious that the euphoria of free enterprise had Matrai firmly in its clutches. He had been grabbing at anything vaguely resembling a new moneymaking opportunity, and he had the red ink to prove it.

The no-nonsense American consultant working with Bross Security instantly recognized the potentially terminal threat to the business from uncontrolled expansion and prescribed some bitter medicine. Overhead would have to be slashed to the bone, unprofitable clients would have to be given their walking papers, an aggressive sales force that knew a potentially profitable high gross margin customer when it saw one would have to be recruited, and Matrai as the company's sole owner would have to recognize the importance of accountability (perhaps by recruiting a strong board of directors to help keep him on the straight and narrow). Do all these things and a few more, promised the consultant, and Bross Security might be able to approach breakeven in 1994. At last report, Matrai was pulling in his horns in the hope of staying alive.

Bross Security is not a prime candidate for help from the Hungarian-American Enterprise Fund. Quite a few other companies, however, are making good use of its millions, with more to come now that a management problem has been resolved and its ongoing solvency is back on track.

THE HUNGARIAN-AMERICAN
ENTERPRISE FUND

The Hungarian-American Enterprise Fund with offices in Washington, D.C., and Budapest is headed by two men with wide-ranging experience in government and investing. Its chairman, John C. Whitehead, also chairs AEA Investors and served as U.S. deputy secretary of state and co-senior partner and co-chairman of the Wall Street investment banking firm of Goldman Sachs. The fund's recently elected president and CEO is Eriberto R. Scocimara, who has been a general partner of G. L. Ohrstrom and Company, chief financial officer of Leach International, and treasurer of Cummins Engine.

The Hungarian-American Enterprise Fund is a not-for-profit corporation devoted to strengthening Hungary's private sector with equity investments and term loans ranging from $500,000 to $3 million in small and medium-sized businesses. The fund began operations in July 1990, after receiving a three-year grant of $60 million from the U.S. Agency for International Development—plus another $10 million for technical cooperation grants—including a series of basic business lessons called "Business az Biznisz." The series includes reports such as how to start a business and how to succeed in a market economy, brought to life by Hungarian actors and contained in a set of videotapes, trainers' manuals, and individual-study materials. Hungarian television has been airing the videos nationally three days a week, and the fund receives royalties on copies sold and expects to eventually recover most of its production costs.

Hungarian firms with a seasoned management team and a solid track record can approach the fund for money by putting together a detailed business plan emphasizing finance and marketing, which it will help them write. If the Hungarian firm is joining forces with a foreign partner, the fund will expect it to help strengthen the firm's management team by providing it with experienced managerial and technical assistance. The $43.3 million the fund invested from its inception through its fiscal year ended September 30, 1993, provides a vivid snapshot of how Hungary is moving onto capitalism's fast track.

The fund has invested $3 million, for example, in the exclusive Hungarian franchisor of Pizza Hut, Kentucky Fried Chicken, and Dunkin' Donuts outlets, and recently added a Baskin-Robbins "31 Flavors" ice-cream franchise.

Still more millions have gone into the first privately owned Western-style dry cleaning service in Budapest; Hungary's leading private retailer with 4,500 employees and more than $100 million in sales; a major sheep breeding company; a joint venture manufacturing customized security vehicles, armored vans, and personal cars; a high-tech company providing online financial data services for Budapest's stock and commodity exchanges; and a meat processor known for its locally famous "Pick Winter Salami."

One of the fund's more interesting investments was the $380,000 it paid in 1992 for 30 percent of Budapest's Recognita company, which had developed optical character recognition software capable of identifying the complex series of dots and dashes printed above fourteen different vowels in the Hungarian language that are essential to understanding their meaning. Recognita's revenues have soared from $600,000 in 1989 to $4 million in 1993, with 75 percent coming from exports and 50 percent from the United States alone. Recognita has opened a subsidiary in Silicon Valley, California, and is continuing to develop new products, including a quality control machine drug manufacturers can use in the production of antibiotic pills.

The Hungarian-American Enterprise Fund has augmented its Small Loan Program, which makes local currency loans of from $10,000 to $100,000 for up to five years, with a Micro Loan Program targeting those with needs of only $1,000 to $20,000. As of the end of its 1993 fiscal year, the fund had made small loans to 109 borrowers and micro disbursements to eighteen it says "have few alternative sources of capital, and limited access to loans exceeding one year's maturity."

A big payoff from all this is when the fund has picked a winner and can then take its investment and profit and sink the money into another venture. This started happening in 1992 when it sold the major portion of its shares in a private classical and pop music recording company called Quint Records Kft. to the big British music conglomerate EMI. The fund immediately wrote up the value of its remaining shares in EMI-Quint Ltd. by 28 percent above cost. It posted an even larger percentage gain when it purchased additional shares in Hungary's third largest printer at a price 45 percent above the cost of its original shares. These gains are then recycled into new investment opportunities so its "planting and harvesting" can continue.

In April 1992, the Hungarian-American Enterprise Fund invested $4 million to establish an investment banking and financial advisory services affiliate headquartered in Budapest, called EurAmerica Capital Corporation.

The new affiliate was set up to consult with companies in areas such as "their capital structure and funding, the attraction of private capital, mergers and acquisitions, privatization, and the raising of equity capital for emerging private-sector companies in Hungary and throughout central and eastern Europe." It also played an advisory role in "raising private investment funds, asset management, and the representation of major American, western European and Asian companies in the region."

EurAmerica's financial experts working out of its Budapest office have filled a unique niche by providing investment banking and financial advisory services to small and medium-sized Hungarian, Czech, Slovak, and Polish companies; regional governmental authorities; privatization candidates; and even international investment groups "often overlooked by major international institutions." According to the fund's 1993 *Annual Report*, "EurAmerica has already attracted $37 million new investment dollars into Hungary and Eastern Europe, representing a total of approximately 1,100 jobs."

The Hungarian-American Enterprise Fund also hopes to raise fresh investment capital for two equity funds that it will manage through a private securities offering for a Hungarian bank and other financial institutions, and a second one for U.S. and foreign pension funds and other international investing institutions.

The fund is looking forward to working closely with the Japanese Export-Import Bank and with a private group financed mainly by industrial companies called the Japan International Development Organization Ltd., which has already joined it in one equity investment with others being explored. The fund is currently looking at the possibility of purchasing a 25 percent interest in a small well-capitalized Hungarian bank through which medium-sized loans could be made to promising local businesses through a $100 million loan pool established by the Japan International Development Organization.

Despite this record, the Hungarian-American Enterprise Fund recently came in for wide-ranging criticism from *Barron's* weekly, published by Dow-Jones, Inc., which also owns the *Wall Street Journal*. The "Editorial Commentary" included an extensive interview with the fund's former president Alexander C. Tomlinson, who had spent thirty years as a Wall Street investment banker with such prestigious firms as Morgan Stanley and First Boston.

What annoyed *Barron's* was that Tomlinson had used the very management techniques it regularly covers in depth when reporting on profit-making U.S. firms to expand the services of the fund, whose money comes out of the pockets of the American taxpayer. Tomlinson's first transgression, said *Barron's*, occured in 1993 when the fund attempted to accelerate the pace of privatization in Hungary, and thus the number of firms available for investment, by paying a Hungarian-American named Pal Teleki "$130,000 a year on the side so that he could afford to take a key job in the privatization ministry as head of the State Holding Company. The government salary was to be $1,000 a month. Although the Hungarian government privately agreed to the arrangement," says the paper, "it caused a political scandal in the Hungarian press and Teleki was forced to step down."

Tomlinson's second goof, says *Barron's*, was hiring a hotshot group of young Wall Streeters to run the $4 million EurAmerica Capital Corporation. The group was headed by a young man named Marc Holtzman, who had worked for the investment banking firm of Salomon Brothers, "and had been very successful during four years in Eastern Europe." Tomlinson, says *Barron's*, offered "a deal that provided Holtzman and his partners a chance to earn up to $400,000 apiece in the first year, depending on financial results."

This deal came to the attention of Congressman David Obey of Wisconsin, who headed the powerful House Appropriations subcommittee that oversees foreign aid including that in the coffers of the Hungarian-American Enterprise Fund. Obey immediately froze the fund's 1993 appropriation (a subcommittee aide had confided to *Barron's* that "we think all investment bankers are overpaid"). Marc Holtzman and partners are out of there, Tomlinson retired, and the Hungarian-American Enterprise Fund's appropriation has been restored. It is back in business, and in its 1993 *Annual Report* it admits to making the two errors in judgment, which it insists have been resolved to the satisfaction of all.

6

Ennui Haunts
Romania, Albania,
and Bulgaria

*"More than half (Romania's) population of 23 million live
below the poverty line—an income of $160 a month for a
family of four. Most households spend up to 70 percent of
their income on food. In contrast, a thin layer of newly
rich, most of them well-placed members of the former
Communist party with access to state assets, flaunt cars
and expensive clothes, and eat at high-priced restaurants
in the capital. Industry remains in state hands; the government has moved less toward privatization than any other
country in Eastern Europe."*

New York Times, December 25, 1994

Eastern Europe today faces a "revolution without glam-
our," said Britain's Prime Minister John Major during
his welcoming speech to the 1993 annual meeting of
the board of governors of the European Bank for Reconstruction and Development. "We in western Europe," he
continued, "have a clear and inescapable moral duty: to
demonstrate in practice our solidarity with those who lived
under communism, who had the courage to overthrow it,
and who are now paying the price of its political and economic depredations. This is not simply a moral duty: it is a
debt of gratitude."

Three of the countries John Major is talking about are Romania, Bulgaria, and nearby Albania, which have a combined population of about 36 million and occupy a landmass totaling some 145,000 square miles, with Romania accounting for more than half the people (23 million) and most of the territory (close to 92,000 square miles).

ROMANIA'S TROUBLED LEGACY

Romania is one of the two poorest countries in Europe (the other is Albania). Much of its current troubles are the legacy of megalomaniacal dictator Nicolae Ceausescu, who came to power in 1967, turned the nation inward, launched madcap projects including his 600-room presidential palace, and was shot by a firing squad on Christmas Day 1989, along with his equally hated wife, Elena.

Romania has been plagued by inept and timorous leadership under the regime of President Ion Iliescu, which has been afraid to liberalize prices and hesitant to close bankrupt state firms or stop woefully inefficient ones from running up huge debts with each other. It has also kept real interest rates negative, stood idly by while the managers of state firms made off with their assets (to the consternation of those who hoped to take them private), and indexed wages to inflation while keeping thousands of workers in nonjobs in state firms. Romania's economy is riddled with negative numbers from industrial output and exports to real wages, which have fallen sharply since 1990. In recent months, however, there has been some evidence that the government may be ready to act, although action is not its long suit.

Romania's State Ownership Fund has been selling off hundreds of the 6,000 state-run enterprises slated for privatization. It is also liquidating unprofitable commercial companies, beginning with three firms the fund said were "without markets for their products, without sources of supply and thus without chances for an economic-financial recovery."

In December 1993, the government succeeded in convincing the International Monetary Fund and the World Bank that it intends to mend Romania's broken economy by, among other things, liberalizing the exchange rate, ending preferential credits, restructuring state enterprises so they can compete in the free market, and increasing the privatization of those companies with enough left to keep them going.

Help from the IMF and the World Bank cannot come soon enough for Romanian workers—some 3.7 million of whom are organized and stand solidly behind economic reform. It might end the chaos that has meant weeks of payless paydays for an army of workers, who are rebelling and attacking the government, backed by communist and extreme-nationalist parties.

Recently, some 3,000 railway repair workers stoned the windows of the transport agency's headquarters in Bucharest, which had to be defended by riot police. The railroad maintenance workers, who had not been paid in two months, joined the battle—and why not? The buying power of the average Romanian's wages—when he or she is paid—works out to less than fifty dollars a month in an economy where 300 percent inflation is an all-too-recent memory.

This is fertile ground for Ponzi schemes, and Romania was recently hit by a fantastic one that conned several million people into paying its promoters an astronomical $1 billion—equal to half the state's spending in 1993—on the promise that they would get back seven times their money in just three months.

Yet economic progress is visible, and foreign companies are taking notice. Romania's Minister of State and Finance Florin Georgeseu told the 1993 annual meeting of the European Bank in London that his country was making substantial progress toward creating a market economy, particularly in the implementation of a sound legal and institutional framework, in privatizing agriculture, and in improving the financial and banking systems along with the social safety net. Attention was also being given, he added, to speeding up industrial restructuring and the privatization of small and medium-sized enterprises.

The Daewoo Corporation of Korea believes in the coming of capitalism to Romania and announced in 1994 that it will pay $156 million for a 51 percent interest in a joint venture with the state-owned automaker Oltcit, with the goal of turning out 200,000 Daewoo cars a year by 1998 for sale in Europe.

Philip Morris also sees promise in the Romanian market and in 1994 said it would pay $4.4 million to buy 82 percent of the country's leading manufacturer of chocolates, hard candies, and caramels (the remaining 18 percent is being reserved for purchase by employees). The deal is being done by the company's Kraft Jacobs Suchard Division in Europe, which plans to invest some $17 million to modernize two of the company's manufacturing plants. It is interesting to note that since 1992 Kraft Jacobs Suchard has bought food companies in Hungary, the Czech Republic, Slovakia, Poland, Lithuania, Bulgaria, and now Romania.

A WOULD-BE GARDEN OF EDEN

One of the mysteries of this part of the world was whether Moldova—a predominantly agricultural country of more than 4 million people nestled between Romania and Ukraine—would turn toward Romania or Russia in early 1994 following its first legislative elections since gaining independence in 1991.

Moldova belonged to Romania until the Soviets annexed it in 1940, and this plus its large percentage of ethnic Romanian citizens led many to believe the country would lean in Romania's direction. But with inflation roaring along at 1,500 percent in late 1993 and living standards collapsing, Moldova was doing everything it could to become a member of the Russian-dominated Commonwealth of Independent States, and voters favoring reunification with Romania were soundly defeated.

Moldova's economy is based on agriculture, wine making, textiles, leather, and light industry. This tiny country produced 40 percent of all the tobacco grown in the former Soviet Union; 30 percent of all the wines, champagnes, and cognacs; 10 percent of the fruits; and 5 percent of the vegetables. Top Western firms are beginning to appreciate the country's potential and moving in. French and Australian companies, for example, are importing the latest wine-making equipment to produce a variety of primarily low-cost labels for export. Britain's B.A.T. Industries PLC is improving the quality of Moldova's tobacco. A German-Moldovian joint venture is turning out perfumes and flavorings. And America's Monsanto is selling the country pesticides for its corn fields and vineyards and hopes to begin processing its fruits and vegetables.

Moldova also hoped to strengthen its economy by slashing its budget deficit from 6 percent in 1993 to 3.5 percent in 1994, reducing inflation to 2 percent a month, privatizing close to a third of its state-owned enterprises, and wisely investing the more than $250 million in assistance it hopes to receive from the world's wealthy industrialized nations and the International Monetary Fund.

The country recently introduced its own currency called the leu—pronounced "lay"—and appears to be steadily improving its impoverished economy, which has only been modestly helped so far by foreign private investment totaling well under $75 million as of early 1994. One priority need? A plant to make good quality wine bottles to replace the inferior ones it has been importing from the Ukraine.

THE POOREST NATION IN EUROPE

The smallest of the Balkan countries, and by far the poorest of the former Soviet empire lands, is Albania, most of whose 3.5 million people live in poverty with their main source of income the roughly $400 million sent home each year by some 300,000 Albanians working as black market laborers in neighboring Greece, plus another 40,000 to 50,000 laboring in Italy, just a short boat ride across the Adriatic Sea.

The Greek government says some 1,600 Albanians who attempt to enter the country illegally every day of the week are turned back, but they keep returning since their own country has little to offer. An International Monetary Fund study found that as Albania has struggled to join the reform movement sweeping through Eastern Europe, its already feeble economy has undergone a further major contraction. There has been a sharp deterioration in its external accounts, a virtual exhaustion of its foreign exchange reserves, and a building up of external debt and arrears.

Albania is isolated from Europe by surrounding mountains, which has helped preserve its natural beauty, ancient archaeological sites, and wild habitats that are home to bears, jackals, wolves, lynx, and eagles (the name Albania is derived from the indigenous word for eagle). A guidebook to Albania published in 1994 recommends that even experienced travelers visiting the country for the first time should take an organized tour since there are "very real security risks in Albania at the moment, and in the foreseeable future. . . ."

The United States has classified predominantly Muslim Albania as the "least developed nation" in Europe. The country's economy is in a shambles, it is unable to pay its foreign commercial debts, and Parliament passed a 1994 budget that proposed to spend $741 million in the coming fiscal year, or well over 40 percent more than the government was expected to take in from taxes and foreign aid.

Parents have little money to clothe their children, who drift in and out of schools that frequently lack windows, heat in the winter, or even textbooks since the old ones spouting communist ideology were destroyed in an orgy of retribution following the death of Enver Hoxha. He founded Albania's authoritarian communist regime and ruled the country as a despot from 1944 until his death in 1985 (after taking power he said his only loyalty was to Stalin, decreed that God had died, and turned the country's mosques and churches into warehouses). A colossal gilded statue of Hoxha in its capital city of Tirana was demolished in 1991 as part of the effort to erase his memory from the Albanian national consciousness.

"Albania's economic model," according to the IMF study, "was based on two principles: complete reliance on central planning and rejection of private ownership of means of production." The report went on to say that "enforcement of these principles was carried to an extreme unknown in many other socialist countries since almost *all* forms of private property were eliminated," and Albania idealized the principle of "national self-reliance as a guiding tenet of economic policy, which, in practical terms, gave a central role to the pursuit of economic autarky."

It has been estimated that up to 60 percent of Albania's urban population is unemployed, and the average wage of those lucky enough to find work is about thirty dollars a month. Dr. Sali Berisha, a movie-star-handsome cardiologist who was elected the nation's first non-communist president in March 1992, with a reported salary of $120 a month, has embarked on a program of privatization and building a free market economy. This is not the easiest thing to do as the country's entire national income from taxes and foreign assistance in its latest fiscal year is expected to total little more than $450 million.

The aid Albania receives from the West is augmented by 30,000 to 40,000 tons of wheat a month used to make bread, the country's staple food. Farm productivity in this land—where the average farm totals an inefficient 3.5 acres—amounts to only 10 percent of the European Union's yield since the country also lacks farm machinery and is heavily dependent on hand tools to sow, tend, and harvest its crops. Albania's land privatization program is virtually complete, although many deeds have yet to be delivered and it is questionable whether this will have the hoped-for result of raising productivity considering the woefully inefficient size of the average farm.

Albania is blessed with natural resources, beginning with a hydroelectric generating capacity sufficient to meet its own needs with enough left over to export through grid connections to its neighbors. The country is largely self-sufficient in petroleum and natural gas and has rich deposits of metals and minerals including chromium, copper, iron, nickel, coal, and bauxite. These resources are not being aggressively exploited, however, because of the declining productivity of existing mines, poor transportation facilities, and the lack of capital to upgrade old mines and open new ones.

Albania's industrial sector turns out relatively high-cost, low-quality goods acceptable for domestic consumption, but little else. Housing has been privatized but continues to be in short supply, with overcrowding the norm for apartment dwellers and with few Albanians in a position to buy a home of their own. It is worth noting that despite its undeniable difficulties a recent survey conducted by the European Union ranks Albania highest among all post-communist societies in overall popular satisfaction with the country's general direction and economic reforms.

This satisfaction could conceivably increase even further thanks to the opening on May 19, 1994, of a $10 million Coca-Cola bottling plant outside the capital, which is providing much-needed jobs for several hundred Albanians and a new taste sensation for locals accustomed to drinking beer and a powerful national drink called raki, made from grapes in the lowlands and from plums in the mountains.

BULGARIA'S SLOW ROAD
TO A MARKET ECONOMY

Bulgarian President Zhelyu Zhelev seems constantly frustrated by what he calls the "barbaric war" in neighboring Bosnia, which has shut down his best trade routes to rich West European markets at a cost of about $1 billion a year. To make matters worse, the country's Bulgarian Socialist Party, with roots in its old Communist party, and the Union of Democratic Forces, which includes a mixed bag of splinter groups from monarchists to neo-fascists, have failed to rush the nation toward privatization even though they say they are committed to it, as is the Bulgarian Confederation of Independent Trade Unions.

The economy of this still heavily agricultural country, including its famous Valley of the Roses where mile after mile of the flowers are grown for their oil, has failed to emerge from state ownership and management by government bureaucrats, who have privatized only about 40 percent of Bulgaria's GDP. Prime candidates for future privatization are Bulgaria's big state-owned trucking company, its flag-carrying Balkan Airways, and its popular tourist resorts even though little effort has been made to get them into private hands.

Alexander Boshkov, executive director of the Privatization Agency in Sofia, has said one reason things are moving so slowly is that "Bulgaria was probably the best kept secret in Europe." He feels this could change, however, because of recent financial, legal, and tax reforms, along with the slow but steady economic growth he sees ahead.

Ignoring Sales and Marketing

If you had to choose the moneymaking tool that is the least-appreciated throughout the former Soviet empire, including Bulgaria, it would have to be sales and marketing, and that is understandable since it was like a third leg under socialism—you simply did not need it.

Kent Manning, former group vice president of international operations for Aeroquip Corporation in Jackson, Michigan, was struck by this cavalier attitude toward marketing soon after he began working with Gamakabel, a cable and wire manufacturing company in the southern Bulgarian city of Smolyan.

"Instead of actively promoting sales and then making deliveries to its customers," says Manning, "Gamakabel relied on its customers to place orders themselves and then drive to Smolyan to pick them up. While the company's purchasing department had two employees who traveled regularly, sales were left to the person in charge of manufacturing."

Manning discussed this situation with Gamakabel's General Manager Ilya Duevski, who agreed that the company should immediately establish a marketing department and name a full-time sales manager to run it. Manning also showed Duevski how to track the delivery status of every sale by entering new orders directly into the company's computer instead of writing them down in a small book by hand. He also recommended that Gamakabel develop brand loyalty and name recognition by aggressively protecting these valuable assets along with its familiar logo (a distinctive coil of red cable). He further suggested Gamakabel create an eye-stopping design for its stationery, business cards, and so on, as a reminder that it is an outstanding company with high-quality products.

While these strategies were designed to increase Gamakabel's business in Bulgaria, Manning felt they would also help the company do battle with its competitors in the West. With this in mind, Manning took Gamakabel's thirty-nine-year-old general manager aside and suggested he begin thinking about training a younger successor—someone who would be ready when today's trading barriers come down, Bulgaria gets a shot at joining the European Union, and hungry Western competitors really begin going after its business with tooth and claw.

The Endless Search for New Business

The Tcherno More Company manufactures high-tech marine and river systems at its factory in the Black Sea port city of Varna, Bulgaria. Like so many other companies in this part of the world, its production capabilities dramatically exceed its orders in hand. One obvious reason, immediately apparent to consultant Charles Drummond, a marketing expert from Portland, Oregon, was Tcherno More's serious loss of business—and cash flow—following the breakup of the Soviet empire.

The company has a multiyear contract to produce its low-cost, high-precision electromechanical systems for Holland's Sperry Marine N.V., but this contract uses only 5 percent of its manufacturing capacity. To get more work, it has launched an all-out marketing blitz pushing both its products and inexpensive production facilities.

A sales letter to a U.S. electronics company, for example, states flatly that "we offer some of the lowest-cost, skill-based production and assembly in the world. Skilled, highly trained machinists for $1.10/hour. Circuit boards assembled for under $3. A 10-function automobile computer with an F.O.B. price of less than $10. No, these costs are not for manufacturing in Mexico, China, or Thailand, but in *Europe*. Specifically, in modern, centrally-located, and politically stable Bulgaria."

Tcherno More—which means Black Sea in Bulgarian—is using its research and manufacturing strengths to develop a variety of new products including a low-cost search and rescue marine transponder that is in production after several years of development. It is also testing a new ground control radar system for medium-sized commercial airports, along with a fixed-base river navigation system, and is beefing up its marketing prowess using ideas suggested by Drummond.

The company is determined to become profitable in three years by restructuring its organization and developing a targeted marketing plan. The plan will stress using existing business as a source of new business, particularly for its radar systems, and bringing its considerable capabilities in the design and development of nonstandard custom tooling to the attention of prospective customers.

Tcherno More produces a variety of stamping tools, cutting tools, molds, and spray forms, as well as small machines for cutting and tooling metals, test stand equipment, and customer-specified equipment. It believes this business has great potential in both Bulgaria and its neighbors Greece, Turkey, and Macedonia, and it is going after it on all fronts with the help of trade shows, trade magazine advertising, and direct mail.

If Tcherno More can get its negative cash flow turned around by doing more business with existing customers, and if its marketing drive begins bringing in a steady flow of new customers, this anomaly of a high-tech company in Bulgaria has a good chance of making it in style.

A Tendency toward Passivity

Karen Johnson of West Hartford, Connecticut, is an experienced marketing consultant who noticed a Bulgarian tendency toward passivity when she visited Bryag-Print, a printing and publishing company in Varna, Bulgaria. In the old planned economy, says Johnson, a favorite expression among employees was "they pay me enough not to die, and I work enough not to fall asleep."

"Under the old system," she adds, "innovative, questioning employees were weeded out of government-owned businesses, and it took a while to change people's minds about how they should view themselves and their jobs. The whole process was a switch from a passive, reactive approach, to an active, questioning mentality. From ignoring problems to accepting responsibility for fixing them."

Johnson says this mindset was visible in Bryag's production standards, which she found to be unnecessarily low. Workers were accustomed to ignoring the most obvious factual errors in the copy they set in type, she says, because their salaries were based on the quantity of work they produced without regard to quality. Satisfying customer's needs, she adds, did not even enter their minds. Johnson helped change this attitude with the result that today Bryag's customers are sometimes shocked to find they are actually getting first-class work.

Pricing—the Key to Survival

Pricing was the key factor in the survival of Optical Technologies, which is part of the Bulgarian government's Institute of Laser Technology. It had been selling most of its output of industrial and medical lasers to customers behind the old Iron Curtain. These customers all but disappeared after the collapse of the Soviet Union in August 1991.

Optical Technologies knew it needed help and got it from James Mitchell, former president of Connecticut's Milford Products Corporation, which does $35 million a year making blades and saws. Mitchell flew into Plovdiv, in the heart of Bulgaria, and went right to work proselytizing the company's management on the critical need to build an aggressive sales and marketing team dedicated to winning new customers in the West. Then he showed it how to ferret out existing and potential laser users, along with the price, service, and advertising strategies used by competing companies. He also emphasized that this market research had to be followed up by building a sales team that knew its products inside and out, was supplied with technical literature on the product line, and kept informed of improvements to old products and announcements of new ones.

"Western Europe, Japan and the U.S. have produced industrial lasers that are more sophisticated than those manufactured by Optical Technologies," says Mitchell, "but they are also priced two to three times higher." The company's greatest opportunity is breaking into Western markets, which Optical Technologies is attempting to do. "Unless new customers can be found," says Mitchell, "the manufacturing facilities in Plovdiv will eventually be closed or converted to produce other equipment assuming other products can be manufactured and sold."

The Bulgarian American Enterprise Fund

The Bulgarian American Enterprise Fund, with offices in Chicago and Sofia, received its initial funding in January 1992, with authorization to invest up to $50 million in the country's private sector, plus an additional $5 million for technical assistance and training. But as Chairman Stephen W. Fillo, head of Fillo & Company, Inc., and President Frank L. Bauer admitted in the fund's 1993 *Annual Report*, they have only been able to make a few investments totaling just a few million dollars for the following reasons (among others):

1. American-style venture capital investments are difficult to find. In fact, the interest rates, taxes, falling demand and anti-competitive state monopolies discourage the start-up of new businesses.

2. Experienced operating partners and managers are difficult to find.

3. Investment decisions are highly judgmental even by the standards of venture capital . . . and it is sometimes not clear that people really understand the idea of paying back money.

4. Many state companies which would have been attractive as privatized investments a year ago are on the verge of disintegrating.

Fillo and Bauer note that economic output was off again in 1993 and shows no evidence of getting back on track. "Official unemployment is about 16 percent and continues to grow at a declining rate. Inflation for 1993 was about 60 percent. And despite some improvement toward the end of 1993, the recent doubling in the price of milk and an upcoming 60 percent increase in energy prices signal new pressure on prices." (Inflation actually hit 122 percent in 1994.)

Having said that, however, Fillo and Bauer insist that "the fundamental preconditions for a highly successful economy are in place," with the private sector now accounting "for as much as 20 percent of the economy, up from just 5 percent a couple of years ago. This is mostly in small business," they add, "because the large enterprises that dominate the economy are still controlled by the Bulgarian state. The 80 percent state sector, which includes the entire banking system, has been slated for privatization for more than two years. However, little has been accomplished to date."

This has made it tough to find attractive investments, but the fund has uncovered a few, including:

♦ Just over $1.6 million in debt and equity financing was provided to refurbish and equip a factory in Gotze Delchev to produce bread and pastries.

♦ A new wholesale food and dry goods distribution company located in the center of Bulgaria received $383,000 in debt and equity.

♦ A micro-loan program called "Nachala"—the Bulgarian word for "beginnings"—was established with a successful not-for-profit organization called Opportunity International. The fund put up $500,000 in debt, and by the end of 1993 Nachala had loaned or committed funds ranging from $1,000 to $25,000 to thirty small businesses including a bakery, telephone switchboard manufacturer, soft drink producer, dental clinic, and real estate office.

Other investments are being pursued, of which one of the more interesting is making loans to eight small hotel owners in the Pirin Mountains region of Bulgaria so they can upgrade and expand their accommodations.

"Despite the easily enumerated problems," Fillo told me in early 1994, "the situation in Bulgaria is quite attractive. The fund has seen an increase in the number of plausible projects in recent months, many with qualified managers or joint venture candidates."

The Lure of Emerging Markets

A fascinating fund that appeared in early 1994 but has yet to reach the market is the $60 million Morgan Stanley European Emerging Markets Fund, created to invest in any of twenty-two countries, which together have a "population of approximately 415 million people and produced an aggregate GDP in 1991 of approximately $1,300 billion." The fund, which is planned as a New York Stock Exchange-listed closed-end fund, would seek long-term capital appreciation and initially focus on investing in the Czech Republic, Poland, Hungary, and Turkey—the most developed capital markets of the European emerging countries whose major stock indices "have generally risen since 1992."

The "fund planned to invest as much as 50 percent or more of its assets in issuers located in Turkey for at least the first year" since its stock market has a large capitalization relative to the markets in the other European emerging countries. At some point the fund said it might also invest in any of the other eighteen emerging countries stretching clear through to "the eastern border of Russia," including such currently questionable depositories for investment capital as Georgia, Azerbaijan, Croatia, and Serbia.

The fund believes these countries represent an "Historic Window of Opportunity" since "most European emerging countries have undergone an ideological shift from communism to capitalism. Nationalized industries are being privatized in many countries, economies are shifting from quota-driven command economies to free market, supply and demand driven economies and, for the ex-communist countries, trading partners are no longer limited to former Warsaw Pact members."

The Morgan Stanley European Emerging Markets Fund would be managed by a subsidiary of Wall Street's big Morgan Stanley Group, which manages some $47 billion, of which about $5.5 billion is invested in developing or emerging countries that it is quick to admit involve "certain special considerations not typically associated with investing in securities of U.S. companies," such as:

1. Currency exchange matters, including fluctuations in the rate of exchange between the U.S. dollar and the various currencies in which the Fund's portfolio securities are denominated, exchange control regulations, currency exchange restrictions, and costs associated with conversion of investment principal and income from one currency into another.

2. Restrictions on repatriation of capital.

3 Differences between U.S. securities markets and the securities markets of European emerging countries, including potential price volatility in, significantly smaller capitalization of, and relative illiquidity of some of these non-U.S. securities markets, the absence of uniform accounting, auditing and financial reporting standards, practices and disclosure requirements and less government supervision and regulation.

4. Political and economic considerations, such as less social, political and economic stability and the possibility that recent favorable economic developments may be slowed or reversed by unanticipated political or social events.

5. Certain national policies which may restrict the Fund's investment opportunities, including, without limitations,

restrictions on investing in issuers or industries deemed sensitive to relevant national interests.

6. The absence of developed legal structures governing private or foreign investments and private property.

7. The absence, until recently, in certain European emerging countries, particularly those in Eastern Europe and the former Soviet Republics located in Europe, of a capital market structure or market-oriented economy.

8. The possibility of the loss of all or a substantial portion of the Fund's assets invested in European emerging countries as a result of expropriation. The Fund may be subject to withholding taxes, including withholding taxes on realized capital gains that may exist or may be imposed by the governments of the countries in which the Fund invests. Investors should also consider the risks arising from unlisted securities, the use of currency and interest rate hedges, stock options and futures contracts and certain anti-takeover provisions in the fund's articles of incorporation. These risks may be heightened in the case of investments in smaller securities markets. In addition, there can be no assurance that any of the economic, market or other trends discussed above will continue, or that the Fund will benefit from these trends.

Although the Morgan Stanley European Emerging Markets Fund remains on hold, a spokesman said in July 1995 that its availability to investors hinges on conditions improving in the countries it has targeted for investment.

7

The Blossoming
of Free Enterprise
in Russia

*"If the economic situation worsens further, society will
be prepared to sacrifice democracy for even modest
economic growth."*

Alexandr Yakovlev,
Mikhail Gorbachev's adviser and ideologist

I had been warned by Sergei Dardykin, a correspondent
for *Isvestia* working in Washington, D.C., that Moscow is
as dangerous today as Al Capone's Chicago was in the
1920s, and that when I arrived at Sheremetyevo Airport I
should be met by someone with a car who was big and
tough and could get me out of there quickly and in one
piece. Sergei said foreigners like me who were unfamiliar
with Moscow and the Russian language were occasionally
lured into cars posing as taxis, never to be seen again.

These thoughts were racing through my mind as I was
en route to Moscow from Kiev aboard an Air Ukraine flight
packed with people encased in heavy coats and hats, when
an obviously deranged young man seated directly behind
me started firing a pistol in the air accompanied by mania-
cal laughter. Everyone around him was alarmed until the

copilot walked back and grabbed his gun, which turned out to be a cap pistol. But it was made of metal, and it had gotten through what passed for an X-ray machine back in the Kiev airport.

"Par for the course," said a middle-aged German seated next to me who spoke perfect English, had a family back in Bonn, and worked for a mining company that forced him to spend four or five months of the year in places like Kazakhstan and Siberia. "When I'm here, I work seven days a week," he said, "because there's nothing else to do. Back home we work thirty-seven hours a week with six weeks paid vacation, which worries me because I think we're getting soft while in Russia they're getting tougher."

I had no idea what to expect as I prepared to step onto an icy set of metal stairs that had been pushed up to the door of the plane amid the swirling snow. As I started to leave the airplane, a Russian guard dressed in a thick, double-breasted, blue overcoat and fur hat took my passport.

Waiting on the tarmac leading to Moscow's nondescript main airline terminal building was a woman holding a big Intourist sign who pointed me toward an empty bus pulled up beside the plane, while everyone else was rushing through the freezing night toward a second bus off to the right. I was immediately joined by my newfound German friend, two other Germans, an Englishman, an African, and a world-traveling businessman from India who said he spent as little time in Moscow as possible, lived in London, and would soon be off for "a long holiday in sunny Australia." The bus with the seven of us aboard took off for a small private terminal beside the madhouse main one where our passports were returned, our luggage was waiting, and we were free to leave.

I was wondering what I was going to do next when I spotted a man who could have doubled for Hollywood tough guy Charles Bronson holding up a sign with my name on it. I immediately relaxed, learned that the name of my driver (arranged for by the Citizens Democracy Corps office) was Slava, and within minutes we were seated in his car with the radio playing rock and roll music and a six-inch-high plastic soccer player doll attached to the dashboard bobbing its head back and forth as we sped along a well-lit highway toward the bright lights of downtown Moscow.

"Good evening, how are you, Mr. Henderson?" Slava said in halting English just before turning off the highway onto a side road leading into the woods. We drove through the darkness for about ten minutes before pulling up beside what looked like an abandoned gas station. I figured this was it for me when Slava got out of the car, walked inside a ramshackle hut, and emerged with a can of gasoline that he poured into his car, and we were off again. Slava was my driver day and night for the next week, and we never once pulled into a gas station. He would simply appear from time to time lugging a can of gasoline that seemed to materialize out of thin air.

Slava had been a cab driver in Moscow, took pride in his encyclopedic knowledge of the city, and had recently set himself up as a car and chauffeur for hire—usually to well-heeled Americans who can afford his five dollars an hour rate, which for a forty-hour week adds up to twice what most Russians earn in a month. Slava knew about a hundred words of English, was quick to mention points of interest, and if he liked you would present you with a white, plastic ballpoint pen with *Moscow Times* written on the side in Russian after you had paid your final bill and no longer needed his services.

MEETING RUSSIAN ENTREPRENEURS

Slava was the first entrepreneur I met in Russia, and in a minute I would meet two others who were waiting for me in the small apartment in a working-class area of Moscow that I would be living in for the next week. Slava grabbed my bags, carefully locked the car, and led me up cracked and dirty stone steps into a relic of an elevator with the numbers long since worn off its buttons with the exception of floor number "4," where my apartment was located.

I pressed the doorbell, heard the unlocking of multiple chains, latches, and deadbolts, and was invited into the small flat by a balding middle-aged man named Kirile and his stunning dark-eyed wife, Natasha. The apartment opened onto a tiny linoleum-covered vestibule dominated by a refrigerator, then ran past a compartment with a toilet, another with a tub, and ended up in a little kitchen with a two-burner gas stove, sink, wooden table with two stools, and a window overlooking a busy road and railroad tracks that began feeding commuter trains into downtown Moscow at the rate of about one every fifteen minutes beginning around 6 A.M.

The living room was packed with a double bed, telephone stand, overstuffed chair, coffee table with two side chairs, television set, and plastic chandelier. The small adjoining room held a couch, desk, large chiffonier, and glass-fronted bookcase. This is how most Russians live in Moscow, including Kirile, Natasha, and their 16-year-old son.

Kirile and Natasha own a small one-room apartment occupied by a full-time tenant, and rent three additional two-room flats. Their family lives in one, and they rent the others out for forty-five or fifty dollars a day to foreigners like me—people who are passing through town and don't want any part of the $200 a day and up it costs to stay at a four-star hotel and are eager to get a taste of how most Russians actually live.

Kirile and Natasha say they are in the bed and breakfast business, which means they must stock the apartment's refrigerator with eggs, bread, juice, yogurt, cheese, and the like, and come around every day to clean up and make the bed. "It can be exhausting," Kirile says, "and the work never ends since people we rent to call us at all hours of the day and night wanting something done yesterday."

This little business is a godsend since Kirile lost his government job a little while ago, and caring for the apartments now keep his wife and him busy virtually full time. They like the money even though they say their apartments are vacant an average of two weeks out of every month. They like it so much that they are actively looking to expand the business by getting one more rental unit, which would allow them to hire a young woman part time to look after their little empire, which they hope to keep expanding. Their dream is to one day own a small hotel. "It's possible," says Kirile, "and we can do it. But it will take years of hard work, and we're not getting any younger."

After everyone had left, I did as Kirile warned me and secured all four locks, which I was not to open again until he or Slava knocked on the door and identified himself. "Right now nobody knows an American is staying here," said Kirile, "but in a day or two after you've gone in and out a few times they will and somebody might try to get in so they could rob and possibly hurt you." I took this warning seriously and was glad I did since only a few days later a young American working for the U.S.-based Ernst and Young accounting firm was found murdered in his bathtub and an estimated $15,000 he had on hand to buy a car was stolen.

After Kirile left, I poured myself a glass of tasteless Algerian orange juice, propped myself up on the living room bed, and turned on the television using a handheld remote control. There were four channels offering a badly dubbed Hollywood gangster film, a children's cartoon, a political discussion, and the Moscow nightly news featuring heavy-duty coverage of an uproar in Kiev triggered by a self-proclaimed messiah named Maria Devi Khristos, who with hundreds of her White Brotherhood followers had invaded the magnificent blue and white Saint Sophia's Church I had visited only a few days earlier and destroyed some of its most sacred religious objects.

Slava knocked on my door at 9 o'clock the next morning and drove me to the Citizens Democracy Corps office, headed by "entrepreneur-in-residence" Bob Jacoby, thirty-five, who holds an M.B.A. from Stanford, has managed several Massachusetts companies, and was part owner and general manager of a Jacksonville, Florida, refrigeration company, whose market share he boosted by 50 percent in the two years before leaving for Moscow with his wife, Donna, and two young children. Bob and his family live in a small apartment adjoining the CDC office. After I had met his Russian staff, he invited me to join him on a visit to a little start-up company in the brick-making business whose owners had asked for a successful CDC consultant from the States who was in the same business and could spend a month or two showing them the tricks of the trade.

We were driven outside of Moscow where the city suddenly gives way to the countryside and the road is lined with small wooden houses, usually painted green. After a few more miles our driver turned into what in the United States would be called an industrial park, but was in reality a wasteland of dirt roads surrounded by weeds, derelict dogs, snakes, and rusting pieces of machinery of every description, from giant gears ten feet across to a huge white plastic tank big enough to hold a car.

The factory buildings looked like they might have been prime targets for Nazi bombers during World War II and had remained gutted and unrepaired ever since. The building housing the brick-making company we were to visit was completely open to the elements, which didn't seem to bother either the man who had started the business with money earned from selling 5,000 tins of canned meat in Uzbekistan or the one running it who had been a top Russian space scientist before the breakup of the USSR and the scaling back of its adventures in the cosmos. "We had powerful boosters," he said, "but after a rocket was launched, we would always tune in the Voice of America's Russian language service to get a news report on whether it had gone into orbit or not since we wouldn't hear from our own people until three days later. I eventually lost my job and decided to try my luck as an entrepreneur."

We were ied into the building past an old white truck whose engine had been removed and was being worked on in the hope that the truck could be restored to duty as a company vehicle. Then we walked through the rubble to a rickety wooden ladder leading up to the structure's open-air second floor where the brick-making kiln was located. The kiln was heated by electricity from a thick black cable the partners had run into the building that they said had just been repaired after being cut by someone they figured was opposed to free enterprise.

The ingredients to make the bricks were mixed by a huge machine with a big rotating drum lined with metal teeth that had been bought secondhand in Germany. The machine had broken down, and two men covered with grease and grime were trying to get it running again by hammering on a fat black chain that was broken in two. First one would bang on the chain, then the other, with no visible results. But they kept at it all during our visit. This is the way it works in Russia today. You take whatever you can find, try to get it working again, and hope for the best since there's no Russian equivalent of the *Thomas Register of American Manufacturers*, listing the names and addresses of suppliers ready to sell you just about anything you need.

The two men in their fifties running this Rube Goldberg business are absolutely confident they are going to succeed. To prove it they said they had already sold five brick-making machines to farm cooperatives for use in putting up buildings of various sorts, while using the one we were being shown to make bricks for use in and around Moscow.

What impressed me time and time again as I talked to entrepreneurs in Russia—where until recently all private commerce was known as "speculation" and was illegal—was their innate understanding of capitalism. You think up something people might want to buy, you make it as good as you can, and then you let them know it is available. This is happening throughout the former Soviet bloc, and its implications are enormous.

The next day Slava drove my interpreter Kataya and me about sixty-five miles southwest of Moscow to the city of Obninsk, in which the Soviet atomic bomb was developed in the 1940s and which until fairly recently was off limits to outsiders. Today the city is dominated by the Russian Atomic Energy Ministry and contains a dozen military research institutes, a factory that makes instruments for nuclear reactors and employs about 5,000 people, and another with 120 workers turning out circuit boards for Polaroid cameras.

Some 120,000 people live in Obninsk, whose town square contains a lighted electronic sign showing the time, temperature, and radiation level. The city is a collection of huge high-rise apartment buildings with shops of every description from supermarkets to intimate restaurants on their ground floors. Kataya and I had a three-course lunch at one with an apple green decor, an aloof maitre d', and American rockers entertaining on the color television screen. Our bill came to 11,850 rubles—about ten dollars—and Kataya suggested I leave 12,000 rubles including a 150-ruble tip for the waiter, which she felt would be quite adequate although it amounted to less than fifteen cents. At a twenty-two-dollar lunch of hamburgers and fries several days later at the posh Radisson Slavyanskaya Hotel with the Moscow bureau chief of the *Wall Street Journal*, it was suggested I leave a three-dollar tip equal to about 3,600 rubles—but that is another story.

Slava was waiting for us in the car, and we set out to find Victor Klysha, who owns and manages a clothes and construction business. Klysha turned out to be a jovial, heavyset man of forty-eight who welcomed us with open arms and with great pride walked us over to a small red brick shed where he had launched his business three years earlier using money raised from selling his house.

The next stop was his little factory in a larger building where nearly three dozen women were hunched over Japanese sewing machines turning out women's dresses and children's clothes using patterns found in German fashion magazines. A slim young woman wearing a body-hugging, white, knitted pants suit was overseeing the operation where red and black checked wool fabric was being cut for delivery to the seamstresses. The dresses struck me as being circa 1950s, but Klysha insisted he was selling everything he produced and was even in negotiation to export some to America.

We then strolled over to what was Klysha's obvious pride and joy: a red brick apartment building close by his clothing factory that was being finished by his construction crew for occupancy by himself and fifteen of his top executives. Russia is woefully short of decent housing. It is estimated, for example, that 180,000 of the Russian soldiers brought back home from Eastern Europe and the Baltic States lack proper housing, with many of them and their families obliged to live in a single cramped room with shared kitchen and toilet facilities.

Klysha insisted we first stop by the construction shack to meet his foreman, who was in high spirits since he was one of the lucky ones for whom these luxurious flats were being built. We then entered the building by walking on boards thrown over mud puddles surrounding the construction site and were shown a typical apartment consisting of two bedrooms, bath, and a huge living room with dining alcove. There were large, triple-paned windows in every room, along with doors leading out onto wide balconies. Klysha then showed us his apartment, which resembled the rest, only considerably bigger with a huge glass solarium that he planned to fill with tropical plants (creating a warm, artificially sunlit oasis where he could escape Russia's depressing winters where temperatures plunge below zero for weeks on end).

As we were leaving the building, Klysha took a detour into the basement, which he said would be filled with laundry equipment, game and meeting rooms, and anything else he could think of to make life more pleasant for his top management team and himself. I then asked him the question I asked every entrepreneur I met on my journey from Prague to Kiev: "What are your biggest problems?" His reply: "I don't have any!" And I believed him.

EXPLORING MY MOSCOW NEIGHBORHOOD

My first two nights in Moscow were spent in my little apartment making my own meals from whatever was left in the refrigerator from breakfast. The third night I decided to explore the shops and sidewalk kiosks several blocks away in the hope of finding something exciting to eat for dinner. It was dark outside, the temperature was below freezing, and little old ladies were huddled together alongside the building talking animatedly, while people going home from work stood stoically in a makeshift shelter waiting for rush-hour buses so packed it was a toss-up whether they could squeeze on or not.

My first stop was a brightly lit kiosk selling daily newspapers, romance magazines, cigarettes, Barbie dolls, cheap vodka, lipstick, sanitary napkins, and countless other items people buy on the fly. My eye was caught by two cans of imported Heineken beer going for 900 rubles apiece, or less than one dollar per can. I pointed to the cans, held up two fingers, shoved 1,800 rubles through a little window, and was handed the beer. What I had forgotten was that in this part of the world people are expected to have their own shopping bags, and I had none. So I stuffed the beer in my coat pocket thinking of the good old bag-rich United States where supermarket checkout clerks always ask, "Do you prefer paper or plastic?"

My next stop was a kind of hole-in-the-wall general store selling sausages, eggs, shoes, condoms, vegetables, mittens, and—praise be to God—one giant-size can of Heinz baked beans and another of Dole pineapple. This was to be my dinner, but first I had to attract the attention of the two shopgirls leaning against the cash register puffing on cigarettes. I approached them, smiled, pointed to the beans and pineapple, handed them 1,400 rubles, deposited the cans in two other pockets, and headed home to dinner.

That weekend I decided to become a tourist and on Saturday morning had Slava drive me to Red Square for a visit to Lenin's Mausoleum, Saint Basil's Cathedral, and the giant GUM department store where frozen Snickers bars are sold everywhere you look and Russia's first automated currency exchange was installed on February 16, 1994, offering dollars, francs, marks, pounds, and rubles at the official daily rate.

You enter the vastness of Red Square through a narrow opening where you are examined by soldiers on the lookout for verboten cameras. You then stroll over to Lenin's squat stone tomb and enter a sloping corridor that soon brings you face-to-face with the waxen corpse of the revolutionary who led Russian workers in an uprising against the czar in 1917, proclaimed "the worldwide socialist revolution" from atop an armored car, and used brutal force to collectivize and terrorize the Russian people until his death of a cerebral hemorrhage in 1924. Nikita Khrushchev once said that Lenin, along with Marx and Engels, would "not be forgotten until shrimps learn to sing." Yet Lenin, at least, seems earmarked for oblivion. Moscow's Central Lenin Museum just off Red Square, jammed with mementos including his Rolls-

Royce, has been closed, and the goose-stepping guards were removed from Lenin's last resting place on October 6, 1993, by order of Boris Yeltsin. The betting is that any day now Vladimir Ilyich Lenin's mummified remains will be shipped off to Saint Petersburg—possibly by sealed train—and buried next to his mother and sister as he requested in his will.

As we were driving back to my tiny apartment from Red Square, I asked Slava to stop near an entrance to the Moscow Metro so I could see this world-famous tourist attraction for myself. Slava treated me to the ride, which cost several pennies, and I waited expectantly to see such wonders as the subway's famed statuary, stained glass, ceiling murals, and magnificent crystal chandeliers that adorn the Komsomolskaya and other major stations that make up the inner ring encircling the city center. But no such luck. We were in the sticks where paint was peeling off the walls, lightbulbs were out in the ceiling, and tiles were missing everywhere you looked.

After lunch at my apartment, I decided to investigate the hullabaloo of entrepreneurship that I was told takes over my local town square every weekend. The crowds of shoppers were so thick that it was difficult to move through what had to be several hundred people hawking just about anything imaginable, from audiotapes to nesting *matryoshka* dolls. The most numerous were women, who account for most of the unemployment in Russia. They were bundled up against the cold selling items to raise a few rubles to help make ends meet: a pair of knitted wool socks, a sack of carrots, a well-worn man's jacket, or even two empty plastic spray bottles. The most entrepreneurial were women holding bags filled with long loaves of bread they were selling at about double the price they had paid for them after standing in line at a state-owned bakery.

More aggressive vendors had staked a claim on a bigger piece of the sidewalk by opening up folding, three-feet-tall, plastic boxes containing cut flowers; others stood behind carts filled with fresh fruit, ice cream, or soda pop; while the most fortunate sat inside the relative comfort of their often-heated kiosks.

Every street vendor I saw during my journey, but especially those in Kiev and Moscow, was standing out there in the often-freezing cold because they desperately needed the money. American vendors may spend their Saturdays selling at a nearby flea market because it is something to do, they enjoy the camaraderie with other dealers, and they may take home a little mad money. But once you get into Ukraine and Russia it is very serious business indeed.

RUSSIAN HISTORY
GOES TO THE HIGHEST BIDDER

I was reminded of this again when the New York headquarters of Sotheby's, the big British international auction house founded in 1744, sold $6,817,197 worth of unique artifacts from Russia's space program, primarily owned by those intimately connected with the artifacts, or their heirs. More than 200 items to be auctioned were lavishly depicted in a half-inch-thick color catalog selling for twenty-five dollars in the United States and thirty-nine dollars overseas.

When a reporter for CNN asked why Russians would put such national treasures up for sale, Mikhail Gorbachev's former science adviser said, "I think they are desperate. Many of them simply are trying for sheer survival, and a little bit of money they would earn from this auction would be helpful to them."

Sotheby's representatives spent years traveling back and forth to Russia examining articles of potential interest to American and other Western collectors and convincing their owners to put them on the auction block. What they ended up with was an eclectic collection of pieces including a cosmonaut mannequin named "Ivan Ivanovich" with a painted face, glass eyes, and jointed arms and legs that went into space on March 23, 1961, and sold for $189,500; a survival knife cosmonauts could use to protect themselves if they were attacked by wild animals when they returned to earth that sold for $9,775, and a child's "mama" doll that cosmonaut Victor Patsayev autographed—even though it was considered bad luck—before he and two others were killed on their return flight when their capsule's descent valve opened prematurely and they were suffocated. "The catastrophe," according to the Sotheby's catalog, "was followed by a wave of public mourning that has been compared to America's after the assassination of John F. Kennedy." The doll fetched $3,450.

Among the items at Sotheby's attracting the most attention from bidders throughout the world were the Kosmos 1443 capsule designed as a crew-carrying spaceship and used only once in 1983 as a cargo vessel, which sold for $552,500; and the Soyuz TM-10 space capsule launched on August 1, 1990, with two Russian cosmonauts aboard to link up with the MIR space station, and returned to earth a little over four months later, which commanded a record bid of $1,652,500.

Three other items of importance to historians were the slide rule used by the legendary "chief designer" of the Soviet space program, Sergey Korolev, which sold for $24,150; the "extraordinarily frank" private diaries and notebooks of Dr. Vasiliy P. Mishin, who steered the Soviet space program for years, which went for $211,500; and a letter written by Yuri Gagarin describing his historic first manned flight in space on April 12, 1961, which was knocked down for $354,500.

These five irreplaceable pieces of Russian space memorabilia were purchased for a total of $2,795,150 by an unnamed American who Sotheby's says regards himself as their temporary custodian, would like to see them publicly exhibited someplace such as Washington's National Air and Space Museum, and "hopes that one day it might be possible for these objects to find their way back to Russia."

The desperate need for money behind Sotheby's New York sale of Soviet space history was repeated six months later in its London auction rooms by the impoverished Russian widow of British superspy and traitor, Harold Adrian Russell Philby. "Kim" Philby spent nearly two decades as a Soviet double agent passing the most-sensitive secrets to the KGB before fleeing to Moscow, where he lived for the last quarter-century of his life. Sotheby's sold everything from eleven letters Philby received from the British writer Graham Greene, which fetched $41,300, to a plastic model of a spy satellite the KGB had given him as a present on his seventy-fifth birthday, which went for $9,340—all for a total of $238,332.

THE TURMOIL UNLEASHED
BY THE COLLAPSE OF THE USSR

"Never before in history has such a huge empire come un- glued so fast," said *Business Week*, following the breakup of what it called the "Soviet monolith."

Yet this is just the start of the turmoil ahead for the new republics created by the collapse of the USSR, according to John Edwin Mroz, founding president of the Institute for EastWest Studies in New York City. "The peoples of eastern Europe and Russia," says Mroz, "continue to deal simulta- neously with four distinct but related sets of problems: dis- mantling the shell of communism; navigating the transition to new political and economic systems; coping with the chal- lenges intrinsic to building and maintaining a democracy; and facing up to the endemic problems that preceded both communism and the transition to civil societies."

Reports released at the end of 1993 by Russia's Eco- nomic Ministry and State Committee on Statistics contained a few rays of hope. They predicted that the country's GNP would contract by only 3 percent in 1994 compared to 12 percent in 1993, that citizens' actual income in 1994 would be 3 to 5 percent less than in 1993, and that 1994 produc- tion would fall by 6 percent (a decided improvement over the precipitous 29 percent collapse in 1993).

Roughly half of Russia's 1993 exports went to the Euro- pean Union's twelve member countries, which bought more than $17 billion worth of minerals, metals, and wood, while sending Russia machinery, spare parts, and food valued at $13.5 billion. The European Union is giving Russia time to restructure its key industries to meet free market competi- tion by protecting her against its powerhouse companies.

At the same time, Russia is allowing European companies to set up shop inside its borders and repatriate both their investments and profits.

The hope so many see in Russia (despite its undeniable problems including spending more bailing out antiquated industries than on education and health combined) is that it is a vast land stretching 5,500 miles across multiple time zones (nearly twice as large as the United States), boasts vast mineral resources, has a still-powerful industrial base, and possesses awesome intellectual wealth as its historic achievements in the black vastness of space make abundantly clear.

Russia's most readily available source of major wealth is its mineral resources. The country is the world's largest producer of natural gas with vast untapped reserves, is a major producer of petroleum and coal, and is rich in non-ferrous metals (copper, manganese, bauxite, uranium, etc.), as well as diamonds, gold, silver, and platinum.

The country is an important industrial power today, with the potential of becoming a superpower tomorrow. It is already a big producer of machinery, steel, trucks, weapons, chemicals, timber and wood products, paper, and petroleum products with a current crude oil refining capacity of about eight million barrels a day. Raw materials and manufactured goods dominate Russia's exports, but its intellectual resources are also beginning to earn desperately needed foreign currency. This brainpower is concentrated in Russia's great universities and scientific institutes where it is being sought out by research-minded corporations such as DuPont, Monsanto, and Perkin-Elmer, along with brokers who understand its value in terms of commercially promising new technologies.

One of the most lucrative of these technologies with tremendous upside potential is Russia's prowess in space, exemplified by its massive Proton rocket that has lifted well over 200 payloads into the heavens since its introduction in the 1960s. The highly cost-effective Proton has proven crucial in winning Russia's government-owned Khrunichev State Research and Production Center more than $1 billion in space contracts from Western companies and governments in recent years. This business includes rockets to launch the Iridium global telephone system being built by Motorola in a joint venture with the Loral Corporation, in which Khrunichev has actually purchased a 5 percent interest for $40 million. America's National Aeronautics and Space Administration (NASA) is also a good customer for Russian rocket technology, having announced its intention to spend $400 million over the next few years, with most of the money going to pay for flights by U.S. astronauts on Russia's MIR space station.

CAPITALIZING ON RUSSIAN BRAINPOWER

Two of the best-known brokers selling Russian scientific brainpower are East/West Technology Partners, Ltd., of Arlington, Virginia, and Scientific Dimensions in Lexington, Massachusetts. The fact that cutting-edge Russian scientific advances were available for commercialization was practically unknown until these and other Western agents began searching them out and presenting them to prospective buyers hungry for ways to improve old products and develop new ones. Today, hundreds of these advances are on their way to being patented with millions in eventual profits to be split between Western companies and Russian inventors.

East/West Technology Partners, Ltd., is a joint venture combining the scientific know-how of BDM International, Inc., of McLean, Virginia; INTEX (International Technology Exchange Corporation) of Washington, D.C.; and a new joint stock company called Technology Exhibition and Investment, Inc., organized and managed by many top Russian scientists and academicians and located at the Russian Academy of Sciences.

"During the past thirty or more years," said BDM's Chairman Frank Carlucci, former U.S. secretary of defense, "the former Soviet Union graduated more scientists and engineers from their universities and institutes than almost all the rest of the world. Much of the research and development work in the country was devoted to military projects and was not available for the commercial market. As a result, there is a huge store of technologies that has never seen the light of day, some of which have great commercial value." A headline-generating example of BDM's global reach is the top-of-the-line Russian S-300 missile defense system—equivalent to the U.S. Patriot system—whose components it recently arranged to have delivered to the U.S. Defense Intelligence Agency in a Russian-built transport plane flown into Huntsville, Alabama, from the former Soviet republic of Belarus for an undisclosed price paid by the Pentagon.

East/West Technology will identify and evaluate new technologies for licensing and marketing, provide inventors and institutes in the former Soviet Union with a partner through which they can exploit their technologies, and perform the due diligence necessary to assure "chain of title" to the potential licenses and intellectual property rights to the inventors.

East/West Technology is currently marketing well over fifty Russian technologies to Western companies and expects this business to boom in the years ahead. A subsidiary of Unisys Corporation called Paramax, for example, has optioned a new advanced electronic packaging method for multilayered printed circuit boards and electronic devices made entirely of aluminum. Solarex Corporation, a division of AMOCO, is negotiating to license a technology that could significantly cut the cost of manufacturing photovoltaic cells while increasing their efficiency. Semimetrics, a British manufacturer of silicon test equipment, has made a firm offer to license a technology for the nondestructive testing of silicon wafers using a patented electrolytic probe.

A large number of other new Russian technologies available for exploitation by East/West licensees are coming on stream each month, including a device that can instantly sterilize medical and dental instruments instead of today's method that takes about thirty minutes, a way to greatly improve the detection of precancerous tissues at a very early stage, and a new discovery for the treatment of human papillomavirus that may offer relief to tens of millions of people, many of whom suffer from genital warts.

Scientific Dimensions in Lexington, Massachusetts, founded by a small group of young Manhattan attorneys, is on the lookout for promising Russian technology with offices throughout Russia and Ukraine and others planned for Belarus and Kazakhstan. Its two top officials are President Charles Gamer, Jr., who has worked for several high-tech firms including Digital Equipment, where he was international marketing manager; and its manager of operations in the former Soviet Union, Dr. Andrei Panasyants, who headed the Department of International Scientific and Technical Cooperation for the Shemyakin Institute of Bioorganic Chemistry in the Russian Academy of Sciences and speaks fluent Russian, English, and Japanese.

Scientific Dimensions says it is in the business of:

1. identifying institutes and researchers in the former Soviet Union that are conducting leading-edge work in areas of strategic interest

2. compiling in-depth profiles of identified technologies

3. assisting in assessing the competitive advantages of identified technologies

4. providing full legal services in acquiring clear title to, and protecting ownership rights to, technology from the countries it covers

5. providing ongoing communications, logistical, and security services to support successful technology transfer

The company's main interest is in disciplines such as biotechnology, materials science, and high-energy physics, but it also claims to review hundreds of new technologies in order to find the handful worth pursuing. It has identified sources of technology of strategic interest to a major aerospace manufacturer, brought a prominent U.S. sports equipment company together with a leading Russian institute in the forefront of titanium technologies, and has numerous Russian technologies under review by U.S. companies including Motorola, TRW, and Bristol-Myers.

Another fascinating use of Russian intellectual firepower was described in a recent *Business Week* report on a $300 million money-management company called Yield Enhancement Strategists, which takes leading Soviet-trained scientists and puts their knowledge of mathematics, physics, and probability analysis to work in Israel and the United States analyzing risk-adverse investment strategies including the mispricing of securities options. The former Soviet scientists' work has been so profitable that the company refuses to give out their last names for fear of having them lured away by competitors, as some already have.

INVESTING IN RUSSIAN BUSINESS

A sensitive barometer of Russia's economic or, more crassly, moneymaking potential is whether or not sophisticated foreigners who have cash and a world of safe havens to invest it in will give this problem-plagued land a flutter. Until very recently, the answer has been "no" with far more foreign money going into Hungary with 10 million people, for example, than in Russia with 148 million. But now that is beginning to change, and the change may well be gathering speed. Gillette, Caterpillar, Procter & Gamble, Lockheed, and Unilever P.L.C. are among the dozens of Western manufacturers staking their claims in Russia's economy, but they are doing it with caution because of numerous uncertainties, from punitive taxes to intimidating mob-controlled crime.

In early 1994, for example, the huge British-Dutch company Unilever P.L.C. acquired a 90 percent interest in Severnoye Siyaniye, a Russian cosmetics and fragrances company with 1,000 employees located in Saint Petersburg. Unilever said it plans to invest $10 million or so refurbishing the firm's production facilities and expanding its business.

Caterpillar, to mention another example, is negotiating with the International Finance Corporation and the Overseas Private Investment Corporation to underwrite two joint ventures with a top Moscow-based Russian truck manufacturer named Zil, which has experienced serious financial troubles triggering massive layoffs. One venture would turn out 150- to 500-horsepower Caterpillar engines for Zil trucks, and the other would produce fuel systems for Zil's new line of mid-range diesel engines. Caterpillar has said little about its proposed commitment to Zil—famed for its long black limousines used by top Kremlin officials during the Soviet era—but estimates are that it could be in the neighborhood of $100 million.

There is a tremendous need for equity financing in Russia today, and it is believed that some of the roughly $40 billion thought to have fled the country from 1991 to 1993 is beginning to trickle back, lured by the prospect of large and reasonably fast profits. But infinitely more capital is needed to rev up Russia's prostrate economy. So much so that many companies are turning to barter—euphemistically dubbed "reciprocal accounting"—to get the resources they need.

In the meantime, once-proud but now cash-strapped and drastically downsized Russian companies that used to make heavy industrial equipment, farm machinery, and weapons are keeping their remaining workers employed turning out anything they can sell—from toys to wheelchairs. Help for such embattled manufacturers, along with promising start-ups, is on the way from Western investors, including funds that commit their money to Russian companies rather than their securities.

A recent *New York Times* "World Market" report noted that the investment firm of CS First Boston had "purchased more than $500 million in Russian stocks and privatization vouchers" as of mid-June 1994 and that the head of the company's Russian operation was predicting that "foreign portfolio investment could reach as high as $3 billion by the end of this year, compared to almost nothing last year." One reason is that the securities of some firms in key Russian industries are seriously undervalued. "While stocks of American oil companies are pegged to about $7 per barrel of proven reserves," says CS First Boston, "Russian oil shares have been valued at the equivalent of 17 cents per barrel."

The few billions in high-risk money currently seeking opportunities in Russia will be followed by billions more if these early investments prove profitable, as seems likely judging by the country's urgent and limitless needs.

Framlington Investment Management, Ltd., for example, has started a fund of more than $60 million to help capitalize small and medium-sized Russian businesses.

PaineWebber Group, Inc., America's seventh-largest securities firm, which has operated in Russia since 1990, has launched the Russian Country Fund and is raising $100 million from U.S. institutions for investment in energy, manufacturing, and export-related industries in Russia and other republics of the former Soviet Union. PaineWebber and Russia's International Economic Corporation will manage the fund through a closed-end investment company. The Overseas Private Investment Corporation is guaranteeing $50 million and the Russian government $25 million of the fund.

Former White House chief of staff and Senate Republican leader Howard Baker has also entered the Russian investment sweepstakes. He and his partner Richard C. Jacobs, a former assistant to the late chairman of Occidental Petroleum, Armand Hammer, rounded up $20 million from the likes of the American Telephone & Telegraph and General Motors pension funds and have started a Washington, D.C.–based company called Newstar that has invested in several small and medium-sized Russian businesses. One is a manufacturer of advanced electronic components called Aurora, which was purchased through an auction sponsored by the Russian government in which Newstar expects to invest more than $5 million.

A Russian fund similar to those already up and running in the Czech Republic and Slovakia, Hungary, Poland, and Bulgaria was incorporated on September 27, 1993, following a talk President Bill Clinton had five months earlier at the Vancouver summit with President Boris Yeltsin. The Russian-American Enterprise Fund, with an initial $340 million in capital, is chaired by E. Gerald Corrigan, an executive with the Wall Street investment banking firm of Goldman Sachs and ex-head of the New York Federal Reserve Bank. It will be run on a day-to-day basis by A. Robert Towbin, formerly a managing director at the New York–based investment banking firm of Lehman Brothers. The fund has offices in New York and Moscow, and is establishing one in the Russian far east.

The fund is currently concentrating on small and medium-sized companies, which it says in the Russian context might include some firms with as many as 2,000 to 2,500 workers. The fund is offering a series of seminars throughout the country, beginning in Volgograd and Omsk, telling private companies and entrepreneurs how to use the fund, including its investment criteria, application procedures, and specifics on how to write a business plan. Fund chair Corrigan, incidentally, takes offense at anyone who suggests Russians are not entrepreneurial. "That view is simply bunk," he said during remarks to the Economic Club of New York on February 9, 1993. "In many ways, the Russians wrote the book and that is how they survived seventy-five years of tyranny and repression."

Still another venture is the Fund for Large Enterprises in Russia, which has been initially funded by Congress through a $100 million grant from the U.S. Agency for International Development, with additional money and resources available through its cosponsor, the Overseas Private Investment Corporation, and other government agencies such as the Export-Import Bank and the U.S. Trade and Development Agency.

W. Michael Blumenthal, who was U.S. secretary of the treasury in the Carter administration, is the fund's chair, and Austin M. Beutner, who was a general partner of the Blackstone Group, a New York–based merchant bank, is its president and chief executive officer.

The fund, with offices in New York and Moscow, "will offer financing packages and management assistance in the form of equity investments, loans. . . . and technical assistance and training to medium and large-sized enterprises in Russia including those emerging from mass privatization." The fund says it "welcomes any ideas or proposals from enterprises, individuals or advisors which involve projects that will help further private enterprise in Russia," and "is prepared to respond quickly to any inquiries or ideas."

At the Tokyo summit in July 1993, the G-7 countries of the United Kingdom, Germany, France, Italy, Japan, Canada, and the United States decided to create a Russian Small Business Fund with assets estimated at $300 million. Half the money will come from the European Bank for Reconstruction and Development, and will provide newly created small and micro enterprises in Russia with access to badly needed capital.

This fund will specialize in supplying equity capital, loans, and loan guarantees, mainly for the purchase of fixed assets (in some cases it may advance working capital as well). The fund's first job will be to launch a $10 million pilot program to determine the future course of its lending activities with emphasis on improving lending practices in existing financial institutions, creating small finance companies to serve micro enterprises, and establishing regional companies to make small-scale investments.

Many private and public groups interested in strengthening Russia's economy are also exploring ways to capitalize on the leverage of donor contributions in getting money into the private sectors within the Commonwealth of Independent States. One approach under discussion would be to inject capital into small and medium-sized enterprises that have recently undergone privatization and show reasonable prospects for operating successfully on a commercial basis, such as Russia's exploding computer industry.

"The Closet Capitalists of Russia and Ukraine"

All this talk about the risks big, sophisticated American investors are prepared to take in Russia, and to a lesser extent in Ukraine, raises the question of how courageous ordinary citizens living in these countries are about taking a risk in hope of making a little money. The answer, published in *Business Week* under the headline "The Closet Capitalists of Russia and Ukraine," is surprising if not downright shocking.

The question was studied by economists at Moscow's Institute of World Economy and International Relations, the Kherson Pedagogical Institute in Ukraine, and Yale University, and the findings published in *Brookings Papers on Economic Activity*. What the researchers discovered was that the Russians and Ukrainians surveyed were just as ready to launch a business as Americans, and their eagerness to invest in other people's ventures was even greater.

"In Moscow, for instance, 51% said they would be tempted to invest a substantial portion of their savings in a new business started by friends, knowing that the business was very risky and could fail—or make investors rich. In Omsk, a city in western Siberia, 42% indicated an interest in making such investments. In New York, by contrast, the figure was 33%." The study concluded by noting that people in Russia and Ukraine "concede that workers do not do quality work—not because they are unable to, but because there is a lack of incentives to do so. If incentives are offered, the authors argue, behavior could change rapidly."

One incentive that is largely missing in today's Russia is serious worker input to the management of the firms employing them. Trade union power has largely vanished, says Joseph Blasi, a professor at Rutgers University's School of Management and Labor Relations and an adviser on privatization to the Russian government, and fewer than 5 percent of the 200 recently privatized companies he visited had any rank-and-file employee representation on their boards.

These companies are among the 14,000 large, nonmilitary enterprises employing some 15 million people that are being privatized. Quite a few of them says Blasi, have cut their payrolls by 20 percent, increased their efficiency, attracted foreign investors, and changed their product mix to emphasize things Russian consumers actually want to buy.

One serious weakness Blasi's study revealed is that too many recently privatized Russian companies have such poor accounting systems that they do not know which of their products are making money and which are not. "One engine manufacturer in southern Russia with 5,000 employees," says Blasi, "makes more than 100 types and sizes of engines without having the accounting tools to pin down costs and profits model by model."

RUSSIA'S TWO HISTORIC PRIVATIZATIONS

Russia's historic first steps toward putting state-owned businesses into private hands took place when the first 3,000 small enterprises were sold to the highest bidders for cash on April 4, 1992, followed by an auction of 8,000 trucks and 735 buses for both cash and 10,000-ruble privatization vouchers over the weekend of October 31, 1992. The auctions were held in Russia's third largest city, Nizhny Novgorod (formerly Gorky), which has a population of nearly 1.5 million, was founded in 1221, has long been a major river port some 250 miles east of Moscow, and is celebrated in the proverb: "Saint Petersburg is the brain, Moscow is the soul, and Nizhny Novgorod is the pocketbook of Russia."

Dimitri Vasiliev, deputy minister of Russia's Ministry of Privatization, met in Moscow with a special task force from the World Bank's International Finance Corporation at the outset of 1992 to begin drafting new laws and regulations to govern the privatization of small-scale enterprises in Russia. The IFC staff was convinced that auctions were the way to go based on earlier successes in Poland and Czechoslovakia.

The next step was to select the kickoff city, and Nizhny Novgorod was chosen because it was a typical Russian metropolis that could serve as a model for the rest of the nation, its local authorities were committed to the privatization process, and the city's ongoing commercialization of its wholesale distribution network provided a foundation on which a private retail sector could be built.

Throughout February and March 1992, working through snows and thirty-degrees-below-zero weather, each small business to be auctioned was evaluated, local auctioneers were trained, and staff people were sent to Prague to learn the mechanics of auctions from experienced professionals. Decisions were also made as to the auction format, starting prices, who should be allowed to bid, and what special incentives should be given to employees of the companies about to go under the hammer.

The auction got under way on Saturday morning, April 4, 1992. When the dignitaries took their seats, then-chief of Russia's privatization program, Anatoly Chubais, announced that "today marks the breakthrough point of the privatization process;" and auctioneer Arseny Lobanov, wearing a red bow tie and white silk shirt, described the first business to be sold.

For the next few hours nearly fifty Russian citizens bid against each other for twenty-two going businesses, including a cheese shop, an old bookstore, and a glass and crystal shop. Marian Bortman, thirty, realized her dream of owning a hairdressing salon. And two young construction workers bid $22,200 they borrowed from a bank to buy an electrical goods shop.

Prices ranged from the equivalent of $700 to $100,000 per business, winners on Saturday took over the management of their purchases on Monday morning, and more than a third of the businesses were sold to their own employees, who were allowed to knock 30 percent off the amount of their winning bid and take an extra long time to pay the city what it was owed.

Weeks before the 3,000 businesses were auctioned off, the IFC experts began work privatizing forty-two large state-owned transport companies whose 18,000 employees were responsible for 8,000 trucks that accounted for 90 percent of the haulage in and around Nizhny Novgorod, plus another 735 buses.

What made this auction of nationwide interest was that Russia's woefully inefficient trucking system was about to be upgraded by private ownership and competition, and successful bidders could pay half the price of their trucks with privatization vouchers and the rest with cash.

The privatization began by setting aside 1,200 trucks to be auctioned off to the public, thereby creating new businesses while helping existing ones to grow. The money-losing bus operation was separated from trucking and taken over by the city. All newly privatized trucking companies were obliged to make their repair and maintenance facilities available to new entrants into the industry at a "fair market price."

The first sixty trucks to be sold were lined up for inspection around a statue of Lenin; they were snapped up at prices ranging from a battered old-timer that sold for $300 or so to a brand new KamAZ model that went for about $6,000. The high bidder for the first truck was thirty-one-year-old Sergei Demyanov, who said he was more than satisfied with the $625 purchase price and tickled that he was the first person in Russia to have used a privatization voucher.

Life after Privatization

Just how far privatization has come, and what it means to the new businesses it has created, is detailed in a study of ninety-nine randomly selected firms in Saint Petersburg, Russia, conducted in late 1992 by the European Bank for Reconstruction and Development and the World Bank.

What the banks found was that "entrepreneurial activity was flourishing throughout Saint Petersburg. In the streets, in retail and service storefronts, in run-down, often abandoned factories leased by new private manufacturers, and within many state enterprises." The banks noted that these companies were "typical of private firms in other Russian urban settings, making research findings more representative than expected."

The total number of enterprises in Saint Petersburg as of mid-1992 was 44,700, of which approximately 30,000 were already private or quasi-private. The banks' study focused on investor-owned manufacturing companies with seven or more employees turning out three major types of products: low-tech consumer goods such as books and cigarettes, low-tech industrial goods such as construction materials and spare parts, and high-tech goods such as precision testing equipment and optical devices.

The Russian entrepreneurs studied in this first wave of privatization were practically all men. Their average age was forty-two, they had solid technical educations (over 60 percent were university graduates), they had worked for the state before striking out on their own, and almost a third had been previously employed in research and development or manufacturing within Russia's huge military-industrial complex.

An aeronautical engineer, formerly employed by a state enterprise manufacturing turbines for power-generating stations, started selling spare parts to power stations throughout Russia while inventing new parts for airplane engines. The former chief designer of spectral equipment at a state research lab is producing microscopes and other optical equipment. The ex-head of the acceleration lab used in Russia's "Star Wars" program has invented and franchised a process for regenerating and recycling television picture tubes. A chief designer of submarines and ships, faced with cutbacks in shipbuilding, began producing car batteries. And a specialist in cryogenics and space research is making garden and household tools, "anticipating growing demand in do-it-yourself home improvement and an increased reliance on private gardens."

Only about 10 percent of the entrepreneurs in the banks' sample could be classified as novices, but they too were embracing private enterprise. A husband and wife team had started a printing company. A former taxi driver was making auto parts. An ex-sailor was manufacturing cast aluminum products. An old Army officer was in the religious icon business. A one-time electronics worker was making money producing plastic headlight covers for trolley buses throughout Russia.

All of these new entrepreneurs face what the banks believe is an uncertain future brought on "by a high rate of inflation, continually changing relative prices, and unpredictable interest rates and exchange rates—all of which obscured the economic signals necessary for properly functioning markets."

The legal forms of these enterprises were concentrated in limited liability companies (29 percent), joint stock companies (25 percent), cooperatives (19 percent), and private small businesses (16 percent). The average firm had sixty-three full-time employees and generated sales equivalent to $14,810 a month. Many entrepreneurs were running several businesses at once, a phenomenon I noticed again and again during my travels throughout the former Soviet empire.

When it came to raising start-up capital, these Russian entrepreneurs tapped the same sources as aspiring business people do in the West. About 66 percent used their own savings, 47 percent got loans, and nearly 40 percent relied on advance payments from customers. One source of money for which demand was extremely low was short-term credit available at a crushing nominal interest rate of between 100 percent and 200 percent a year.

What sets these entrepreneurs apart, however, is that virtually all their capital equipment was either bought or leased through state-owned enterprises where, according to the banks' survey, "the opportunity to purchase depended heavily on personal connections and substantial bribes. Illegal practices were rampant and costly. Bribes reportedly were required to obtain leases, lower raw material prices, and lock in contracts. And mid-level local government officials were said to offer paid 'consulting services' to businesses for expediting paperwork that might otherwise take months."

The entrepreneurs in the banks' study were quick to admit that "pervasive corruption was costly to them," yet they accepted it. The obvious reason is that there was little else they could do since the state-owned enterprises had what they needed to get into business, and often to stay in business. To make matters worse, many of the most desirable productive assets of state enterprises had been grabbed by their managers at what the banks suspect were below-market prices even as their liabilities and responsibilities were being "transferred back to the state."

An interesting sidelight on all this noticed by the banks' survey team was that these Russian entrepreneurs appeared isolated from one another, as well as from the state and the outside world. Only three of the companies surveyed did any exporting, for example, and that only to countries of the former Soviet Union. What they have not yet realized, as Western businessmen did long ago, is that there is a lot to be gained from regularly getting together in organizations such as the Rotary or Kiwanis, or by lobbying lawmakers for what you want from government through an industry group or the equivalent of the Chamber of Commerce.

Would-be female entrepreneurs in Saint Petersburg are getting a much-needed helping hand from the nonprofit Alliance of American and Russian Women, based in Washington Depot, Connecticut, and founded four years ago by Alexandra Chalif, a psychotherapist of Russian descent. Since then, according to a January 22, 1995, report in the *New York Times* some fifty American women have traveled to Saint Petersburg to conduct small business conferences and begin setting up a business incubator in nearby Volkhov.

The problems the American women found in teaching entrepreneurship to their Russian sisters (many of whom had lost their state jobs and were desperate to create new ones) mirror experiences encountered by Russian men, from the difficulty of obtaining working capital to dealing with the Mafia. A few of these Russian women, however, have actually succeeded in launching a jewelry-making cooperative, a doll manufacturing company, and a firm assisting foreign visitors who need help. One budding Saint Petersburg fashion designer was even brought to New York and introduced to prospective buyers who gave her several thousand dollars worth of orders even though she resisted their advice to replace her clothes' handmade silver buttons with less costly substitutes.

THE SEARCH FOR JOINT VENTURE PARTNERS

Western companies are looking for attractive joint venture partners in Russia and are finding a few that know the territory and are blessed with good managers capable of getting things done in this vast and uncertain new market economy that is eager to do deals—particularly with hard currency partners.

Russian government statistics show that the United States leads in the number of joint ventures with close to 400 valued at well over $400 million, ranging in size from relatively small alliances—such as the satellite launching venture between the tiny Rimsat Corporation of Fort Wayne, Indiana, and the privately owned Informcosmos company of Russia—all the way up to the long-term monster deals between giant international oil companies and sovereign states.

The outlook for U.S.–Russian joint ventures is examined in some detail in an incisive article in the *Harvard Business Review* written by Harvard Business School professor Paul Lawrence, who has studied Russian organizations since 1987; and senior research fellow Charalambos Vlachoutsicos, who had done business with Russian and Eastern European countries since 1956 and is a member of the joint Russian–International Chamber of Commerce task force on investments in Russia.

The authors are quick to point out that most of the thousands of would-be Western investors flying into Russia these days are immediately turned off by what they see as these unfamiliar obstacles to business success:

1. the current impossibility of converting profits earned in Russian rubles into American dollars

2. the lack of the most basic business services including banking, transportation, communications, security, insurance, and production materials

3. the constantly shifting regulatory and legal environment throughout Russia

Yet the authors discovered, after interviewing the Russian heads of thirty-three successful joint ventures with Western companies, that making money still mainly depends on having a solid business concept, an in-depth knowledge of the market, and the ability to get the most out of available resources.

The authors also found that successful joint ventures in Russia (and probably in Ukraine and Belarus as well) are driven by three factors:

1. Russia has many terrific managers, and successful joint ventures know how to put them to work and give them the freedom to make things happen.

2. Quality is now every bit as important in Russia as it is in the West.

3. The key to successful joint ventures in Russia is the capacity to adapt quickly to problems of economic turbulence and social change, which in no time begin to look like opportunities for growth.

While the authors heap praise on Russia's highly skilled and educated workforce, they are even more in awe of its "wealth of managerial talent." Russian executives, they insist, "are often strong, personal leaders who practice hands-on, walk-around, face-to-face management. They'll also know more about indigenous markets and suppliers, networks and ministries, regulations and cultural patterns, and work force strengths and weakness than a Western manager could learn in years on the job."

This makes for highly profitable joint ventures, and at the top of the heap are those in which Russian managers have "entered into new businesses, expanded operations into new cities, and launched construction projects all without advance approval of the Western partner."

If Russian managers have a weakness, and the authors say they do, it is the years they spent under communism where headquarters bureaucrats told them what to produce and the reward for professional success was "the freedom to exercise authority while avoiding responsibility." As a result, "getting a Russian general manager to take on full responsibility for a joint venture often calls for firm measures (such as) insisting on complete and candid reports at regular intervals," while sweetening the pot with a financial stake in the business commensurate with its profitability. The Harvard business experts go further and recommend that majority ownership of new companies be put in Russian hands even though local law permits 100 percent foreign ownership. Only five of the thirty-three Western joint venture partners they studied own more than 50 percent of the Russian companies (and none more than 55 percent). Allowing Russians to own the company, they say, encourages management responsibility, adaptability, and hard work. Since the Russian owners can end up very rich, giving them control of the business hypes their will to win, even as the risk of failure puts a razor's edge on their intellect.

Russian managers are also more likely than their Western partners to reinvest earnings back in the business since they are eager to see it grow (what their Western partners lose in repatriated earnings is often partially offset by profits on components sold to these ventures). Not only that, but Russian managers are constantly on the lookout for attractive places to invest the company's ruble profits. The authors tell of one Russian manager who considered repatriating 12 million rubles worth $100,000 at the time. Instead, he took the 12 million rubles and bought a plant his Western partner estimated would have cost $15 million in the United States.

Finding crackerjack managers is a lot more difficult in Russia than it is in the United States, the authors say, because an American candidate's background and references are easy to check, everybody plays by the same ground rules, and if a mistake is made in hiring a manager it can be corrected even though it may be difficult and expensive.

A management candidate's professional history in Russia "is often clouded in obscurity, compromised by politics, or simply inaccessible." His or her business knowledge is likely to be limited (for example, Russian managers tend to define profits as surplus cash). Once hired, managers are extremely difficult to dismiss, which is a holdover from the traditional Soviet system of full employment and lifetime tenure.

Ferreting out the ideal Russian manager not only takes time, but involves the building of personal relationships. The authors mention one case where an American investor met a Russian manager at a Moscow cocktail party, liked him, and eventually invited the manager and his wife to visit his home and business in the Midwest. The American introduced them to his friends, gave the Russian manager a chance to wander around his business and ask questions, and quickly realized that the manager had a firm grasp on what made his business tick. The next time the American visited Russia, the two men began developing a joint venture plan.

Ballet Shoes, Wigs, and Joke Noses

United States and other Western companies can bring a host of strengths to joint venture deals with Russian partners, from sheer management savvy to global contacts and money. To understand the kind of Russian company that might benefit from such an arrangement (while also bringing a great deal to it), consider the case of Russia's Union of Theatrical Workers.

The Union of Theatrical Workers had no idea what it was getting into when it decided to begin offering some of the items it had been making for its members to the general public. It wasn't long, however, before it had more than 800 workers toiling in a factory near Moscow Airport turning out ballet shoes; folk dance ensemble costumes; theater stage curtains; theatrical wigs; plastic cases for lipsticks, cosmetics, and creams; puppets (and the little furnished stages on which they performed); scarves; linen flowers; albums for business cards, photos, and stamps; light filters for use on the stage; and even joke noses.

The business had sales of about $700,000 a year, but it was in deep trouble for reasons ranging from its dependence on a major customer that was not paying its bills, to soaring utility costs that threatened to exceed its total revenues, to having just one man engaged in selling its products (and he only responded to inquiries that came in over the transom since he had no financial incentive to go after new business). To make matters even worse, the product line had not changed in more than a decade.

The upshot of all this was that very few areas of the company had materials to operate more than one day a week, its workers had not been paid in two months, and simple improvements such as weather-stripping its plant, which could slash its near-runaway heating bills by at least 25 percent, were not being made.

It was at this point that the Union of Theatrical Workers' general director approached the Moscow office of the Citizens Democracy Corps for help. It arrived in the person of Gerald Berstell, forty-five, who lives in Chicago, has a B.S. and M.S. in architecture from MIT and an MBA from the Harvard Business School, and has spent years advising financially troubled overseas organizations on how to invigorate their operations—from Japan's Osake Apparel Manufacturers Association, to Bulgaria's National Management Center, to Indonesia's Clove Cigarette Industry.

Within hours after sitting down with the Union of Theatrical Workers' general director, Berstell understood the magnitude of the problems he faced, beginning with the company's reliance on a handful of customers who showed no eagerness to pay their bills. Most of its plastic makeup cases, for example, were bought by the Moscow Factory of Theatrical Cosmetics; its main customer for scarves was the Russian Gallantry distribution company; almost all its ballet shoes went to two outlets in Moscow and Saint Petersburg; and its puppets, linen flowers, and albums were sold to schools throughout the country by a single wholesaler.

These problems exploded when the Soviet Union collapsed and the company had trouble doing business with its old customers in Ukraine, Kazakhstan, and Russia's other suddenly independent neighbors. To make matters worse, hard-charging competitors from the capitalist West began going after its customers with tooth and claw (including some customers in Russia who started rejecting its utilitarian cosmetics for more sensuous ones from Revlon and Chanel, dull scarves for the latest from Yves Saint Laurent, and old-fashioned toys for Barbie dolls and Nintendo video games).

Berstell knew that the company's loss of major customers, the obsolescence of many of its key products, and the price hikes for its basic materials and components were "absolutely normal," and that "there are few Western companies that do not experience all of them every day of the week. Yet they survive and grow despite these nonstop upheavals by intensifying their sales efforts, increasing new product development, and installing advanced technology. The cause of the theatrical union's problems was that its factory management's use of these mechanisms—particularly the critical first two—was virtually nonexistent."

To solve the company's pressing current problems and give it the capability to deal with future ones, Berstell recommended that management replace its lone salesman with a sales force by having at least two reps hawking each of its major products, such as ballet shoes and cosmetics cases, and at least one salesperson pushing each of its lesser products, such as puppets and plastic flowers. Berstell also suggested that salespeople receive a commission of 15 percent on everything they sell. This idea, as we've seen with other Russian companies, was not well received. Typical of the objections, says Berstell, was that "it would be very difficult to pay salespeople three or four times what factory workers earn."

The Union of Theatrical Workers' expanded sales force should not only be out there beating the bushes for new customers, Berstell advised, but should be on the lookout for other companies to whom it might become a supplier. Since its inception the theatrical union has waited patiently for customers to somehow find it (as a manufacturer that needed containers to hold its herbs and spices recently did). But now, said Berstell, the company should begin aggressively canvassing for new customers who could buy its products in quantity—such as ballet schools for its shoes, shampoo companies for its plastic containers, and new folk dancing groups for its traditional folk costumes.

Russia is also beginning to compile business directories to help customers and suppliers find each other, Berstell told the theatrical union, but it does not appear to be listed in them. The latest *Business Directory for the Soviet Region* has categories for ballet shoes and plastic containers, but the union is not represented.

The U.S. Department of Commerce offers free listings in its *BISNIS* publication for Russian companies interested in selling in the United States, and Berstell told the union it would be well worth seeing that its name, address, and products are included.

The theatrical union should do a lot more advertising, said Berstell, which it knows works because a small ad it ran mentioning its ability to dye fabrics pulled in a new customer. If a small ad works in a particular publication, he added, consider running a bigger one. And begin getting involved with trade exhibitions in the same way.

Berstell also stressed the fact that while the company has a catalog, it is more than four years old and has more pictures of factory workers than products. It also shows many products it no longer makes, while presenting few facts on those it does. It fails, for example, to mention the sizes and colors of its shoes or scarves, or the shape and composition of its plastic cosmetic cases. The company should immediately begin developing simple product specification sheets on each of its products complete with drawings and detailed information. Expensive color photography and reproduction is unnecessary, said Berstell. But the sheets describing items, such as ballet shoes, that are of potential interest to foreign customers should be translated into English, German, and French (possibly also Spanish and Italian) and should spell out how to get in touch with the company to place an order.

The general director of the Union of Theatrical Workers and his staff were also advised to work with their salespeople to develop ideas for selling its products in new markets. Berstell suggested they consider:

♦ selling scarves in theater lobbies and at the All Russian Exhibition Center

♦ selling costumes to small circuses, ballet groups, orchestras, bands, and student music and dance groups

♦ selling curtains to managers of new hotels, office buildings, and apartment houses

♦ selling puppets and related products to all thirty of Russia's teaching collectives instead of the eight currently serviced

♦ selling shoes to the hundreds of ballet schools all over Russia, instead of the relatively few it does business with today (perhaps approaching one ballet school in each city to serve as its distributor)

Berstell then suggested that company management dream up wild ideas for a whole new series of products, such as:

♦ ballet shoes in different colors

♦ plastic plates, glassware, ashtrays, flowerpots, wastepaper baskets, children's blocks, and plastic flowers for cemeteries

♦ puppets representing popular figures such as Boris Yeltsin and Mikhail Gorbachev, whose likenesses are already for sale all over Moscow in the form of nesting *matryoshka* dolls

♦ painted T-shirts for sale to Western visitors, including Bolshoi Ballet T-shirts to be sold in the Bolshoi Theater lobby, Kremlin Ballet T-shirts to be sold in the Kremlin Palace of Congresses, Moscow Circus T-shirts, Tchaikovsky Conservatory T-shirts, and so on

New product designs should be tested by setting up displays at the Moscow Metro station or other high-traffic spots so interest in them can be evaluated. If a new product requires a significant up-front investment, such as new molds for plastic flowers, Berstell cautioned, the company should get a few dozen samples from foreign suppliers, display them in the same high-traffic locations, and copy the designs receiving the greatest amount of interest. Developing new products, Berstell said, will mean spending money for investment in new designs, product prototypes, molds, and test marketing, which will cut into profits. If successful, however, they will fatten long-term profits and thus help ensure the company's continuing growth.

A more promising future is clearly in the hands of the general director of Russia's Union of Theatrical Workers and its workers. The company, as Berstell emphasized in his final report to management, has large production facilities, easy access to Moscow's airport and Outer Ring Road, large numbers of sewing and plastic molding machines on which most of its products are made, and an abundance of craftspeople skilled in making ballet shoes and costumes.

"This combination of assets," says Berstell, "is extremely scarce in Russia because of its past emphasis on central planning, and could not be easily assembled by any new competitor." But to make maximum use of its assets will require management to launch an all-out effort to expand sales while upping its investment in new technology and product development.

It will, in other words, have to show some entrepreneurial energy, and it does not have to go far to see it in action in today's Russia. "Several Russian entrepreneurs," says Berstell, "have actually brought several closed-down areas of the company's factory back to life by leasing space and equipment to create new ventures. Many of these Russian go-getters are called 'traders,' and their ability to get things done is awesome even though most Western aid organizations look upon them with contempt."

If the theatrical union's management is unwilling to get out there and hustle, then Berstell recommends that it "increase the number of joint ventures with Russian and foreign enterprises that know how to find customers." These joint ventures, he quickly adds, should meet the following two criteria:

1. The company's joint venture partners should compensate it for the use of its facilities, machinery, and workers by giving it a share of the products produced. The union, however, does not know how to sell these products, so it would be better if it received its share of the joint venture profits in *cash*.

2. The joint venture should be prohibited from competing with the company for its current customers. Instead of helping the union open up new markets for its ballet shoes, for example, its English joint venture partner is trying to steal its only Moscow customer.

Russian entrepreneurs are gradually learning about the importance of good design, worker incentives, an emphasis on quality, and finally the fact that nothing happens until somebody sells something. This means throwing off decades of simply making products and then shipping them off to distribution centers. Those days are gone forever. The Age of the Consumer has finally arrived in Russia, and there is no turning back.

8

Communism's Terrible Legacy

"Workers of the World, Forgive me!"
Graffiti on a monument to Karl Marx
around the corner from Red Square

Everywhere you look in today's Russia you are confronted by momentous change whose outcome in every case is impossible to predict. The mighty Red Army has been downsized. Crime is out of control. Agriculture is leaving the comfort of state ownership and venturing into the icy waters of dog-eat-dog free enterprise. Religion banned under communism is coming back with a rush. The people's health is deteriorating. The vital oil industry is stagnant from a lack of capital. Russia's death rate is soaring while its birthrate is plummeting, putting the nation's future in question. And some of the republics that make up Mother Russia are flirting with independence.

The autonomous republic of Tartarstan is leading the drive for political freedom within the Russian Federation to the point where it has its own constitution, parliament, president, flag, and army, whose soldiers are forbidden to fight outside its borders, located some 500 miles east of Moscow. Tartars make up about 48 percent and Russians 43 percent of Tartarstan's roughly 4 million people—making it bigger than sovereign nations such as Albania, Estonia, or Slovenia—and both the Tartar and Russian languages are considered official. Tartarstan puts a high priority on demonstrating its independence from Russia, and one of the major ways it does it is by paying her only a fraction of the taxes it collects (although it has offered to pay a little more to help cover the cost of maintaining the railroads and the Red Army).

The new Russian constitution drafted by the Yeltsin government gives Tartarstan and the other republics symbolic privileges such as their own flags and emblems (for Tartarstan it is a griffin with the head and wings of an eagle and body of a lion). But Tartarstan and these equally independence-minded regions want to be co-equal with Russia within the Commonwealth of Independent States. The Republic of Chechnya, as we know, recently declared its full independence from Russia. The Sverdlovsk region where Boris Yeltsin launched his political career says it is now the Urals Republic. The Primorski territory, whose capital is Vladivostok, washed by the Sea of Japan, is determined to become the Maritime Republic. And neighboring Khabarovsk—a territory one and one-half times the size of France—is debating whether to become the Far East Republic.

THE DOWNSIZING OF THE RED ARMY

It was the former Soviet Union's decision to devote the lion's share of its industrial production and scientific brainpower to its insatiable military machine that eventually proved unsustainable, hastening its collapse as a world superpower on a par with the United States.

In commenting on the disintegration of the Soviet empire, Harvard University professor of Russian history Richard Pipes says, "I cannot think of any parallel to this kind of collapse. Great empires usually wear down or are defeated in war, but this kind of implosion is unprecedented. But then the whole Soviet experiment was unprecedented."

The current Russian military establishment is but a problem-plagued shadow of its old self—reduced, among other things, to selling rides to well-heeled Westerners in its supersonic MIG-25s and other advanced fighters at $10,000 a pop and unloading forty old attack submarines from its Pacific Fleet on the North Koreans, who insist they have been bought for scrap. The military has watched its sales of military hardware to primarily third world nations collapse to $1.8 billion in 1993 from $27 billion in 1987 when it was part of the old Soviet Union. Spending on defense has been slashed, but now seems headed higher in part because of the Yeltsin government's calamitous decision to crush the separatist uprising in Chechnya. Hundreds of poorly trained eighteen- and nineteen-year-old Russian soldiers have lost their lives at a projected cost to the national treasury of $3 billion to $6 billion—or up to 2 percent of the country's anticipated 1995 gross national product, virtually ending any hope of its near-term economic stabilization.

Endless rows of once-powerful assault tanks quietly rust in Siberia, and warships of the Black Sea Fleet do the same. Thousands of soldiers are forced to live in tents during the fierce Russian winter. Military gear is routinely swapped for cigarettes or soap. Young Russian men are successfully using every trick in the book to escape the draft. And the Russian air force is so poor, says *Aviation Week and Space Technology*, that by 2005 it may be unable to afford new combat aircraft and by 2010 new warplanes could "cease to exist."

"Not a single army in the world is in such a catastrophic state," Russian Defense Minister General Pavel S. Grachev told Parliament on November 18, 1994, adding that he needed three times the $14.5 billion allocated for the military in the country's 1995 draft budget if its armed forces are to avoid collapse. Military training is being slashed, Grachev warned, many pilots are not flying, warships are stuck in port, 2,600 young officers left the service in 1994 alone, and only 40 percent of the army has modern equipment which could plummet to 10 percent by the year 2000 if its budget is not increased.

Ethan B. Kapstein, codirector of the Economics and National Security Program at Harvard University's John M. Olin Institute for Strategic Studies, says in the May/June 1994 issue of *Foreign Affairs* that "by the early 21st century, the United States will be the sole producer of the world's most advanced conventional weaponry, as other countries discover—like the Soviets did—that the costs associated with financing new defense programs are too heavy to manage."

Kapstein goes on to note that "during the Cold War, the only other country that financed a defense budget equivalent to America's was the Soviet Union, which spent far more as a percentage of its gross national product. While reliable statistics on current Russian expenditures are hard to come by," says Kapstein, "every observer agrees that defense spending has fallen through the floor. It is now a small fraction of the American defense effort."

An arresting analysis of the collapse of Soviet defense spending is contained in a *National Review* article called "Who Broke the Evil Empire," written by Peter Schweizer and based on his new book *Victory*. Schweizer, who completed the work while a media fellow at the Hoover Institution, credits President Ronald Reagan for the Soviet downfall, thanks to his decision to drastically inflate U.S. defense spending, which the Soviets went bust trying to match, while slashing the price of their two most important sources of hard currency—oil and arms. Schweizer says Reagan got Saudi Arabia's King Faud to flood the market with petroleum, causing prices to plunge from thirty dollars a barrel in November 1985 to twelve dollars a barrel five months later. This cost the Soviets billions in lost income, while eviscerating arms sales to their big Middle East customers whose own oil revenues had also been gutted.

Russia's weapons sales have been on a downward trajectory since the end of the Cold War, with the situation so bad today that the country is selling its most advanced weapons, including MIG-29 fighters and Kaman-50 attack helicopters, to anybody with ready money from Moscow gangsters to the Bosnian Serbs.

All this has led the Russian military to begin converting the army from a conscript to a well-paid and motivated volunteer force. Gabriel Schoenfeld, writing in *Post-Soviet Pros-pects,* published by the Center for Strategic and Interna-tional Studies, says that "although a volunteer army had been the subject of a desultory debate for several years, the decision to move forward came in the wake of the Gulf War and the USSR's collapse. The accomplished performance of smart weapons manned by smart soldiers left Russian generals stunned. An army of resentful conscripts, they con-cluded, is not what it takes to win a silicon-chip war."

The move toward a professional army, Schoenfeld says, has been speeded up by the unwillingness of young men to serve and the poor quality of those who for some reason fail to escape the draft. Only 40 percent of the men drafted in the autumn of 1992, he notes, had "completed seventh or eighth grade."

"Russia's volunteer army," Schoenfeld concludes, "is designed to halt this hemorrhaging of numbers and brains. Volunteers will have to sign up for a minimum of three years, but in return will earn generous salaries, plus bonuses as they accumulate seniority and higher proficiency ratings. They'll also receive excellent fringe benefits including guar-anteed housing, free use of public transportation, free uni-forms, liberal portions of free food, plus bath and laundry services." Some 100,000 volunteers have already joined up under the plan, but the lack of money to pay new re-cruits has apparently put it on hold at least temporarily.

Russian generals are determined to maintain the most powerful peacekeeping force in the region, ready to deploy fast-reacting airborne troops and helicopter assault units wherever they are invited, as they recently did in the Trans Dniestria region of Moldova and in South Ossetia, Georgia.

While the Russian military is shrunken in size, and its generals no longer giants bestriding the earth, it is still a key player—perhaps the key player—in the troubled country's national life. Defense Minister Pavel S. Grachev, a battle-hardened airborne commander in his mid-forties, backed Yeltsin during the abortive 1991 coup attempt against Mikhail Gorbachev. He came to Yeltsin's aid again in October 1993 to put down the abortive putsch led by Aleksandr V. Rutskoi, whom the Parliament had named to replace Yeltsin as acting president (along with parliamentary chairman Ruslan Khasbulatov), and commanded the forces Yeltsin dispatched to put down the secessionist uprising in Chechnya.

Russia's declining military threat to the West would be further reduced if the United States succeeds in buying billions of dollars worth of highly enriched uranium extracted from dismantled Russian warheads. In the meantime, both Russia and the United States have agreed to retarget their nuclear-tipped ICBMs at the empty vastness of the ocean rather than at each other. The United States is so confident the Cold War is finally over that it is scrapping its $8 billion Doomsday Project, built years ago to keep the government running for six months following a surprise Soviet attack on Washington, D.C. On the Russian side, defense contractors with fast-evaporating order books are frantically—and so far none too successfully—converting factories designed to build weapons of war into those turning out water purification systems, earthmoving equipment, and even sailboats.

RUSSIA'S COSTLY EPIDEMIC OF CRIME

"Corruption is devouring the state from top to bottom," said Boris Yeltsin recently; and if estimates in investigative reporter Claire Sterling's new book *Thieves' World* are accurate, the Russian Mafia is a union of racketeers without equal, consisting of 5,000 gangs and 3 million people who work for or with them. Sterling goes on to quote Alexander Gurov, head of the Soviet Interior Ministry's Sixth Department to Combat Organized Crime, as having predicted back in 1991 that in the next five years organized crime will "control 30 to 40 percent of the country's GNP."

Yet for what it is worth, I felt completely safe during my visit to Russia. I was an instantly recognizable American who frequently walked the streets at night and could be seen emerging from expensive places like the plush Plaza Hotel near my apartment, yet I was never bothered. This may be because in today's Russia over 90 percent of criminal defendants are convicted.

A special report prepared for President Yeltsin concluded that up to 80 percent of the private enterprises and commercial banks in major Russian cities are forced to pay a tribute of 10 to 20 percent of their sales to organized crime through payoffs, kickbacks, debt collection, money laundering, and the like, which in turn generates about a quarter of Russia's inflation rate.

Another report issued by Russia's Interior Ministry and summarized in *Isvestia* said criminal gangs are holding the country's emerging private sector by the throat with Saint Petersburg alone at the mercy of 10,000 hoodlums, of whom 500 are hardened criminals. The report goes on to say that organized crime in Russia controls all types of activity compared with the United States and Western Europe, where it is usually limited to gambling, prostitution, and drugs. The paper said the situation has gotten so bad that there has been a call for an elite anticrime unit answerable only to the president, whose handpicked members would receive exceptionally high salaries of $250 to $300 a month and be given special police powers such as the right to make preventive arrests.

Russian commentators often attribute the crime wave to public indifference (or perhaps despair), too few policemen including quite a few on crime's payroll, and the lamentable absence of an effective court system able to put evildoers behind bars in the country's hellish prison system.

The upshot is the emergence of protection services, including those supplied in Moscow by U.S. companies such as Honeywell Security, and elsewhere throughout the country by heavily armed guards (the Moscow manager of Honeywell Security told me he knew of one entrepreneur with sixty guards on his payroll).

There has been an explosive growth in security guard firms offering to protect businesses with guard dogs, strategically placed video cameras, Kalashnikov machine gun–wielding young ex-Red Army combat troops wearing black berets and bulletproof vests, and even armored personnel carriers. These companies, reminiscent of Pinkerton here in America that has been in the protection business for more than a century, are being hired by frightened entrepreneurs throughout Russia as protection against freelance gangsters and the Russian Mafia, whose latest terror weapon is the remote-controlled car bomb.

Russia's Interior Ministry claimed in a statement released in early 1994 that organized crime—loosely defined to include racketeers, shady business executives, and corrupt bureaucrats—committed 355,500 crimes in 1993, up 27.8 percent from 1992. It also reported that about one-third of these groups specialize in large-scale embezzlements, financial and property manipulation, and the laundering of illegal profits, and that 40,000 businesses are controlled by these gangsters—who are not adverse to using such tried and true techniques as kidnapping and murder to frighten their victims into paying up. The ministry said ninety-four entrepreneurs who apparently did not pay were murdered in 1993 (an estimate considered to be much too low).

Russia has apparently had all it can take of rampant crime, according to a recent Reuters news dispatch from Moscow describing how the heads of Russia's main security agencies have developed a $1.5 billion anticrime program "to stop gangsters from terrorizing people and businesses." The government has spent months preparing the program, which involves "everyone from counterintelligence agents to volunteer policemen," and includes several new draft laws to replace Soviet-era ones that "did not reflect new realities and prevented the police from acting resolutely."

In early June 1994, President Yeltsin announced a decree to "cleanse the country of criminal filth." The decree was immediately blasted by human rights activists, according to a *New York Times* report out of Moscow, and attacked by Parliament, which Yeltsin had failed to consult before swinging into action.

Yeltsin's preemptive decree "grants the police the right to detain people suspected of involvement in organized crime for up to 30 days without charges or bail, permits officials to root through the bank accounts of anyone suspected of criminal involvement without a court order or approval, and allows the police to use anything they obtain in these searches in court. There is even a provision that permits the authorities to investigate anyone who has lived with a suspect for more than five years."

Yeltsin's action, for all its controversial ferocity, suggests the Russian Mafia's salad days may be drawing to a close as the Interior Ministry and armed forces—backed by the fast-growing number of private security guards—begin using their superior firepower to ensure public safety and fight organized crime, which has estimated revenues of $10 billion a year.

THE BACKBONE OF THE RUSSIAN ECONOMY

Agriculture is Russia's biggest occupation with some 27 million people living on the country's more than 26,000 state and collective farms, which are gradually being transformed by the transition from communism to capitalism.

At one point Russia's top economist Yegor Gaidar suggested that Russia's agricultural outlook was brightening even though the production of meat, milk, grain, and vegetables had fallen every year since 1989, but that optimism was questioned in early March 1994, after Boris Yeltsin predicted that cash-strapped Russia wouldn't import any grains for the first time in thirty years, according to a report by the respected Bloomberg Business News service. Traders on the Chicago Board of Trade, where both wheat and corn prices reacted to the news by falling sharply, said the problem was a lack of money, while some others insisted it was a ploy to get grain and corn prices down since the year's poor crops meant Russia would have to buy millions of tons of both commodities, although not nearly as much as in some recent years.

Letting farmers own land has proven to be the key to raising agricultural output throughout the world. But there was no legal basis for privatizing land in the Soviet Union, and the Parliament wanted to keep it that way. What little land had been placed in private hands was done under two government decrees issued in December 1991.

The first simply obliged state and collective farms to choose the form of ownership they wanted, including rejecting state ownership if they wished. Just under one-third of the farms did so, turning themselves into limited-liability partnerships, according to a Moscow report in *The Economist*.

The second decree said members of a farm collective were entitled to receive equal shares of its land and assets if they left the farm, without specifying who was to get what. So farm managers did the obvious and gave those who left pieces of the worst land on the property.

This may soon change thanks to a decree Boris Yeltsin signed on October 27, 1993, allowing Russian agricultural land to be freely bought and sold for the first time since the Bolshevik Revolution and authorizing an agricultural experiment now under way in Nizhny Novgorod.

Boris Nemtsov, the province's governor, says what they are trying to do is create viable farms that those living on them could divide up quickly and fairly. Six farms were chosen for the experiment, and the acreage of each one was then divided by the number of workers and pensioners living off it with each receiving a land-entitlement certificate for that many hectares. Entitlements to the farm's other assets—its cowsheds, tractors, and so on—were calculated according to how many years each individual had worked on the farm.

At the 3,616 hectare (8,932 acre) Pravdinsky farm, which was the first to distribute the certificates, an auction was set up allowing certificate owners to bid for income-producing assets such as a tractor-repair facility or land. Eight bidding groups emerged led by farm managers and directors, who competed for the support of certificate holders by offering them either active partnerships, which shared in any profits, or passive ones, which received a fixed income and were usually preferred by pensioners.

The Nizhny Novgorod experiment is still in its infancy, but it seems to have solved the allocation problem in an equitable manner. Only time will tell if privatization will unleash enough energy among the farm's new worker/owners to significantly increase production of all farm commodities in the face of seemingly intractable problems, from widespread soil damage caused by years of bad farming techniques to the lack of scientific and industrial support essential to efficient modern farming.

In the meantime, Russia's farmers are using their considerable clout to pressure Moscow for ever higher prices. Farmers warned government bureaucrats right before harvest time that crops would be left to rot in the fields unless they received massive subsidies totaling a promised 6 trillion rubles in 1994 of which one trillion was paid before they agreed to return to work. This weakened the government's ability to deny price hikes to workers in other critical industries such as coal and nuclear power who were promised cash subsidies shortly after the farmers were paid off.

THE COLLAPSE OF RUSSIA'S HEALTH CARE SYSTEM

Georgetown University demographer Murray Feshbach, writing in *The American Enterprise* magazine, reports that the former Soviet Union's health care system has collapsed and lists these unnerving statistics:

♦ The number of children born to Russian women has fallen from an average of 2.17 in the late 1980s to just over 1.4 today, which means Russia is not reproducing itself and that its population is destined to decline precipitately in the years ahead. A report released by the International Labor Organization in Geneva adds that since the 1980s the life expectancy for Russian men has dropped to fifty-eight years, which it attributes to stress generated by economic factors ranging from the late or nonpayment of wages to the fear of being laid off.

♦ Sixty percent of infants have health problems, and infant mortality rose from 17.8 per 1,000 in 1992 to 19.3 in 1993.

♦ One-quarter of children under age five develop anemia or rickets.

◆ Congenital birth defects such as cleft palates and cerebral palsy appear to have increased dramatically as a
  result of radioactivity released when the atomic power
  plant at Chernobyl experienced a partial nuclear meltdown along with pollution from atomic, chemical, and
  biological facilities plus mines and industrial sites.

◆ One in four adults was chronically ill according to a 1990
  report.

◆ Hospitals and clinics are turning patients away because
  they lack medicines (many sick people will not go near
  them anyway because they fear infection from
  unsterilized syringes).

This last point was the subject of a frightening report by
Dan Rather on the CBS Evening News when he was in Moscow covering President Clinton's January 1994 visit with
Boris Yeltsin. "If you get sick in this town," said Rather, "the
best prescription is to get out of town fast." The CBS television cameras then entered one of the city's oldest public
hospitals, woefully short of medical supplies and equipment.
"Americans have donated a respirator," Rather reported, "but
most of the other equipment is outdated and often doesn't
work. There are no CAT scans or ultrasound machines," he
said, adding that "the X-ray machines are old and faulty,
and the staff doesn't have adequate protection against high
doses of radiation."

"But the biggest problem we have now," said one doctor, "is blood."

"There is a critical shortage of blood for transfusions,"
Rather noted, "because many Russians won't give blood
because they're afraid of getting AIDS from reused needles.
Rubber surgery gloves are in such short supply that they're
cleaned and dried to be used again. Nuns from a local church
volunteered to keep their hospital spic and span when the
regular orderlies quit because of low salaries. Overcrowding is so great," said Rather, that "every nurse has to care
for 40 patients. The corridors are waiting rooms not only for
patients needing care, but for the dead until they're shipped
to the morgue. And this city has become so dangerous that

hospitals have had to improve their security measures by putting bars on the doors because there actually have been instances where Mafia hit men have chased their victims right into the hospital.

"Not surprisingly," said Rather, "these conditions have driven doctors out of medicine." A top hospital orthopedic surgeon, who said members of his family had been physicians for five generations, earns only $200 a month including untold hours of overtime. This is why, said Rather, "Twenty percent of the doctors of this hospital have left for jobs with higher salaries; many of them working as stock brokers, or taxi drivers."

Russia's health crisis is visible everywhere. More than half of Moscow's schoolchildren are infested with lice due to impoverished living conditions and a shortage of soap. Far more serious is the diphtheria epidemic with thousands of cases reported and well over 100 deaths (compared with only several cases in the United States). Dr. Anatoly A. Monisov, Russia's deputy chief epidemiologist, said the country's recently launched mass immunization program should ensure that 75 percent of Russia's adults and 90 percent of its children will be protected against diphtheria by 1995. Meanwhile there have been frightening reports of other infectious diseases plaguing Russia such as cholera, tuberculosis, typhoid fever, and usually fatal anthrax which could easily reach epidemic proportions overpowering Russia's antiquated health care system even though most of these diseases are easily preventable and cheap to cure.

RUSSIA'S CASCADING
ECOLOGICAL DISASTER

In many ways these problems pale beside the continuing assault on the health of more than 300 million people generated by decades of spewing a witches' brew of deadly nuclear, industrial, chemical, and municipal wastes into the Soviet environment. Millions of Russians have lived all their lives beneath blackened skies where the sun rarely shines, downwind from the uncontrolled burning of thousands of tons of deadly chemical weapons, among forests reduced to rotting stumps, and along streams long since transformed into stinking cesspools. Lung and bone cancer, malformed hearts, and spontaneous abortions confront overworked doctors able to offer little but sympathy to hapless victims condemned to live out their lives in ruined environments unfit for human habitation.

With the possible exception of the atomic catastrophe at the Chernobyl nuclear power plant in 1986, no one knows the extent of the human and ecological destruction already caused by the former Soviet Union's devastation of its air, water, and soil. Included in this tragedy is the secret pumping of billions of gallons of nuclear waste into the earth containing up to three billion curies of potentially deadly radioactivity (the accident at Three Mile Island released about 50 curies).

Past Soviet regimes considered the appalling condition of the nation's environment to be a state secret, with even the Aral Sea tragedy—generally considered to be the worst ecological disaster of the twentieth century—kept hidden from the public eye.

Now the true story of the environmental emergency in today's Russia is coming out, and it is a frightening picture. Sergei Bobylev, who is a professor at Moscow State University and a member of the High Ecological Council of the Russian Federation Supreme Soviet, summarized the situation this way in a recent issue of *Demokratizatsiya: The Journal of Post-Soviet Democratization.*

"By expert estimates," says Bobylev, "only 10 to 15 years remain before a general ecological crisis in agriculture, triggered by the degradation of land resources, occurs. Accordingly, this will result in a deep food shortage, and even food aid from the United States and Western Europe will hardly help Russia avert the collapse.

"Soon," Bobylev adds, "Russia may face dire industrial and agricultural consequences due to the growing dearth of water resources from the Volga and Don Rivers, Lake Baikal, Azov and Caspian Seas, and others. They are polluted above all admissible levels with organic compounds, heavy metals, phenol, oil products and other substances. This leads to a rising deficit of drinking water, together with a crisis in water supply for urban populations."

Even more alarming is Bobylev's analysis of the impact on the Russian people both born and unborn. "Only 15 percent of Russia's urban population lives in an ecologically sound environment," says Bobylev. "In 84 large Russian cities, with a combined total population of about 50 million, air pollution exceeds accepted world standards by a factor of 10 or more."

Within the next decade, Bobylev predicts, growing environmental degradation may lead to 80 percent of all Russians having at least one chronic disease. He then quotes Russia's minister of environment and natural resources as believing "the country is close to a critical level of genetic inferiority, beyond which begins national degradation."

"It is clear," Bobylev concludes, "that if the present degradation of the gene pool proceeds at the same pace, the Russian people will degenerate and start to die out in two or three generations." His prediction is made even more alarming by the fact that the Russian birthrate has plunged by 30 percent since 1989 as dispirited young people elect not to have children.

"In the midst of internal political stalemate and economic collapse, wholesale environmental rehabilitation could only be a distant dream," contends Soviet health and demographics expert Murray Feshbach and *Newsweek*'s former Moscow bureau chief Alfred Friendly, Jr., in their new book *ECOCIDE in the USSR*. The reason is obvious. The United States has spent close to $400 billion cleaning up its rivers and lakes during the last seventeen years alone, and that is something that people in the far more seriously polluted ex-Soviet lands can only dream about.

Just about the only good news is that the West, along with Russia's private sector, is beginning to underwrite the start of an admittedly modest program to reverse the deadly pollution of the country's air, land, and water.

On November 8, 1994, the World Bank approved a $110 million loan to help Russia clean up its environment, accompanied by $90 million in donations from the United States and the European Union, and $45 million in investments from newly privatized Russian businesses. The bank said forty-three Russian cities are in urgent need of relief from air pollution, and that the $110 million is just the "first installment" of a large program of environmental lending for the Russian Federation "with nearly half the funds slated to be spent outside of Russia, for foreign environmental cleanup equipment and foreign consultants."

The urgency of international assistance was dramatized by the recent environmental disaster near the town of Usinsk some 1,000 miles northwest of Moscow when an old state-owned oil pipeline developed leaks along its 32-mile length, spewing millions of gallons of oil into the surrounding landscape (estimates range from 4 million to 80 million gallons, compared to the Exxon Valdez spill of 11 million gallons). Alaska Governor Walter J. Hickel, who immediately flew to the site, reported he saw no evidence of an effort to clean up the spill, which threatens to devastate the region's fresh water suppplies and wildlife, and if not corrected could eventually flow into the Barents Sea conceivably reaching the shoreline of Norway or even Alaska.

What all this comes down to is purchasing power: cash or credit that Russia simply does not have for dealing with the firestorms that are racing its way, but won't engulf it until later. You can see this most clearly in the reluctance of Russia and the rest of the former Soviet bloc to close down potentially hazardous nuclear reactors. The reason is that it would force them to generate power by burning coal or gas, which they can export for hard currency, or it would force them to pay hard currency for power if they lack these energy resources.

Ukraine has once again promised the West to eventually shut down Chernobyl's last two working nuclear reactors following its commitment to help in replacing their 1,700 megawatts of lost power. But Ukraine is so heavily dependent on this energy that it is doubtful if they will be retired any time soon. There is even talk of restarting a third reactor that was shut down after a fire in 1991. Atomic energy accounts for about one-third of Ukraine's electricity production, and the impoverished country has few resources left to buy urgently needed power from neighboring Russia—threatened by its own looming nuclear disasters.

Professor Thomas Halverson of England's Keele University, writing in the *Bulletin of the Atomic Scientists*, quotes Boris Yeltsin's environmental adviser Alexei Yablokov as saying that "it's impossible to deliver (our) power stations by missile to some other country, but in reality they are no less dangerous." Halverson goes on to warn that "the 25 most dangerous Soviet-type nuclear reactors should be closed down immediately. The energy they generate may be desperately needed to avoid further economic collapse, but every day their machinery deteriorates and staff quality and morale plummet."

The most alarming of these units are the Model 230 pressurized-water reactors, which Halverson says probably represent "the most dangerous nuclear threat in Europe today" since "they have no containment structure; no true emergency system for cooling the core; inadequate fire protection; poor secondary safety systems, instrumentation, and control; and they have a host of other safety-related problems. Over the years their reactor vessels have become embrittled. Even the nuclear power–promoting International Atomic Energy Agency (IAEA), which is not known for criticizing reactor safety, says, 'It is most probable that no changes or upgrades can reduce the uncertainty on the safe operation of these plants, as understood and accepted outside Eastern Europe.'"

At risk, of course, is another nuclear disaster similar to the one that destroyed Chernobyl's number-four reactor in 1986, spewing radioactivity across much of Europe.

IAEA experts have told Russia that two versions of its pressurized-water reactors are fundamentally flawed and should be shut down within the next several years to reduce the risk of another Chernobyl-type disaster. The West has offered to help finance the cost of mothballing these reactors, but with the money involved running into the tens of billions it is questionable whether anything will be done. "All we can do," said a woman I met in Kiev, an unnerving sixty-five miles from Chernobyl, "is pray it doesn't happen again."

RELIGION RETURNS TO RUSSIA

Karl Marx condemned religion as the "opiate of the people," and communist dictators from Lenin on succeeded in virtually destroying the 1,000-year-old Russian Orthodox Church with its ornately robed priests, complicated rituals, revered icons, and estimated 60 million members. Since the death of communism, however, more than 6,000 churches and monasteries have been reopened as Russians reclaim their faith. President Clinton publicly recognized this fact during his 1994 summit meeting with President Yeltsin when he limousined to Moscow's Central Clinical Hospital to pay a courtesy call on Aleksy II, the leader of the Russian Orthodox Church and Patriarch of Moscow and All Russia, who was ill with bronchitis.

Data collected in mid-1991 by the Russian Center for Public Opinion Research in Moscow, and analyzed by the National Opinion Research Center in Washington, D.C., found that a third of all Russians who once considered themselves atheists now believe in God (although only 8 percent said they regularly attend church).

Religion in Russia is making a comeback with the help of nonstop personal appearances by heavy-hitting American evangelical and charismatic preachers such as the Reverend Billy Graham, Morris Ceriullo, Bob Wilcox, and Jack Finley, along with television appearances by Jimmy Swaggart and Pat Robertson. Jehovah's Witnesses held a revival in Moscow's Locomotive Stadium, and 2,000 or so new converts wearing bathing suits were baptized in three portable swimming pools.

It is open season in Russia for foreign religions—everyone from Hare Krishna devotees in their saffron robes aggressively proselytizing passersby, to the Reverend Sun Myung Moon's disciples quietly working institutions. The inept Russian Parliament couldn't resist getting into the act so it passed a law requiring foreign religious groups to register with a special government board that had not even been formed. The law was immediately blasted as flying in the face of the freedom of conscience formerly granted to the

Russian people in 1991, and no one is taking it all that seriously.

Some Russian lawmakers had wanted to force foreign religious groups to obtain state accreditation or to become affiliated with Russian churches or related organizations. But these efforts, including putting restrictions on the activities of foreign missionaries, were outlawed by the Soviet Parliament following amendments to the Law on Freedom of Religion suggested by President Yeltsin (although preferential treatment is still given to the Russian Orthodox Church).

Weird religious sects have also surfaced in Russia, such as the Mother of God Center in Moscow that worships the Virgin Mary and preaches hatred for mothers and other women who refuse to join the cult. Yet even this bizarre outfit is kid stuff compared to a cult that has surfaced in Ukraine called the White Brotherhood, formed in 1990 by a fifty-two-year-old wild man named Yuri Krivonogov, who claims that he and his wife are gods. Krivonogov preaches the familiar refrain that the end of the world is nigh, and only his disciples will be saved. What gives this a particularly unsavory twist is that Krivonogov has been accused by parents of luring their children into his brotherhood, where they become fanatical slaves.

Russian Jews Rediscover Their Faith

Russia's nearly 1.5 million Jews are rediscovering their faith, and a semblance of normal religious life is beginning to return now that the old Soviet state ideology of atheism has all but disappeared. Russian Jews living in communities without even a rabbi, synagogue, or Torah scroll, are once again celebrating their faith, which was outlawed under the Soviets.

The anti-Semitism that flourished under the czars, Stalin, and their pre-Gorbachev successors has diminished, leading to a sharp decline in Jews immigrating to Israel from the former Soviet Union. Less than 70,000 left for Israel in 1993, which is down slightly from 1992 but off considerably from the 170,000 who left in 1991 and the 185,000 who emigrated in the peak year of 1990. Not only have fewer Jews been leaving for Israel, but many who had already gone are returning home to Russia.

Daily life for Russia's Jews is little different today than it is in other democracies. They can work, live, travel, own a car, worship (even though the vast majority of Russian Jews are not religious), read Jewish publications, and enjoy normal everyday life. Many Jews would much rather live in Russia where they can work and earn money than in Israel where suitable jobs and housing are scarce.

Suddenly, however, Russia's Jewish community is worried about its security, and the reason is the spectacular rise of Vladimir Zhirinovsky in Russia's new Parliament. Zhirinovsky, whose father was Jewish, insists he is not anti-Semitic, but he believes the Jews in Russia have far too much power and that there should be "free immigration of Jews out of Russia to Israel." This, together with the suspicious fire in the only synagogue built in Russia since the Bolshevik Revolution, has Russia's Jewish leaders calling for immediate police protection of their institutions and even their community buildings.

Russia's deteriorating economy, Zhirinovsky's anti-Jewish statements, and the declining authority of Boris Yeltsin, whom they see as a sympathetic figure, have all contributed to the recent increase in the number of Jews leaving for Israel, urged on by the powerful United Jewish Appeal (UJA) via its "Operation Exodus" among others.

The UJA has been running full-page ads in the *New York Times*, the *Wall Street Journal*, and elsewhere beneath a picture of a group of unidentified individuals in uniform giving the straight-arm Nazi salute. The headline reads "For Jews in the former Soviet Union the exit signs are clearly marked," followed by a request to support the UJA's current fund-raising campaign: "The signs are all too familiar. Brown-shirted fascists march. Synagogues mysteriously go up in flames. Right-wing extremist Vladimir Zhirinovsky rants against Jews and 'Zionist plots.' And his party wins more votes than any other in Russia." The ad concludes by asking for support so the Jews remaining in Russia "can leave the hatred and despair behind. Before it's too late."

THE REVOLUTION IN EDUCATION REACHES THE FORMER USSR

A recent dispatch out of Moscow in *The Economist* noted that ". . . only 22 percent of Russians receive some form of higher education. That is no better than Costa Rica or the Philippines and decidedly worse than America, where 60 percent go on to higher education of some sort. Second, much of Russian higher education is not what it seems. Only sixty of the roughly nine hundred institutions that claim to offer it would conventionally be considered universities elsewhere. Most of the rest are technical institutes training skilled workers for a particular branch of industry. 'It is quite easy for a young man here to spend four years studying how to crush stone,' says Vasily Kolesov, the dean of the economics department at Moscow University."

One note of optimism in the former Soviet empire is that educators are gradually dismantling the old highly centralized communist command approach to education and replacing it with Western-style choice, according to a recent "World Education Report" published by the Paris-based United Nations Educational, Scientific, and Cultural Organization (UNESCO).

The newly democratic governments in the former Soviet Union and Eastern Europe are allowing an increasing number of parents the right to choose between public, private, and religious schools, while giving both schools and teachers greater freedom to decide on their own curricula. The upshot has been a proliferation of expensive private schools patronized by Russia's new rich and offering the best money can buy, from luxurious surroundings to a teacher for every two or three students.

The UNESCO report noted that the emphasis on science and engineering education needed to produce technicians to run the old communist regimes' vast commitment to heavy industry has been replaced by today's exploding demand for students who are "specialists in business, finance, economics, law, sociology, foreign languages and the humanities."

The report said that possibly the greatest challenge facing the countries of Eastern Europe and the former Soviet Union is handling their cultural and ethnic diversity including the right of minority groups to run their own schools. The report went on to say that this presents a particular problem for an estimated 25 million Russians living in the new republics outside the Russian Federation that have started using their own languages instead of Russian in their schools.

Literacy is high throughout the former Soviet empire, with a proliferation of newspapers, magazines, and journals devoted to subjects of every kind from science and business to fashion and the arts. Literally thousands of magazines with as few as 50 to 100 readers are being reproduced by ubiquitous photocopying machines that only the elite had access to under communism (just like the now equally commonplace fax).

I was reminded of this difference during a visit with Sergei Dardykin when he was coeditor in Washington of the recently discontinued newspaper *We*, published by America's Hearst and Russia's *Isvestia* and billed as "The First Independent Russian-American Newspaper." "There are some basic differences," said Dardykin, "between what's good in American journalism, and what's good in Russian journalism. American journalism is very news oriented with a strict difference between news and opinion. There is nothing similar to that in Russia. American readers expect news, facts, figures. Russian readers expect to read the journalist's opinion. There is also a huge difference in political opinion between Russian newspapers, but very little difference here in America."

Frank Cook, who was managing editor of *We*, agreed with his colleague. "Russians find our copy dull. We put a news lead on stories, follow with 'He said-She said,' are heavy with quotes, and try to back everything up that's in there. Our Russian colleagues find that very dull. But if I were to put their copy as written into our American paper it would be laughed at, and simply not be an acceptable product on the newsstand."

RUSSIA'S VAST OIL AND GAS RESERVES

Russia's richest material treasure is hidden deep beneath the earth's surface in her vast oil and gas reserves, which add up to more than one-third of the world's total and produce 80 percent of the hard-currency export earnings it desperately needs to buy Western technology and other key imports and to meet the huge payments on its multibillion-dollar hard-currency debts.

Russia's once-prolific oil industry, however, is in shambles because of years of neglect. As a result, says Anatoly Fomin, Russia's first deputy minister of fuel and energy, its investment needs for producing oil, upgrading oil refineries, and manufacturing new equipment add up to nearly $75 billion. This is money that Russia does not have but is now beginning to flow in from Western petroleum companies.

In early 1994 a consortium of Western oil giants including Marathon, Royal Dutch/Shell, McDermott International, Mitsui, and Mitsubishi agreed to invest an estimated $10 billion to develop potentially major oil and gas deposits near Sakhalin Island off the coast of Hokkaido, Japan. The deposits are believed to contain some 750 million barrels of oil—small in comparison to the North Sea's 13 billion barrels and Alaskan Prudhoe Bay's 10 billion barrels—and 14 trillion feet of natural gas, which the consortium will develop under a profit-sharing deal with Russia getting more than half the proceeds. Russia has also signed an agreement with Chevron and Switzerland's Asea Brown Boveri (ABB) to upgrade one of the country's major oil refineries near Saint Petersburg with advanced Western hydrocracking technology used in converting heavy oil into fuels including diesel and high-octane gasoline.

Russia's oil reserves are among the largest on earth, yet its actual production has been falling steadily for more than five years with over 27,000 wells currently idle, according to Wilhelm Bonse-Geuking, member of the managing board of Veba Oel AG, a major German energy company. Crude oil production, according to Russia's Ministry for Fuel and Energy, fell by another 11 percent to 302 million barrels in 1994. What is more, says Bonse-Geuking, budget allocations for developing Russia's energy sector so it can produce more oil "have dropped practically to zero."

Russia's crude oil exports outside the former Soviet Union—its major source of foreign currency earnings—surged about 20 percent in 1993, according to State Statistics Committee figures published by the Interfax news agency as reported from Moscow by Reuters. Crude oil and gas condensate exports rose to 79.7 million metric tons or 1.6 million barrels a day in 1993, up from 66.2 million metric tons or 1.32 million barrels a day in 1992. The value of these sales, however, dropped to $8.2 billion from $8.6 billion in 1992 because of the sharp decline in world oil prices to about their lowest level in five years. One optimistic note was that more valuable refined oil product exports rose by a solid 36 percent to 34.5 million metric tons, or 690,000 barrels a day, up from 1992's 25.3 million metric tons or 506,000 barrels a day.

The highly regarded *Oil & Gas Journal* did a special report in August 1993 on Russia's energy crisis, with articles by Dr. A. Konoplyanik, former deputy minister, Russian Federation Ministry of Fuel and Energy in Moscow; Valeri S. Plotnikov, a top engineer at a big gas processing plant in Western Siberia; and Lucian Pugliaresi, president of LPI Consulting, Inc., in Washington, D.C., which closely monitors energy developments in Russia and elsewhere.

Dr. Konoplyanik paints a depressing picture of Russia's oil production, whose 1993 tonnage he put at 12.1 percent lower than the year before with export volume plummeting 27 percent. "Russia's major high-yield deposits of oil," he said, "are 60 percent to 90 percent depleted, which is largely why production has dropped so much." The situation is so bad "the country may have to import crude oil or products within the next five years."

The disaster that has hit Russia's oil industry is overpowering, making it difficult to know where to begin in describing the crisis. Consider these examples taken at random from several dozen listed by Dr. Konoplyanik:

♦ Many of Russia's oil fields are now idle, and the quality of residual reserves and new discoveries has deteriorated.

♦ Oil production in 1992 was 62.3 million tons lower than in 1991 and 170 million tons lower than the record high of 1988. That is equivalent to revenue losses of $20 billion to $22 billion a year, which is equal to half of Russia's 1993 foreign debt repayment obligations (if existing restructuring deferrals are not taken into account). This decline continued in 1994 with production dropping another 11 percent to 302 million tons.

♦ No highly productive deposit has been found recently, and the average production from new wells drilled in the oil-rich Tyumen region has fallen from 130 tons per day per well in 1975 to between twelve and thirteen tons in 1992. This means the financial, material, and technical costs of producing one ton of oil a day from new wells have risen tenfold in seventeen years.

♦ Financing for geological work and exploratory drilling has dropped significantly, and as a result the growth in development of Russia's oil reserves has stalled.

Russia realizes, says Dr. Konoplyanik, that it does not have the $30 billion needed to revive its oil industry, nor can it rely on debt to get the money, since it would have to produce 50 million metric tons of additional oil exports a year during 1993–1998 to repay the loan. That is over and above the 38 million tons or so it exported in 1993.

So Russia must woo foreign investors, who, Dr. Konoplyanik believes, are ready to invest as much as $70 billion. This presents no problem to the world's big international oil companies, which have the money and are always on the lookout for new reserves. But they can sink as many wells as they want in familiar and hospitable places such as the Middle East, Southeast Asia, and the United States and are not all that eager to go exploring in the wilds of Russia. Among the reasons listed by Canadian oil experts are Russia's high level of political instability, prohibitively high taxes, outrageously high tariffs on oil exports, and a costly and time-consuming legal environment. As a result of these problems, says Dr. Konoplyanik, the "minimal rates of return which would satisfy the U.S. investor should be 25-40 percent higher in Russia than in Western Europe and from 66-75 percent higher than in the U.S."

"Even a few years ago," says Dr. Konoplyanik, "none of the above problems in the relationship with foreign investors existed." That is because the old USSR was a command economy whose oil industry officials were accustomed to dealing with the Exxons and British Petroleums of the world on a regular basis. Now all that has changed, and Russia is scrambling to create an investment climate that will lure Big Oil back again. It could well be succeeding, concludes Dr. Konoplyanik, since 25 percent of all Russian oil fields and 40 percent of the Tyumen fields will be reaching the production stage from 1992 to 2000 with the participation of foreign oil companies active in the development of proved recoverable reserves.

So far, direct investments by foreign companies in the development of Russian oil fields are insignificant with only about four dozen joint ventures operating or being established by what Dr. Konoplyanik calls "forward-based emissaries of western investors. The goal of this task force," he adds, "is to formulate rules of the game and 'show the flag' in the Russian oil business and also to track from the inside changes taking place in the Russian economic balance of forces."

Lucian Pugliaresi, president of LPI Consulting, Inc., in Washington, D.C., and a recognized expert on global oil developments, goes a step further in his article in the *Oil & Gas Journal* by suggesting that "perhaps what is needed now is some demonstration to jump-start western interest as frustrations grow. Whether it is the Barents Sea, Western Siberia, or offshore Sakhalin, a large demonstration of Russian willingness and commitment to do what is necessary to close a large deal could go a long way to get the essential long-term investment under way.

"The Chevron deal in Kazakhstan," says Pugliaresi, "has provided an enormous boost in reassurance and interest among investors there. The Russians have several large projects on the table. Perhaps they should pick one up and make it work. Perhaps they will."

A notable one they have already picked up is a proven field in Siberia above the Arctic Circle. Texaco, Amoco, a subsidiary of Exxon, and a Norwegian oil company named Norsk Hydro plan to spend roughly $100 million over three years analyzing the potential of this field where oil is known to exist. The field is believed to contain some 2 billion barrels of oil, and oil has been found in a majority of the wells drilled in the past, which the Russians lacked the capital to develop—making it virtually a dream situation.

In early 1994, Lukoil, Russia's biggest oil producer, which controls 15.7 billion barrels of proven reserves and was formed by the merger of three leading oil and gas producers, two refineries, and several distribution outlets, held a public auction of its shares to raise money it badly needs to be competitive in today's world markets. The company's wells produced nearly 1 million barrels of oil a day in 1993 or close to one-seventh of Russia's output, of which slightly over 100,000 barrels a day were exported.

Lukoil is determined to become a global market-oriented petroleum superpower in the same league with the Royal Dutch/Shell Group, whose reserves of close to 18 billion barrels are the largest outside the giant state-owned producers in the Middle East, China, and Latin America. Lukoil's reserves could quickly top Royal Dutch/Shell's if it succeeds in raising the billions it needs for expansion and modernization.

Lukoil's major market is Russia where the number of cars on the road is increasing by 15 percent to 20 percent a year, according to company vice president Leonid A. Fudin, who calls his country the energy "market of the twenty-first century." Lukoil dominates the Russian market where it hopes to eventually operate more than 1,000 gas stations partially supplied by a new $1.5 billion refinery to be built by Swiss-Swedish Asea Brown Boveri (ABB). In the meantime, Lukoil has joined a Western oil consortium developing some of the large reserves in Russia's neighboring republic of Azerbaijan, even as it is wrapping up joint-venture oil deals in Italy, Egypt, and Tunisia, and is negotiating one with oil-rich Iraq once United Nations sanctions have been lifted.

A Natural Gas Superpower

Russia is "the biggest natural gas producer in the world representing about 35 percent to 40 percent of total world gas output," says Wilhelm Bonse-Geuking, head of oil and gas exploration for Germany's Veba Oel AG, which is one of the top ten energy companies in Europe.

"Gas has become the primary source of energy for the Russian economy," Bonse-Geuking said during a September 1993 speech to the Ninth Asia Pacific Petroleum Conference in Singapore, "and it's solidified its leading position following the decline in the oil industry and troubles in the coal and nuclear power industries."

"Russia," says the *Oil & Gas Journal*, "will remain the dominant world supplier of gas through the year 2015—and overwhelmingly so." Its state agency Gazprom controls 25 percent of world gas reserves plus yearly exports of $8 billion. Russia is conserving this wealth worth up to $1 trillion by increasing its economy's fuel-using efficiency (Russia consumed four times more energy per unit of GDP in 1990 than the United States) and by capturing the estimated 260 billion to 370 billion cubic feet of gas currently flared each year in Russia's big west Siberia oil fields, which is expected to worsen in the years ahead.

In the meantime, says Veba Oel's Bonse-Geuking, Gazprom is planning to develop Russia's sprawling Yamal gas fields, containing some 450 trillion cubic feet of gas, and build a 1.9 trillion cubic feet per year export pipeline running from Yamal through Poland to Western European markets at a cost estimated at $10 billion.

HELPING RUSSIA PRODUCE MORE CONSUMER GOODS

The well-being of every nation's citizens, in the final analysis, is measured in part by the amount of consumer goods available for purchase. Russia has a long way to go before it can even dream of the riches available in supermarkets dotting the landscape in the United States and other Western countries. But this may be about to change.

An audacious idea for introducing American-style consumer abundance to Russia was described to me by G. William Miller, sixty-nine, who has been chairman of Textron, head of the Federal Reserve Board, and secretary of the treasury in the Carter administration. With a small group of others, including the Brookings Institution's top Russian expert Clifford G. Gaddy, Miller produced a white paper outlining "A Russian-American Partnership for Industrial Development" (RAPID). This intriguing idea has a lot going for it, and to get a little more background I visited Miller in his sunlit suite near DuPont Circle in Washington, D.C., from which he runs a merchant banking firm bearing his name.

"Russia," says Miller, "is short of capital. It's producing the wrong products. Its market needs everything. And from that reality evolves the very simple idea behind RAPID. What we hope to do is bring over American products, along with the tools to produce them, so that many of Russia's no longer needed military plants can be restructured to make consumer goods of every description, including farm machinery, containers, communications gear, road building and food processing equipment, consumer appliances—almost anything you can think of they need. And since there isn't enough time for them to design new products from the ground up, American firms should give them what they need to get into production right away. You can take an American refrigerator, gas turbine, compressor, or even an entire meat processing plant and adapt it for use in Russia. You don't have to reinvent the wheel."

Miller believes the optimum way to do this is by having U.S. investors buy stock in a well-managed U.S. government–guaranteed fund that would then use the money to purchase shares in Russian corporations so they could retool to produce civilian goods. If they succeeded, their market value would go up to a greater degree than the investment in them. And to sweeten the deal, Miller recommends that the United States and Russia each take a 5 percent interest in these companies so they will make money if the companies make money. While RAPID would have its own management and board of directors, it would rely on individual American and Russian enterprises to propose specific investment projects.

RAPID would pay for the American companies' capital equipment, industrial technology, manufacturing know-how, etc., says Miller, "via ruble-denominated shares in the newly created and jointly owned Russian enterprises. And as an incentive for success, the American firms would be required to keep perhaps 10 percent of the shares issued for their goods and services. The Russian side would also have to reserve 10 percent of its equity in the new venture for purchase by its citizens using privatization vouchers with the shares listed on the Russian Stock Exchange."

The great majority of RAPID's shares would become dollar-denominated securities pooled into a fund for sale through underwriters to private investors, with both the American and Russian governments guaranteeing its shares, provided investors hold them for at least five years. Each government would be entitled to receive 5 percent of the fund's profits, in return for its guarantee.

"You'd get all the major U.S. underwriters to line up in a syndicate to sell say one billion dollars worth of shares in the fund this year, another one or two billion more next year and so on," Miller says. "Investors would be promised a worthwhile return on their money, and if it hadn't materialized in five years the fund would give the investors their money back.

"The Russian government would guarantee that the proceeds of sales of Russian shares financed through the fund could be converted from rubles into dollars. This would give

American investors an incentive to buy Russian as well as U.S. shares in the fund. The same would apply if the fund were unsuccessful so U.S. investors in Russian shares could get their original investment back in dollars."

The Russian government would have to do its part, says Miller, by creating a capitalist legal system, along with granting a five-year tax holiday for all the companies in which RAPID invests as Russia's contribution to building capital for reinvestment in the business. Miller suggests that the Russians also draw up a set of modern business laws, using the experience of the United States and Europe, but whose content is strictly Russian and would include these general characteristics:

1. Limited liability for the investor. You put your money in, and you're not going to be called on for more.

2. Transferable interest in a company's shares so you can create markets, raise capital, and pool capital in a constructive way.

3. Perpetuity of existence. Somebody dies, but the corporation keeps on going.

Miller believes this can be done in six months with the help of American legal scholars since the Russians don't have to reinvent the wheel (although he feels they will undoubtedly want to change it). "There is great genius," he says, "in being able to take someone else's ideas, synthesize them, adapt them to your own cultural conditions, and make them your own."

WHAT WORRIES RUSSIA THE MOST

The most worrisome single question facing Russia today is whether it will succeed in harnessing the power of democratic capitalism to enrich its people's lives, or fail and be forced to retreat back into the humdrum austerity of authoritarian socialism. Life before Gorbachev appears enticing indeed to millions of Russians who have lost their jobs, are forced to scrounge for their daily bread, or receive pay-checks for showing up at vast factory complexes that pro-duce little of value except preventing—for the moment—a massive uprising against the government.

Russia is in a race with time. Can it get a free enterprise system up and running fast enough to put food on every Russian table and thus avoid a revolution? Or will a charis-matic politician like Vladimir Zhirinovsky, or former Gen-eral Alexander Lebed, grasp the reins of power during the next presidential election in June 1996—if not before—even though they are bereft of anything approaching a workable strategy for reviving the Russian economy?

There is an old saying—it may well be Russian—that "The fox knows many things, but the hedgehog knows one big thing." The big thing Russia knows is that it must put a cred-ible free enterprise system in place reasonably soon or face a return to economic drift, if not chaos.

The West is finally moving into Russia with its money, know-how, and determination to help it regain its status as a great nation. The next few years are going to be critical.

9

Russia Struggles toward Solvency

"Only a handful of events in this century are as important as the creation and eventual collapse of the Soviet Union."

Professor Stanley Fischer, Massachusetts Institute of Technology

"We must walk along the edge of a razor blade (between hyperinflation and industrial collapse) and we must not fall down on either side."

Russian Prime Minister Viktor Chernomyrdin

When President Bill Clinton ended his whirlwind trip to Moscow on January 15, 1994, he figured all was well. Boris Yeltsin himself had assured him that Russia was on track toward market reform. But within days that assurance had fallen apart, and many figured that Russia was now being run by old-line party hacks more interested in maintaining the failed status quo than in putting the nation on the admittedly rough road to recovery.

Harvard Russian expert Jeffrey Sachs, who for years was a consultant to Yeltsin, asked during a National Public Radio interview on January 21, 1994, "What do you do with a country that is spinning out of control financially and is on the verge of hyperinflation and bankruptcy? "My best judgment," he said, "was that you try to get this explosive inflation under control before it destroys social stability, and before it brings to power a true extremist that's a danger to Russia and the rest of the world."

The ruble seemed to echo Sachs's sentiments by plummeting more than 20 percent against the dollar at the beginning of the year and again toward the end. This was followed by testimony on January 24, 1994, before the U.S. Senate Appropriations Committee's Subcommittee on Foreign Operations, chaired by Senator Patrick Leahy. Members of the media covering the hearing were given a press packet containing, among other things, a rundown on the more than $1 billion the United States had promised to spend in what was called the Newly Independent States (NIS) during fiscal year 1994. Two examples:

♦ $51,891,000 to improve "health care in the NIS by transferring medical knowledge and technology through hospital partnerships, supporting the pharmaceutical and medical supply industries, and encouraging efforts to reform the health care system"

♦ $125,000,000 to provide "financing to Russian importers for the supply of U.S. equipment and materials needed to increase efficiency and productivity in energy production and distribution, and to reduce waste and pollution"

The first to testify before Senator Leahy's subcommittee was Ambassador Strobe Talbott, special adviser to the secretary of state on the NIS—more often referred to as the Commonwealth of Independent States—who had just been nominated to be deputy secretary of state under Warren Christopher.

"When President Clinton was in Moscow two weeks ago," said Talbott, "the principal subject on his agenda with President Yeltsin was the Russian economy. In their discussions, President Yeltsin stressed the good news. Over one-fourth of the labor force is now employed in the private sector. More than three-quarters of Russia's small businesses and retail shops are now privately owned. Over 7,000 medium and large enterprises are in private hands. Roughly 55 million Russians own a stake in a private venture. Prices have been freed on more than 90 percent of goods and services. The old centralized distribution system has been virtually eliminated. The contraction in Russia's economy is slowing. Exports are up. . . ," and although inflation had been easing it now appears to be moving up again. Then Talbott cautioned that "there is still a long way to go. Privatizing firms is only a first step in developing profitable, job-creating enterprises. Production is still falling, and the inflation figures are favorable only in the most relative sense. At 12 percent a month, prices are still doubling every six months.

"In Russia," Talbott said, "inflation has already eliminated people's life savings, impoverished people on fixed incomes, and eroded the wages, morale, and effectiveness of teachers, doctors, police, scientists. While privatization has generated wealth, inflation has driven much of that wealth out of the country to the safety of western banks."

The next day Central Intelligence Agency Director R. James Woolsey told the Senate Select Committee on Intelligence that the Russian "economy is at a critical juncture. President Yeltsin has shattered the incentives and structures of the old system: more than 95 percent of all prices are free, central planning and the State distribution system have been abolished, many controls on foreign trade and investment have been lifted, and more than a quarter of GNP is now produced by a rapidly growing private sector.

"Our major concern," Woolsey went on to say, "is that looser fiscal and monetary policies aimed at easing the pain of reform will unleash forces that could bring Russia again to the brink of destructive hyperinflation."

Woolsey summed up by noting that "the long existence of a system encrusted by decades of inefficiency, coupled with the stresses in an empire once held together by force and one-party rule, have had a profound impact on the Russian people. Thus, he concluded, "it should come as a surprise to no one that the road ahead will continue to be a long and difficult one, and that these problems will exist in some form for years to come."

Yet even as concerns about a return to communism and runaway inflation were being raised in Washington, Russia's

Prime Minister Viktor Chernomyrdin, fifty-seven, who was natural gas minister in Gorbachev's first cabinet was cautioning that "the period of market romanticism has ended for us. We must make our people's life easier." Chernomyrdin expanded on this idea while on a trip to central Russia by promising to spend billions more subsidizing collective farms (in addition to $500 million for a new Parliament building). And as these giant steps toward hyperinflation were being announced, members of Russia State Duma, the country's powerful lower house of Parliament, were voting themselves a pay increase, free travel on trains and planes, free apartments in Moscow, free telephones, and round-the-clock limousine service.

This, needless to say, rang alarm bells in the West, so a few weeks later Chernomyrdin attempted to put things right by telling a meeting of the World Economic Forum in Davos, Switzerland, attended by some 2,000 Western executives and politicians, that "Russia will not turn back. There will be no backpedaling. I know what socialism is all about. There will be no going back to it."

In a report out of Moscow describing the waning of reform and the communists' comeback, the *Wall Street Journal* said that after two years of trying the reformers could not deliver the goods and that the Communist party has reclaimed power, which it realizes may well be its last hurrah since its "600,000 members are drawn mainly from Russia's graying masses: the disaffected pensioners who wax nostalgic for a bygone era that no one seemed to like at the time, but many now recall as the glory days." The *Journal* then went on to wonder "if the Yeltsin era is winding up," and quoted Viktor Linnik, who edits the pro-communist daily, *Pravda*, as saying, "The Yeltsin era is pretty much over." The paper then quoted Communist party head Gennady Zyuganov's remark: "They tried to put an American suit on Russia. But it didn't fit."

CRITIQUING BORIS YELTSIN

An analysis of Russia's current crisis that takes this view into account was given to the Senate Appropriations

Committee's Subcommittee on Foreign Operations by Princeton University's Soviet expert Stephen Cohen on the same day it heard from Talbott.

Professor Cohen, author of the definitive biography of the old Bolshevik revolutionary leader Nikolai Bukharin, told me, "The Senators wanted to hear a different view and they got it," including a scathing attack on Boris Yeltsin, whom he accused of being an "extremist leader" who "since 1991 has tried to impose from above very radical—that is, extremist—policies on a country that never voted for any of them.

"Yeltsin's most extreme policies," said Cohen, "came as three shocks to Russian society. In 1991, he suddenly abolished the Soviet Union, the only country most Russians had ever known. In 1992, his economic 'shock therapy' took away the life savings and standard of living of most Russian families. And in 1993, his tanks destroyed Russia's democratically elected Parliament and constitutional political system that was previously presented to the people as the embodiment of Russia's post-communist future. Yeltsin's shock leadership utterly polarized Russian society, opinion, and politics. But extremism always begets extremism. Yeltsin's extremism led to the extreme nationalist Zhirinovsky's big, but not surprising, victory in the democratic elections."

The man who paved the way for Yeltsin's rise to power was Mikhail Sergeyevich Gorbachev, who became general secretary on March 11, 1985, following the death of the ailing and ineffectual Communist party apparatchik Konstantin Chernenko.

Gorbachev, who had been number-two man in the Kremlin under Cherenko's predecessor Yuri Andropov, unleashed political, economic, military, and social reforms that rivaled Lenin's earlier revolution, including two historic breaks with past Soviet leadership. The first was his somber television address to the Soviet people describing the deadly meltdown that had occurred nearly three weeks earlier on April 26, 1986, in the Chernobyl nuclear power plant's number-four reactor, but had been hushed up by official denials. The second event was the telephone call he made eight months later to dissident nuclear physicist Andrei Sakharov, sixty-five, informing the father of the Soviet H-bomb and winner of the 1975 Nobel Peace Prize that he was being freed from his six-year exile in Gorki—which has been renamed Nizhny Novgorod and is where Sakharov's home is today a national shrine.

One of the more fascinating summations of Gorbachev's career as the last leader of the Soviet Union was given in an address by Andrei Sakharov's wife, Elena Bonner, at the University of California, Berkeley, on March 22, 1990, and later published in English in *The New York Review of Books*.

Dr. Bonner began by telling her audience that the two Russian words most strongly associated with the Gorbachev years—"perestroika," which means "reconstruction" in English, and "glasnost," which means "openness"—were actually used by her husband in his 1972 work *Memorandum to Soviet Leaders*, which also contained the word "stagnation" (which needs no translation).

Dr. Bonner said she believed Gorbachev's leadership passed through two phases, beginning with the first two to three years immediately after he assumed power. These years were "progressive" since he introduced glasnost, released a large number of prisoners of conscience, eased the policies for both emigration and visits to and from the Soviet Union, withdrew Soviet troops from the war in Afghanistan, and set an authentic disarmament process in motion with the West.

The later years of Gorbachev's reign—the second phase in Bonner's opinion—were primarily devoted to increasing his power while virtually ignoring internal crises such as helping the estimated 43 million Russians living below the poverty line.

Seventy Years on the Way to Nowhere

Within weeks after Bonner's talk, a May Day demonstrator in Moscow's Red Square was seen holding up a sign lamenting "Seventy Years on the Way to Nowhere." The month after that, *U.S. News & World Report*'s Moscow correspondents described Russia's economy as "all but dysfunctional," adding that "in the view of Gorbachev's own people, documented in public-opinion surveys, the Soviet Union today resembles nothing so much as a patient opened for surgery by a chief doctor who now has no idea what to do next."

A snapshot of employment in the Soviet Union in 1988—when Gorbachev's glasnost was in flower—highlights the areas of weakness in its economy compared, for example, with the United States and the then German Federal Republic. While the percentage of each country's labor force employed in manufacturing, construction, and community services was roughly equal, there was a profound difference in agriculture, wholesale and retail trade, and finance and insurance.

The precollapse Soviet Union had 20.2 percent of its labor force toiling in agriculture, compared with 5.3 percent in the Federal Republic and 2.9 percent in the United States. The country had just 6.1 percent of its workers in wholesale and retail trade, compared to more than double that in the Federal Republic (15.1 percent) and well over triple that in the United States (22.1 percent). But perhaps most interesting of all is that the Soviet Union had a mere 0.5 percent of its labor force employed in finance and insurance, compared with 6.7 percent in the German Federal Republic and a whopping 11.3 percent in the United States.

Equally unnerving is what happened to key Russian exports and imports in the critical 1990 to 1991 period as the Gorbachev era was drawing to a close, Yeltsin was gaining power, and the realization that democracy and free enterprise were within reach for the first time in decades was gaining momentum throughout the entire Soviet empire. Russia's exports of crude oil fell 50 percent from 2.2 million to 1.1 million barrels a day, in the 1990 to 1991 period, while television set exports plunged 57 percent, from 1.7 million to 700,000 units. Imports showed equally dramatic deterioration, with production equipment for food and light industry plunging 80 percent, leather shoes dropping from 136 million to 40 million pairs, and pharmaceutical purchases from abroad falling 43 percent, from 3.1 million to 1.8 million rubles.

This was the state of the Russian economy on Sunday, August 18, 1991, when Gorbachev, on vacation at his Crimean dacha some 900 miles from Moscow, was taken prisoner by a ragtag group of plotters, including Defense Minister Dmitri Yazov and KGB Chief Vladimir Kryuchkov, who told him that they had assumed control of the Soviet Union. Gorbachev was isolated, all the dacha's phones were cut off, and the briefcase containing the launch codes for Soviet nuclear missiles was missing.

Boris Yeltsin, who had been elected president of the Russian Republic on June 12, 1991, was vacationing at his dacha twelve miles outside of Moscow. When he was told on August 19 what had happened to Gorbachev, he immediately took off for Moscow and Parliament. Tanks and other military vehicles had surrounded the Parliament building, thousands of troops were pouring into the city, and at 11 A.M. Yeltsin held a press conference in which he called the coup "madness," adding, "I will never be removed by anyone except the Russian people." Then around 1 P.M., he left his office, entered the street, and climbed on top of a tank to urge the people to join in a general strike and fight the plotters. Shortly after 5 P.M., Yeltsin signed a decree putting all Russian military units under his command.

Yeltsin slept in the Parliament building that night. The next day, Tuesday, August 20, at a little before 4 P.M. he received orders from the plotters to surrender or face an all-out attack. He refused, the attack never came, and the next day the coup evaporated. Gorbachev flew back from the Crimea on Thursday, August 22, and an estimated 100,000 people gathered around the Parliament building to celebrate the collapse of the coup and their new hero, Boris Yeltsin.

Yeltsin's Brief Honeymoon

Yeltsin's honeymoon didn't last long, and among the reasons was the escalating battle with Parliament, which erupted into a bare-knuckle brawl in mid-1993 between a powerful Yeltsin presidency attempting to move the Russian economy toward a Western-style free market and an increasingly anti-

Yeltsin, communist-dominated Parliament with its own hide-bound ideas about Russia's destiny. This erupted into open warfare when Parliament returned from its summer holiday in August 1993 and Yeltsin called for the early election of a new body, which Parliamentary Speaker Ruslan I. Khasbulatov, fifty, immediately blasted as a "provocation." This triggered a series of historic events that are continuing to unfold to this day:

September 21: Yeltsin appeared on national television to announce that he had disbanded both the federal Supreme Soviet and the far-flung, 1,033-member Congress of People's Deputies and ordered new elections for December 11 and 12. Russian Prime Minister Viktor Chernomyrdin declared the government's support for Yeltsin and urged the country's regional leaders to do the same, which most of them did. The Parliament then immediately and overwhelmingly voted to impeach Yeltsin, ordered the nation's security forces to stop obeying him, and elected Afghanistan war hero and former Yeltsin running mate Aleksandr V. Rutskoi, forty-five, as acting president. Moscow remained calm, and the Russian Army pledged "strict neutrality." Yeltsin retaliated by dissolving Parliament; taking control of its newspapers, radio, and television programs; rescinding his tormentors' diplomatic travel passes; and announcing new presidential elections for June 12, 1994, in which he said he would run again for president.

September 23: Yeltsin was joined for a stroll in Pushkin Square by Defense Minister General Pavel Grachev and Interior Minister Viktor Yerin, and was later seen chatting casually with Security Minister Nikokai Golushko—who all pledged their support. Rutskoi spent the night in the Parliament building called the "White House" and the next day issued additional resolutions calling for resistance to Yeltsin. He then named his own ministers of defense and security. Yeltsin cut off all government telephones in the White House and closed down its radio and television broadcasting facilities. Parliament countered by calling a meeting of the Congress of People's Deputies, which under Russia's Soviet-era constitution had the power to officially oust Yeltsin, but it failed to round up a quorum.

President Clinton threw his support to Yeltsin, as did other Western leaders from Britain's Prime Minister John Major to German Chancellor Helmut Kohl. Russia's Central Bank Chairman Viktor Gerashchenko also sided with Yeltsin, further strengthening his hand at the expense of Rutskoi, whose every decree since becoming acting president had been completely ignored by Yeltsin.

September 28: Security Minister Golushko sealed off the White House and the parliamentarians inside with razor-sharp concertina wire. Trucks and troops surrounded the building, and the estimated 600 fighters inside were told to lay down their arms—thought to consist of 1,000 assault rifles, 2,000-plus pistols, 18 machine guns, 12 grenade launchers, and perhaps a ground-to-air missile.

October 2: Widespread street violence erupted, and former Soviet Army general Rutskoi urged everyone to rise up and rebel against the dictatorship of Boris Yeltsin, who had overwhelming public support according to the latest opinion polls.

October 3: Thousands of protesters gathered in Moscow's October Square, denounced the Yeltsin government and its economic reforms, and broke through a police cordon surrounding the White House—convincing Rutskoi, Khasbulatov, and the others inside that they had won. Yeltsin was at his dacha in the country; at 4 P.M. he declared a state of emergency banning all public meetings and demonstrations. Rutskoi appeared on a White House balcony and urged the crowd below to seize the office of the mayor of Moscow and the nearby television station. Yeltsin arrived at his Kremlin office at 6 P.M. by helicopter. At 7 P.M. Moscow Mayor Yuri Luzhkov went on television urging the masses to "stand against the illegal activities of the provocateurs." At midnight the Defense Ministry decided to storm the White House.

October 4: At 7 A.M. the Yeltsin government issued a final appeal for those inside the White House to surrender. At 9 A.M. Yeltsin appeared on television vowing that "the armed fascist putsch in Moscow will be crushed." At 10 A.M. tanks opened fire on the White House and the upper floors were soon in flames. At 11:30 A.M. crack antiterrorist troops stormed the White House. At 2:30 P.M. three men left the burning building carrying white flags of surrender. At 5 P.M. they were followed by others leaving with their hands in the air. At 6 P.M. Rutskoi and Khasbulatov were marched out of the White House under guard, put aboard a bus, and taken off to Lefortovo Prison. Yeltsin had nipped a potentially bloody revolution in the bud. Still, 142 Russians had died in the worst civil violence since the 1917 Bolshevik revolution.

RULER OF A STAGNATING ECONOMY

What Yeltsin had inherited was a stagnating closed economy run by and for rapacious bureaucrats and biased toward heavy industry while disregarding the needs of its own consumers, not to mention world markets. The economy began stagnating in 1975, and productivity started sagging a year later, virtually assuring the system's eventual downfall and the current painful transition to a consumer-driven, globally-oriented free enterprise economy.

The former Soviet Union's inability to enter the world market, says Gorbachev's economic adviser Abel Aganbegyan in his book *Inside Perestroika: the Future of the Soviet Economy*, created "a hothouse atmosphere for enterprises and organizations." They were "not forced to change their product, improve quality or adopt new technology." Nor did they have to sell their output abroad, or work together with other firms, and as a result did "not participate in the world experience of production. They continue to stew in their own juice. Ultimately, they generally fall behind."

Russia's economic disaster has continued to worsen with signs only now beginning to appear that a significant recovery may be under way. This is true even though real wages and consumption seem locked in a downward spiral, the dimensions of the nation's environmental and health crises are frightening, there has been a serious increase in crime along with social and economic inequality, and hundreds of outmoded and overstaffed plants are finally being closed with the loss of millions of jobs. The famous Zil automobile factory known for its huge trucks and big black limousines, to mention one example, dismissed more than 20,000 of its 85,000 works in May 1994, with more layoffs virtually certain unless the government comes across with the billions of rubles that Zil's management says it needs to survive.

The significance of mass layoffs at Zil and other large Russian factories was brought up sharply in an article by MIT professor Stanley Fischer in a 1992 issue of *Brookings Papers on Economic Activity*, which included a table showing that in 1988 the former Soviet Union had only 1.8 percent of its people working in enterprises with from one to ninety-nine people, compared to 27.6 percent in the United States at about the same time. While the United States had 25.8 percent of its labor force working in factories with 1,000 or more employees, the Soviet Union had 73.3 percent, reflecting its heavy concentration of production in the relatively few plants serving the entire far-flung nation.

The tumultuous events that marked the beginning of 1994 did not materialize out of the blue. They had been building up for months as Yeltsin clung to power in the Kremlin in the face of an increasingly powerful and democratically elected Parliament.

Yeltsin had been struggling to create a new Russia with an entrepreneurially driven market economy and democratic institutions. This was a daunting undertaking since it meant, among other things, enacting inflation-fighting tight money policies at the very moment powerful pressure groups of every kind were demanding financial help, no matter what the cost. This can be seen in the first round of Russia's 1994 budget estimates in which government income was projected at a wildly optimistic equivalent of $107 billion or so, while spending was being outrageously low-balled at $71 billion. It is worth noting while Russia was talking about spending $107 billion, the Clinton administration was getting ready to present Congress with spending estimates totaling $1.5 trillion.

One of the most urgent problems facing Yeltsin is the need to end the huge subsidies being paid to support millions of workers employed by state-owned farms and factories producing little of value except jobs. This would dramatically increase unemployment, which the International Labor Organization in Geneva put at a brutal 10 million as of mid-1994, while 1 million jobless had been the norm in Russia's make-work economy. Equally unnerving numbers come from Russia's own Labor Ministry, which predicts that the people currently living on pensions—360 for every 1,000 at work—will nearly double to 700 per 1,000 by 2010. This assumes the country can find the money to support the additional millions of older people, who traditionally retire at fifty-five in Russia compared with sixty-five in the United States. Out-of-work Russians, along with those getting paid for merely showing up, will have to be kept on the dole until the private sector begins hiring in quantity, which will take years.

What Yeltsin's strategists did do in an attempt to hype the economy is lift price controls on most wholesale and retail goods. They also trimmed the budget deficit by introducing a value-added tax, cutting subsidies for both consumer and industrial enterprises, demonopolizing domestic trade, deregularizing foreign trade, decentralizing the distribution system, and slashing defense spending. Then on July 5, 1995, they finally fixed the ruble's exchange rate—at between 4,300 and 4,900 to the dollar until October 1, 1995.

One hopeful sign is that Russia is gradually becoming a player in international commerce despite the battering of its economy, caused by everything from the country's deteriorating transportation system to the loss of major export markets in Eastern Europe. The International Monetary Fund estimated that Russia's exports totaled $35.4 billion and its imports $37.1 billion within a year or so after becoming a sovereign nation. What is interesting is that 70 percent of this trade was with the West, up sharply from about 25 percent in the mid-1980s. This surge in trade was mainly at the expense of Russia's old allies in Eastern Europe and its client states in the developing world.

The Russian legislature did its part by approving a plan for privatizing 60 percent of all existing small businesses as of late 1992, and according to recent figures from the U.S. Agency for International Development—which is helping to underwrite the effort—some 80 to 85 percent of all Russian state property would be privatized before the end of 1994.

CREATING INSTANT CAPITALISTS

A far more sweeping program to put Russia's productive facilities into private hands was the distribution of privatization vouchers beginning on October 1, 1992. Adults received vouchers valued at 10,000 rubles—equivalent to roughly six weeks of wages for the average Russian—which they could use up until July 1, 1994, to:

1. buy shares in the privatized factories in which they worked, such as the huge KamAZ truck factory.

2. buy enterprises put up for auction by the government, such as tourist hotels, fishing fleets, restaurants, service centers, chemical and car plants, and, with reluctance, some urban land.

3. swap their vouchers for shares in any one of dozens of funds that would use them to make substantial investments in newly privatized firms (although quite a few, such as the Technical Progress Fund, would simply disappear into the night). Boris Yeltsin is said to have invested in a fund called AKKIP, which promptly trumpeted the fact to one and all.

4. sell their vouchers to others—including foreigners—for cash, which a great many did with dispatch.

Investors put a value of $7.3 billion on Russia's 500 largest privatized companies when they were auctioned off with nearly half this amount accounted for by the ten largest firms of which eight were in natural resources—primarily oil. Only 92 companies were valued at more than $10 million apiece by voucher holders, 166 at less than $2 million, and a surprising 13,500 knocked down for next to nothing.

A study by the chief of the Russian Privatization Center Maxim Boycko, and Harvard University professor Andrei Shleifer, found that while U.S. companies have a market value of about $100,000 per employee, in Russia the average is under $1,000. In some cases such as the country's largest car maker Avtovaz it is a scarcely believable $81 per worker. The "most plausible explanation" for the cheapness of Russian manufacturing assets, say Boycko and Shleifer, is that shareholders fear their investments in these companies may be somehow expropriated by their employees, management, or even the Russian government itself.

Russia's Privatization Ministry estimated that toward the end of 1994, foreign investment in Russian companies was running at $600 million a month, and investment analysts in both Europe and the U.S. are touting money-making opportunities in Russia as being absolutely immense despite undeniable risks growing out of everything from the lack of reliable financial information to an increasing nationalistic outcry against foreign ownership of Russian industry (not to mention expropriation).

Richard Greer, a research director at the British investment firm of Baring Securities, has advised its clients that Russia offers "opportunities for investors unmatched in any other emerging market." And Eugene Lawson, president of the Council for Trade and Economic Cooperation that promotes U.S.–Russian business relationships, sees American direct investment in Russia reaching $50 billion in the next ten years (compared with the $316 billion foreign firms invested in U.S. companies alone during the past decade).

PROBLEMS DEMANDING
IMMEDIATE ATTENTION

As Russia gradually converts its vast landmass from the comfort and familiarity of communism to the daunting complexity and promise of capitalism, it must also deal with a host of pressing problems requiring immediate attention. Among the most urgent are maintaining control of some 25,000 nuclear warheads (down from 45,000 said to have existed in 1986 when Western intelligence experts put the entire world total at 50,000); repaying billions of dollars owed by the former Soviet Union; reversing the poisoning of one-sixth of the earth's landmass and potentially millions of people; controlling outbreaks of interethnic violence; and putting in place the new production and distribution arrangements, laws, and government oversight institutions needed to manage a successful market economy.

The great transition to a capitalist economy could have been theoretically accomplished in a remarkably short time using an audacious scheme advanced by radical economist Stanislav Shatalin, which both Gorbachev and Yeltsin temporarily embraced but were unwilling to implement. The Shatalin Plan, says Stanley Fischer in his Brookings article mentioned earlier, would have "transformed the Soviet Union into a market economy within 500 days beginning on October 1, 1990." This would have been accomplished through a series of giant steps, one after the other. Small businesses, housing, and vehicles would be quickly privatized, for example, with the money received for them making a "serious contribution to balancing the budget." Then a market structure would be put in place, wages would be indexed to inflation, imports of consumer goods increased, prices liberalized, ruble convertibility achieved, and so on until the job was done. "Read in the light of hindsight," says Fischer, "the plan did not recognize the imminence of the threat of collapse of the Soviet Union. Moreover, the plan's 500-day target was unrealistically ambitious, although the notion of a sequenced program makes sense."

Yeltsin Fights to Keep Russia "A Unified Force"

The forces that destroyed the old Soviet Union are now buffeting Russia itself as various regional councils—equivalent to state legislatures in America—refuse to send money to the central treasury and threaten secession as they pursue what they see as their own individual destinies. Boris Yeltsin has come out swinging at these semiautonomous republics based on ethnic groups and regional administrations longing to breathe free.

On August 13, 1993, two years after the attempted coup that led to the collapse of the Soviet Union, Yeltsin warned that if Russia could not be held together peacefully, "it could be done by naked force, by a dictatorship."

"The Russian Federation," added Yeltsin's press spokesman, Vyacheslav Kostikov, "is not a piece of Swiss cheese."

Yeltsin is currently demonstrating his commitment to a unified Russia, as we have seen, by putting the heat on Chechnya, a small mountainous republic in southern Russia with just over a million people, who declared their independence from Moscow at the end of 1991. Yeltsin wants Chechnya back in the fold and is doing everything he can to overthrow what he sees as its rump regime.

Yeltsin clearly understands the seriousness of the regional forces threatening to pull Russia apart. In an effort to keep it "a unified force," he has proposed the creation of a Federation Council on which leaders from regional administrations would serve. This proposal, he noted, was first backed by the regions but was blocked by the Supreme Soviet, which—understandably—saw it as a parallel parliament and hence a direct threat to its power.

The Great Leadership Struggle Continues

The titanic struggle between Yeltsin and Parliament continues to fester, exploding again on February 23, 1994, when the Duma approved a wide-ranging amnesty for Khasbulatov and Rutskoi, along with those who had collaborated with them in attempting to overthrow Yeltsin's government. A mixed bag of others accused of lesser crimes were also given their freedom, as were the plotters who had attempted to oust President Mikhail Gorbachev's government back in August 1991.

This amnesty was a savage slap at Yeltsin and unleashed a torrent of reactions, ranging from his spokesman Vyacheslav Kostikov's comment that it was "a challenge to Russian democracy," to his archenemy Vladimir Zhirinovsky's celebration of it as "a historic moment."

Zhirinosky was waiting at the gate of the maximum-security Lefortovo Prison as Khasbulatov emerged followed by Rutskoi, who had grown a full beard and was wearing his "Hero of the Soviet Union" medal. When Russians choose their next president, said Zhirinovsky, the choice would be between him and Rutskoi.

Yeltsin reappeared on the scene when he gave his State of the Nation speech to a joint session of the newly elected legislature, after his followers had been soundly defeated in the election. The president somberly reeled off a long list of problems eating at the heart of Russia with particular emphasis on crime and corruption.

Yeltsin was seriously hurt by the election of a hostile Duma and the release from prison of Khasbulatov and Rutskoi, whom he has not forgotten. "I would like to emphasize," Yeltsin said, "that those who by the decision of the State Duma were amnestied, and pursuant to our laws, will again be arrested if they even begin any political or other action to damage the security of the Russian State."

Yeltsin pushed a new constitution through Russia's Parliament in December 1993 following the country's first multiparty election. It allows him to retain control over the key ministries of Defense, Foreign Affairs, and Interior and the former KGB, while continuing as commander-in-chief of the armed forces with the power to nominate the prime minister. Yeltsin further strengthened his hand by increasing his hold over the State Duma so that he can dissolve it and call for new elections if its members reject two of his candidates for prime minister. Russia's continuing struggle to establish a broad-based, legitimate government that can achieve sustainable economic reform has led to questions concerning what some believe is the West's heavy commitment to Boris Yeltsin. U.S. Senator Richard Lugar, Republican from Indiana and a member of the Senate's powerful Foreign Relations Committee, remarked recently: "Our preoccupation with President Yeltsin appears to be shortsighted. He's simply not up to the job right now."

That remains to be seen. What is certain is that onrushing events impacting Russia and her neighbors will continue to harass an ailing sixty-four-year-old Boris Yeltsin until his term is up in 1996, when he could very well face—should he decide to run again—an unrepentant Aleksandr Rutskoi, the ubiquitous off-the-wall Vladimir Zhirinovsky, or an increasingly popular and energetic Viktor Chernomyrdin.

10

Turmoil in the "Near Abroad"

"The West must understand that the newly independent countries, having brought down the Soviet empire, are still faced with the problem of millions of men and women steeped in parasitic attitudes, naive faith in the State and fear of its enormous power and secret bureaucracy."

Rustan Azimov, chairman,
National Bank Tashkent, Uzbekistan

"Our relationship with Ukraine is more important to Russia than our relationship with any other country in the world."

Yegor Gaidar, economist and
former first deputy prime minister

Russians call the newly independent lands that used to be part of the Soviet Union the "near abroad," and if Russia is in desperate shape economically—and it is—then these countries embroiled in problems from musical comedy political leadership to hyperinflation are certifiable basket cases.

So much so that Princeton University's Soviet expert Stephen Cohen, in his testimony before the U.S. Senate Appropriations Committee's Subcommittee on Foreign Operations, said he believes "some sort of new union is going to emerge there—a Russia plus. If we put it crudely, and a little unfairly, Georgia is now a military province of Russia. Tajikistan is being run by the Russian Army and its political counterparts in return for policing its Afghan border. Half of Moldova is now in Russian hands. Kazakhstan—half of which is Russian and which abuts Russia—has to come to terms with Russia.

"Eventually," Cohen concluded, "a new Russian-centered union is going to emerge. How many of the former republics will be there I don't know. Whether it will emerge through persuasion, in a voluntary way, or through force of arms I also do not know. But you should prepare yourself for this emerging reality."

Alexander M. Haig, Jr., the four-star general who was NATO commander in Europe and secretary of state in the Reagan administration, seemingly agreed with Cohen a few days later at a meeting in the State Department when he criticized Russia for unleashing a barrage of neo-imperialism in Georgia, Tajikistan, Moldova, Armenia, and Ukraine "that's got to curdle your blood."

THE AGONY OF UKRAINE

When former prime minister and missile factory boss Leonid D. Kuchma, fifty-five, defeated Leonid M. Kravchuk, sixty, on July 10, 1994, to become president of Ukraine, avowed nationalists feared he would quickly push his impoverished nation into the arms of Mother Russia, on which it depends for critical imports from raw materials to energy.

But while Kuchma immediately issued a joint statement with Russian President Boris Yeltsin reaffirming the need to get on with divvying up the ships in their jointly owned Black Sea fleet, Kuchma surprised everyone by soft-pedaling his campaign rhetoric about integrating with Russia and instead reached out to the West.

U.S. Vice President Al Gore, who was the first foreign leader to call on Kuchma following his election, assured him of America's support, reminded him that it was President Clinton who had just urged the wealthy industrialized nations to offer Ukraine $4 billion in aid, and invited him to visit the president in Washington, D.C., on November 29, 1994.

Kuchma had promised Ukrainian voters that if elected president he would streamline the government and fight for a quick tax cut in a desperate effort to revive the country's sagging economic output, which dropped a frightening 30 percent during the first four months of 1994 alone. But Ukraine's communist-dominated Parliament showed little interest in Kuchma's decision to stimulate the economy, opting instead to freeze any further privatization of industry, just as it had earlier failed to ratify the agreement then-president Kravchuk had signed in January to eliminate 176 long-range missiles and some 1,800 nuclear warheads.

Ukraine's defeated president Leonid Kravchuk was a senior Communist party ideologist before being elected to his country's top office following its independence from the USSR on August 24, 1991. No sooner had he taken office, however, than he was overwhelmed by a multitude of emergencies. Inflation, for example, was running in excess of 100 percent a month. The all-important rail system was grinding to a halt because of the lack of maintenance and spare parts. Nearly one out of every two Ukrainians was living below the poverty line. And there had been little effort to encourage the transition to a free market economy, already hobbled by a recalcitrant Parliament's orders stalling the privatization of medium- and large-scale industry.

State enterprises had run up unpaid debts with each other exceeding $3 billion, production had collapsed, deliveries had stopped, and workers had gone unpaid for months. To put things right, the Kravchuk government—before it was sent packing—had announced its intention to flood the economy with inflation-hyping credits equal to 10 percent of 1993's GNP in a desperate effort to stimulate industry and agriculture.

Ukrainians were so fed up with Kravchuk's leadership that a year-end poll showed that only 11 percent had confidence in him and that a mere 17 percent were prepared to vote for him. Then–prime minister Leonid Kuchma had seen the light months earlier, resigning on September 9, 1993, following a statement to the Cabinet saying he was "convinced Ukraine needs urgent political reforms without which no economic reforms can occur, and we could well lose our independence."

Ukraine has the second largest population of the former Soviet republics with 52 million people (11 million of whom are ethnic Russians). Its citizens are well-educated, and its abundant natural resources should have put this Texas-sized land on the road to prosperity in the few years since independence. But just the opposite is true. "Our country is now at the brink of catastrophe," says President Kuchma, and it is easy to see why.

Ukraine's economy is in ruins, its hard currency reserves are almost exhausted, energy use has been cut to the bone, many of its factories are operating at only a fraction of capacity, coal miners' strikes in the mineral-rich Donbass region are endemic, and this once agriculturally rich country that used to grow a quarter of the Soviet Union's wheat— and in the nineteenth century was the world's largest grain exporter—must now import grain when it can find the money. One upshot of all this has been the return to barter, where a village trades part of its sugar crop for fuel from a nearby oil refinery, while its residents swap pigs for bricks.

Once flourishing trade with Russia, on which it depends for much of its oil and natural gas, has all but evaporated. In early 1994, Russia decided to end natural gas shipments to Ukraine, which had failed to pay for past deliveries worth more than $700 million. Deliveries have since resumed, following Ukraine's promise to pay half its debt for 1993 in hard currency and half in equipment and parts for Russia's gas transportation network, used to carry its natural gas to customers in Western Europe. All this is reflected in Ukraine's GNP, which the World Bank estimates fell by 18 percent in 1992, 25 percent in 1993, and showed few signs of improvement in 1994. The drop has been so drastic that a Ukrainian toilet paper company has started using the national currency—called "coupons"—in manufacturing its product. "It would not be an exaggeration to call the situation catastrophic," said Volodymyr Cherniak of Ukraine's Institute of the Economy.

Just about the only aces in Ukraine's deck are the $12 billion Ukrainians are believed to have stashed away in foreign banks and elsewhere (compared to an estimated $40 billion for Russians); its arsenal of aging nuclear weapons inherited from Russia, which it has talked about getting rid of in return for what could add up to $1 billion; and the growing attention the country is receiving from the United States as a counterforce to a return of Russian imperialism.

While Ukraine's present is unquestionably somber, its future doesn't have to be, according to a recent in-depth survey in Britain's *The Economist*. Ukraine's black earth is so rich, said the report, that it "enabled Ukraine to produce 1,033 kg of grain per head in 1991 when the Germans produced only 445 kg." Ukraine is also benefiting from the fact, adds *The Economist*, that "some Soviet-era military dinosaurs are learning to live with the market. Antonov, the maker of the world's largest cargo planes, has become a successful operator of charter flights through a joint-venture with Air Foyle, a British company. Yuzhmash, the world's largest missile plant, is producing trolley buses. And the Kharkiv tank factory is making mini-tractors which sell for less than $1,000."

The editors of *The Economist* are also impressed by the fact that Ukraine has the untapped elements "needed to launch successful economic reform: a good plan, people capable of implementing it, some financial help, and the political will to carry it through." The magazine believes the first three of these four elements are already in place since (1) Ukraine has "plenty of able officials," (2) "the World Bank and the IMF are ready to support any plan that looks half-credible," and (3) the country's "economics minister is putting the finishing touches to a plan that might not be perfect, but is at least a good stab at an orthodox stabilization programme." The only question remaining is, Do Ukrainians have the stomach for the sacrifices needed to save their economy and will they find a leader "to forge the political will to do what needs to be done? Without such a leader the future looks bleak."

In the Lap of Ukrainian Luxury

I was introduced to Ukraine's troubles when I strolled into the lobby of what passed for a first-class hotel in Kiev and noticed that only five of the fifty-six overhead lights actually worked. The rest, I was told, had their bulbs snatched for use in other parts of the hotel, were stolen by locals desperate for illumination (and replaced with burnt-out bulbs), or were unavailable because under the Soviets lightbulb production had been concentrated in Azerbaijan, which is at war with neighboring Armenia.

I had arrived at the hotel shortly after 8 P.M., and after freshening up went down to the dining room, which had been converted into a nightclub, ordered a tumbler of vodka, and listened to a three-piece rock and roll band attached to the usual half-ton of amplification equipment blast out the latest hits (about half in English). The dance floor was packed with attractively dressed couples in their twenties and thirties having a terrific evening on the town, which was ending its celebration of the fiftieth anniversary of the liberation of Ukraine from the German Army during the Great Patriotic War.

Ukraine's poverty is instantly apparent on the streets of Kiev—often called "the mother of Russian cities"—where there are few cars during the day and hardly any at night, perhaps because about one out of every three streetlights seems to be missing a bulb. Crowds of people stand motionless in the cold waiting for buses, which are in short supply as is everything else unless you have dollars (I had an excellent chicken Kiev dinner with wine for twenty-five dollars, which is more than many Ukrainian workers make in a month).

Capitalism is slowly emerging in the Ukraine where its most spectacular showcase so far is Seagram's glittering jewel of a store in drab downtown Kiev. Seagram was founded by the Bronfman family, which immigrated from Ukraine years ago, and this store looks like it is saying, "Here's what awaits you if you make it big in the West." Bottles of rare liquors, brandy, champagne, Irish whisky, and vodka stand enthroned on red and purple velvet in the well-lit window. The store had few customers the afternoon I walked by, and I was told they were probably newly rich entrepreneurs or members of the local Mafia who feed off them.

The first entrepreneur I stumbled upon in Kiev was far from rich and would hesitate to even step inside the hushed opulence of Seagram's palace today, although tomorrow could be different. I discovered her the morning after I arrived in Kiev, when I decided to go out in search of an eye-opening cup of coffee. I had walked only a few blocks when I encountered an old woman dressed in boots, a cloth coat tied around her middle with a piece of rope, and a babushka knotted beneath her chin, who was selling coffee, tea, and freshly baked buns in the lobby of a rundown office building. The place was frigid, and none of her cups had handles, yet she was doing a brisk business, making a little money, and obviously pleased as punch with herself.

My next stop was another nondescript building surrounded by high-rise apartments about an hour's drive from midtown Kiev. I had come to see an apple-cheeked man of twenty-six, who greeted me in his office lit by two bare bulbs dangling from the ceiling and then took me on a tour that bordered on the astonishing. As we walked along concrete corridors and through peeling plywood doors, I was ushered into one room after the other filled with state-of-the-art Japanese television equipment. Young men in blue jeans and young women in miniskirts were hovering over the equipment, turning out television shows and ads for sale in Ukraine and Russia.

The equipment had cost $800,000, but it was almost entirely amortized thanks to the company's booming sales, which reached $1.5 million in 1993 and I was told have no place to go but up. The reason is that practically everyone has access to a television set, and the demand for locally produced entertainment and commercials is expected to keep growing for years. As I was leaving, I put my arm around my young host and said, "In twenty-five years you'll be bigger than CBS." Without a moment's hesitation, he replied, "Bigger!"

Businesses like this intrigue the Ukraine Fund, with offices in Kiev and Boston, which began doing venture capital deals with small firms here in mid-1992 when it had less than $1 million in capital, which it has since increased to $10 million. Additional money took little time arriving from sources such as the European Bank for Reconstruction and Development, the Bank of Boston, and the Boston-based venture capital firm of Claflin Capital Management, Inc., which launched the fund.

The fund is being run on a day-to-day basis by George Yurchyshyn, who was born in Ukraine and is a vice president of Claflin Capital, which granted him a leave of absence to serve as deputy chairman of the National Bank of Ukraine (the country's central bank). The fund is focusing on areas that it says "were almost totally ignored under the former Soviet economic regime including building materials, home furnishings, small appliances, communications, hand tools, medical supplies, food products, distribution, publishing, computer services, media and finance."

The fund's first investment was in one of the largest privately owned retail distribution companies in Kiev, followed by a small furniture factory and a food processor that began operations in mid-1993. The fund says it is looking for investments between $50,000 and $250,000, with "ultimate positions in some companies being perhaps as large as $400,000 to $500,000," in which other foreign firms would be welcome as co-investors. The fund is eager to put its capital to work, has no hesitation about the moneymaking possibilities in Ukraine, and is currently looking at what it considers excellent opportunities in marine hardware, wet cell batteries, contract sewing, and ceramic tiles among others.

One company the fund has looked at is Stolichny Enterprise, which is the largest service operation in Kiev and has over 400 employees at work meeting local needs for everything from dry cleaning, hairdressing, and clothing manufacture, to jewelry, printing, and appliance repair.

Stolichny is a state-owned business that was eager to improve its operations so it could attract an outside investor such as the Ukraine Fund and then go private. To do this, it worked with Citizens Democracy Corps adviser Fred Krieger, who spent seven weeks at its headquarters meeting with Director Irina Marinina and her management team.

What Krieger discovered was that Stolichny was doing a lot of things right and quite a few wrong. He felt the company's management team was capable and hard-working, and that its director's prime contacts in business and government were key factors in helping Stolichny deal with bureaucratic regulation and corruption. He also felt the company's inexpensive services appealed to Ukraine's masses of low-income consumers (although a more afflu-ent group was emerging offering opportunities for higher profit margins), that the quality and speed of delivery of its services were good and in some cases better than in the United States, and that being a cash business would help it turn a profit in 1993.

What Stolichny badly needed to change, Krieger quickly realized, were negatives he knew might be beyond management's ability to put right. Among the most critical were the soaring cost of hot water, which tripled in price in 1993 alone; cleaning chemicals, which were difficult to buy; cloth for apparel, which was of poor quality and in limited supply; and the government's insistence that it keep deliv-ering unprofitable services while adding new ones.

Krieger advised Director Marinina to prepare a Western-style business and strategic plan, which he wound up writ-ing himself for her approval (she approved it with few changes). He then suggested that a prospectus be prepared to acquaint investors and lenders with the potential value of the company following privatization. This meant drawing up a profit and loss statement and a balance sheet. "I found," says Krieger, "that while these are very elementary principles in Western business, the types of reports developed under the communistic system and perpetuated by the State today do not provide a clear analysis of revenues, costs, profits, or losses over any time period. In addition, the re-cording of sales revenues and customer counts by individual businesses at Stolichny was lacking. While the Accounting Department insisted it had records of this information, it could never produce one unified report that recorded these important statistics over the past year."

Krieger believes the financial prospectus and reporting system he prepared for Stolichny will help investors and lenders to better evaluate the business, while pinpointing those areas that would benefit from increased management attention, including bringing in experts—hopefully volunteers from the United States—to suggest ways to strengthen the company's apparel design and manufacturing operations, its dry cleaning and laundromat services, and its financial reporting and overall control mechanisms.

The U.S. Agency for International Development has proposed a $100 million Western NIS Enterprise Fund to stimulate the creation and expansion of newly privatized—or privatizing—businesses in the emerging economies of Ukraine, Belarus, and Moldova, with emphasis on economic reform in Ukraine and Belarus. Ukraine's Parliament has approved the sales of a large chunk of state-owned businesses by the end of 1994. The deal would increase the private sector's share of Ukraine's economy from 2 percent to 28 percent by selling 20,000 small enterprises, 8,000 medium-sized and large firms, and 1,400 unfinished construction projects. Most of these assets will be exchanged for privatization vouchers, which were distributed free to Ukrainian citizens.

Making Money Selling Apples in Ukraine

Steve Minsky is the general manager and principal owner of CDC Ltd., headquartered in Kiev, which is the sole distributor of Apple Computer products throughout the entire Ukraine. CDC provides Ukrainian language hardware, software, and documentation solutions to a customer list ranging from newspaper and advertising agencies to banks and engineering firms. Although Minsky will not reveal CDC's sales and profits, he says the company was "tremendously successful" within months after it opened its doors.

Minsky grew up in Boston, graduated from Tufts University, worked for General Foods in the United States and Japan, moved over to Procter & Gamble in Taiwan, and went on to the University of Pennsylvania's Wharton School, where he received a master's degree in 1991.

He then went to work as director of sales and marketing for Apple Computer in Czechoslovakia. "When I started there," he says, 'sales were $240,000 a month. When I left a year later, they were averaging $650,000 a month. We were successful in Czechoslovakia during a time when it was going through the same kind of upheaval and privatization that is happening in the Ukraine today."

Getting his own Apple Computer business up and running in Kiev, where he had to go head-to-head with heavyweights such as IBM, Hewlett-Packard, DEC, and Compaq, took Minsky four months of working twelve to sixteen hours a day, seven days a week, before he felt he could take an occasional day off.

"The people in the Ukraine have tremendous technical backgrounds and are highly qualified programmers," says Minsky, "in part because they haven't exactly had the latest technology to work with. Much of their software, for example, was outdated and came without documentation.

"People here had heard of Apple," Minsky says, "but they had never seen the Apple logo and they didn't know much about us. One of the reasons we've been successful here is that we take a long-term approach. In the education field, for example, we show users how a computer can support classroom instruction, how it can be used as an educational tool. Training and consulting is a very important strategic aspect of our business."

An understanding of what Minsky has accomplished can be better appreciated when you realize that Apple's efforts to break into the huge Soviet market failed back when President Mikhail Gorbachev was in power, even though the company had presented him with a free Macintosh computer. Today, Apple is solidly on the ground in Russia and aggressively tapping what it sees as a terrific market.

Apple is breaking new ground in Ukraine by setting up a software and development project with the National Academy of Sciences of Ukraine to capitalize on the country's 500,000 or so programmers, who it believes could be writing 2 percent of the world's software sometime around the year 2000. The select group of Ukrainian programmers initially chosen to write the software will be paid 25 percent of what they would earn in the United States. Nearly half of the profits from the joint venture's foreign sales will be used to buy more Apple computers and related hardware.

The Rusting of Ukraine's Big Steel Industry

Typical of Ukraine's many problems is its once-powerful steel industry, whose ten mills, which used to produce 40 percent of the Soviet Union's steel needs, make it the world's fourth largest producer despite its antiquated, overstaffed, and badly polluting plants. Ukraine's 1993 steel output plummeted to 4 million tons from the prior year's 7 million because of crippling coal strikes in the nearby Donbass region, and the situation seems destined to get worse before it gets better.

Ukraine's big Stalin-era Azovstal steel plant, located in the southern city of Mariupol on the Sea of Azov, operates old-fashioned open-hearth furnaces yet still produces steel plate whose price and quality allowed it to sell 40,000 tons to the United States in 1992, which shot up to nearly 200,000 tons in 1993. The company's management has no idea how many man-hours it takes it to produce a ton of steel because it says "we don't have the methods to calculate this figure."

An estimated 10,000 of the Azovstal plant's 25,000 workers are involved in nonsteelmaking activities (such as running a hospital and football stadium), and its newest production facility is more than twenty years old in a hotly competitive global steel industry that routinely spends billions a year on new facilities.

To make matters worse, steel consumption has dropped sharply in Ukraine, whose formerly communist-dominated government demands that its steel factories exchange half the hard currency earned from sales to the West for virtually worthless coupons. This means it is extremely difficult for the industry to find the dollars, Deutschemarks, and so on needed to modernize its facilities in order to remain competitive.

Fear of a Nuclear Disaster

While the West is content to see Ukraine's steel industry stew in its own juice, it is decidedly concerned about its nuclear power industry, which it sees as a distinct threat because of the Chernobyl disaster. In April 1994, Ukraine promised to shut down the two nuclear reactors still operating at Chernobyl, but it has apparently changed its mind, as these units are still producing power. It is also talking about restarting in 1995 a third Chernobyl reactor, which was turned off in 1991 following a fire, leaving only the fourth reactor—the one that was consumed by an explosion in 1986 blanketing much of Europe with radioactive dust. Chernobyl's two working reactors produce a mere 3 percent of the country's electricity, yet Ukrainian officials see these nuclear plants—along with their stockpile of nuclear ICBM warheads—as heaven-sent bargaining chips with which to squeeze hundreds of millions out of the West.

The European Union has offered to help Ukraine finance the completion of three half-built Soviet-style reactors experts regard as flawed, providing it agrees to shut down Chernobyl's two working reactors and not restart the third. But Ukraine is unlikely to do this since it needs nuclear power, which currently supplies a third of its electricity, is likely to supply even more in the future, and is far cheaper than power generated by oil- or coal-fired plants (let alone juice provided by renewable resources such as wind power, being pushed by the West).

This is true even though Ukraine's demand for energy fell sharply between 1990 and 1993 along with an even steeper drop in industrial production, which shows few signs of improving. One of Ukraine's problems is that it has been delivering electricity to industry at about half of what it costs to generate, and to households for considerably less. This is unfortunate since if power were sold at cost plus a profit— still an off-the-wall concept in the backwaters of the old communist bloc—it would be an incentive for Ukrainian industry to become more energy efficient, hence more productive, while providing power stations with the money they need to upgrade their personnel, maintenance, and equipment.

Dismantling Nuclear Weapons

One of Ukraine's most valuable assets is its deteriorating nuclear arsenal, which it is in the process of swapping for desperately needed help from the United States and Russia, which will reprocess the missiles' nuclear innards. Details of this were discussed during former president Kravchuk's visit to Washington, D.C., in March 1994, when President Clinton pledged to double aid to Ukraine during the year to $700 million contingent upon the dismantling of its arsenal of long-range nuclear missiles.

Ukraine's army of half a million men is second only to Russia's in Europe, and its nuclear arsenal is the third largest in the world after the United States and Russia, with something like 130 Soviet-built SS-19 long-range nuclear missiles each carrying 10 warheads, 46 of the more modern SS-24s also equipped with up to 10 warheads apiece, and some 564 air-launched cruise missiles.

The important point is that this country wants to cut military spending in order to free up the resources it needs to build a strong market-driven economy. Former president Kravchuk said he wanted Ukraine to be a non-nuclear power, although it has yet to ratify the Strategic Arms Reduction Treaty, known as Start One, calling for the destruction of its missiles. Ukrainian officials said they are removing the warheads from their big SS-24 missiles and storing them away from the launchers and have also begun dismantling the aging SS-19s. Under the terms of the agreement, Ukraine would ship its nuclear warheads to Russia, where their uranium would be extracted and then sold by the United States as fuel for nuclear reactors around the world. Ukraine would get an estimated $1 billion or so of these revenues, plus low-enriched uranium for use in its civilian reactors, reducing its dependence on costly oil and natural gas imported from Russia. The first sixty of these nuclear warheads were put aboard a train for Russia in early 1994 as promised.

Ukraine's desperate need for Western aid and investment, should convince it to gradually do away with all of the old Soviet nuclear weapons on its soil under a proposed fixed timetable running for the next seven years. Right now the ball is in the Ukrainian Parliament's court. The United States, Russia, and Britain have stated that if Ukraine ships its nuclear weapons for dismantling it will never be threatened with an atomic attack, and before leaving office Kravchuk urged Parliament to approve the transfer, or risk "international isolation" and a nuclear calamity from "corroding warheads."

Turning Old Weapons into Cash Cows

Ukraine has already started profiting from the destruction of its obsolete conventional munitions, which are turning into something of a cash cow. Ukraine has commissioned Alliant Techsystems, Inc. of Edina, Minnesota, to convert 200,000 tons of its surplus ammunition, including artillery shells, mortar rounds, and tank projectiles, into valuable products for sale on the world market. The metals, representing 88 percent of the reclaimed munitions' value, will be sold as scrap, with the remaining 12 percent of explosives converted into fuels, fertilizers, and explosives used in mining operations.

The weapons will be dismantled and their valuable components reclaimed at ammunition depots throughout Ukraine, which are expected to create 100 or more badly needed jobs for local people and generate in excess of $100 million in sales for Alliant over the next five years. "Ukraine has inherited massive armed forces and military stockpiles of ammunition from the former Soviet Union," said Minister of Defense Konstantin P. Morozov. "Not having any territorial claims on others, and believing that issues can only be resolved through peaceful means, Ukraine has embarked on a major demilitarization program."

While Ukraine is seemingly committed to getting rid of its nuclear missiles and recycling its old ammunition (some dating back to 1905), it is sparring with Russia over control of the rotting Black Sea fleet at anchor in the Crimean port of Sevastopol, which neither of them really need. Both countries have repeatedly agreed to divide up the fleet, which should take several years to complete since it consists of some 300 vessels from submarines to helicopter carriers, about 500 naval combat and support aircraft, and anywhere from 70,000 to 100,000 people. Russian naval officers say the fleet is worth $330 billion, while others say $16 billion is closer to the mark, if that. In the meantime the blue and yellow Ukrainian flag is flying over a few small ships, even as the Russian Parliament proclaims that both Sevastopol and the entire Black Sea fleet should be controlled by Mother Russia alone.

On June 9, 1995, Boris Yeltsin and Ukraine President Leonid Kuchma, meeting in the Russian Black Sea resort of Sochi, agreed that Russia could buy up to 82 percent of Ukraine's share of the fleet and pay rent mostly in energy supplies and debt forgiveness for the right to berth its ships in Sevastopol. In the meantime, Ukraine is building its own fleet of warships in its own huge naval shipyards.

Crimea Wants to Dump Ukraine for Russia

All this maneuvering may become somewhat academic if Crimea, an autonomous region within Ukraine with its own president, 196-seat Parliament, militia, and control over its own budget, continues to call for independence so it can reintegrate with Russia, which looks almost affluent compared with Ukraine. Crimea is no lotus land itself. Its seedy capital of Simferopol is blessed with statues of Lenin, but little else—including privatization, which has been lighting fires under the economy of Russia but is virtually invisible in this Black Sea city whose sun and beaches have long made it the favorite vacation spot for Russian czars and later Communist party elite.

That is why the January 1994 election of separatist candidate and former lawyer Yuri A. Meshkov as Crimea's first president could prove significant. "I have made the choice many in Crimea made long ago for unity with Russia," said Meshkov, who is an ethnic Russian, received 73 percent of the vote in the presidential runoff, and should get plenty of support from Moscow as he is decidedly pro-Russian along with the majority of Crimea's 2.7 million citizens who are of Russian extraction.

Ukraine has threatened "decisive action" to keep Crimea, which has watched the collapse of the Ukrainian economy with horror. This is a tough call for Russia, which recently signed an agreement with the United States guaranteeing Ukraine's existing borders in order to encourage the country to give up its nuclear weapons. To make matters worse, then-Russian premier Nikita Khrushchev only gave Ukraine "the jewel" of Crimea in 1954 as a gift; and if its big ethnic Russian majority insists on it being returned to their motherland, it might be tough for Yeltsin or his successor to say no. But in 1995, Ukraine abolished Crimea's constitution and Meskov's role as president. Russia showed little interest in the move, making a separatist Crimea virtually a lost cause.

THE WHITE HOUSE HONORS BELARUS

Belarus is a Kansas-size country of nearly 11 million people that sits on Ukraine's northern border. It was catapulted into the headlines in January 1994 when President Clinton stopped off on his way from Moscow to Geneva to visit its capital of Minsk and then-chairman of its Supreme Soviet, Stanislav Shushkevich.

The president had months earlier honored Belarus by making Shushkevich the first head of a former Soviet republic to be invited to visit him in the White House, because of the country's willingness to get rid of its nuclear arsenal of old Russian-built SS-25 missiles. While there Shushkevich signed an agreement giving him $59 million of the $65 million he had been promised, with part of the funds going to convert one of Belarus's missile bases to civilian use, including housing for the officers who manned the facility.

Belarus declared its independence from the Soviet Union on August 25, 1991, and a few months later joined Russia and Ukraine in founding the Commonwealth of Independent States, with Minsk as the capital of both Belarus and the commonwealth. Belarus's pro-Russian, apparatchik-dominated Parliament, which had been elected when the country was still part of the Soviet Union, never thought much of Shushkevich and ousted him on January 26, 1994. Parliament was fed up with his reformist free-market policies that had done little if anything to improve the fortunes of this agricultural nation whose means of production are still overwhelmingly state owned although moving slowly toward privatization.

The man who replaced Shushkevich in a landslide victory was thirty-nine-year-old former farm manager, crusader against corruption, and member of Parliament Aleksandr Lukashenko. After taking office as the first elected president of Belarus, he said he was "shocked" to discover just how bad off his country really was. He then publicly vowed to put things right by freezing prices, taming inflation, giving everyone a job, aiding the elderly, slamming the brake on the privatization of business, sacking the old Communist party bosses who had actually been running the government, and aligning Belarus far more closely with Russia both politically and economically.

Belarus's GNP has been declining nonstop despite a skilled and highly educated workforce and a reasonably advanced manufacturing sector whose three top exports were recently refrigerators, wristwatches, and television sets. The trouble is that Belarus's biggest trading partner by far is Russia, whose imports have fallen sharply denying it—among other things—the rubles it needs to import energy and other supplies. Recently, Belarus's ambassador to the United States commented, "We're in for a long, long struggle on our way to a new society."

The question is what shape that society will take, and whether Belarus can remain independent of Russian entanglements long enough to achieve it. In the meantime, price increases are running at close to hyperinflation levels, goods are in short supply, stealing is becoming endemic, most of the country's citizens live below the official poverty line, and manufacturing is taking place under conditions frequently bordering on the primitive.

A Scary Lack of Safety Precautions

A delegation of top U.S. safety experts recently toured factories in Moscow, Saint Petersburg, Kiev, and Minsk, and what they saw at a huge tractor plant just outside the Belarus capital was both typical and unnerving. Among the delegation's findings, reported in the American Society of Safety Engineers' official publication *Professional Safety,* were:

- No worker wore any type of eye protection despite the high degree of machining taking place.
- Many young people on the assembly line were wearing sandals, even those on stations where heavy objects were moved and positioned around the tractor frame.
- Noise levels were extremely high, but we saw no one wearing hearing protection. We had to stand nose-to-nose and shout to be heard.
- No smoking signs were seen everywhere. However, people were smoking throughout the plant.
- We saw no fire protection in the facility—no extinguishers, sprinkler heads, sensors, alarms, or hose reels/racks.
- Hydraulic fluid was evident on the floor, equipment, assembly line tracks, and the area we walked in. Cracked oil lines leaked fluid all over individual work areas.
- At one station, several of us witnessed a worker precariously placing his hands into an operating punch press. On several cycles of the machine we thought he'd lose a hand.

While the U.S. delegation found that the former Soviet countries they visited are making headway in devising labor safety and environmental standards, they believe the objectives of these regulations are not being seriously enforced.

Belarus Enters the Air Cargo Business

One industry in which Belarus is making solid progress is air cargo through a company called TransAviaExport, which began operations in May 1993 with a fleet of four-engine Ilyusian 76s built at a factory in Tashkent, Uzbekistan, which is also supplying it with aircraft repair and technical support.

TransAviaExport, according to an *Aviation Week* report from Minsk, is approaching a million dollars worth of business a month through scheduled cargo flights to destinations from Belgium to Somalia. The lack of insurance facilities in Belarus forced the carrier to create a new company called PromTransinvest to provide insurance coverage for its fleet, with reinsurance handled by a firm in Russia.

The new cargo carrier was started by three government-owned manufacturing companies, which make trucks, electronics, and appliances and which put up about $6.5 million of their excess cash to get TransAviaExport off the ground and flying.

The critical question facing Belarus today is whether it will remain independent or reunite with Russia. "Today," says a reporter for the *Wall Street Journal* who recently visited the country, "Belarus is on its way to making history as the former Soviet republic willing to shrug off sovereignty and resubmit to Russian rule."

OIL-RICH KAZAKHSTAN

Of the fifteen new nations spun off from the old Soviet Union, only Kazakhstan—the ninth largest country in the world—appears to have a shot at becoming fairly well-off by Western standards. Its 17 million people live in an area spread out over a million square miles. Kazakhstan is being hailed as the next Kuwait, thanks to its vast, undeveloped oil and natural gas resources. "The people of Kazakhstan may someday be the richest in the world," said the head of the Price Waterhouse consulting firm in the Kazakh capital. "But right now, all of Kazakhstan's riches are still behind glass."

These riches are beginning to be exploited by the world's major petroleum giants, led by San Francisco-based Chevron Corporation. Chevron has already invested several hundred million dollars in Kazakhstan's big Tengiz field, thought to be one of the ten largest on earth, on which an estimated $20 billion may be spent over the next forty years (although in May 1994 Chevron announced that it was reducing its outlays, at least for now).

While Kazakhstan is blessed with massive oil deposits, it is burdened with a crushing lack of capital, modern oil drilling technology (and the skills to use it), refineries, and access to the open sea and world markets. Kazakhstan is landlocked, and all of its oil will likely be exported through Russia since alternate pipeline routes through war-ravaged Georgia, Azerbaijan, or Armenia and then on through Turkey to the Mediterranean would be far too dangerous.

The day after Kazakhstan was given observer status by the Organization of Petroleum Exporting Countries, a huge oil consortium including British Gas, British Petroleum, Italy's Agip, Norway's Statoil, France's TOTAL, America's Mobil, and Netherlands' Shell Exploration won the right to conduct geophysical studies on a huge stretch of the North Caspian Sea's outer continental shelf, believed to hold more oil than Alaska's Prudhoe Bay.

A serious problem with this site, although not serious enough to stop future oil production, is that its waters are part of a nature preserve that is rich in wildlife, including seals, several hundred species of migrating birds, and sturgeon (it is the world's largest breeding ground for these fish, whose roe is a leading source of caviar). Kazakhstan's minister of ecology and bioresources says his country will not allow commercial oil production to begin until it is satisfied these environmental riches will be protected.

The riches everyone sees flowing from Kazakhstan's vast treasure of black gold has attracted the attention of multinational corporate giants such as Hyundai, Samsung, Mercedes-Benz, and the big oil-equipment companies, which have been setting up shop in Kazakhstan to cash in on the prosperity they see following in its wake. The Overseas Private Investment Corporation understands this fact; when Kazakhstan President Nursultan Nazarbayev visited President Clinton in February 1994, it organized a big investment conference attended by more than fifty companies, from Amoco to Procter & Gamble, that are prime candidates for bringing their capital, know-how, and products to Kazakhstan. Several days later, General Motors announced that it had already made that decision and was about to dispatch the first shipment of Chevrolet cars and trucks along with some Cadillacs. The food and tobacco giant RJR Nabisco has so much confidence in Kazakhstan's future that it is planning to invest upwards of $100 million over the next few years, supplying this country with its Camel and Winston cigarettes, and has purchased a controlling interest in the Shimilent Confectionery Enterprise, which produces specialty chocolates, cookies, and other products. And the Central-Asian American Enterprise Fund will be deploying 150 million to encourage small and medium-sized businesses in Kazakhstan, as well as in Kyrgyzstan, Tajikistan, Uzbekistan, and Turkmenistan to its south.

Some sixty U.S. companies were actively involved in Kazakhstan's economy as of mid-1994, and several of them are at work building a modern communications system to serve this vast land. AT&T signed a ten-year, $500 million contract in March 1992 to install a telephone network in the capital of Almaty and the rich Tengiz oil field, and the German subsidiary of the French communications giant Alcatel received a major contract to interconnect another section of the country. These two big networks will be augmented by Kazakhstan's first cellular phone system, which will serve Almaty and is being built by Motorola in partnership with the Canadian Wireless Technology Corporation at a cost that is also expected to reach $500 million.

Living on the Edge

The prospect of billions from oil sales can't materialize fast enough for the Kazakh people who, like their neighbors, are living on the edge. "The number of elderly beggars is growing, as is the number of rural families who come to the city to beg because they have nowhere else to go," said Eric Rudenshiold with the International Republican Institute in Almaty, writing in *Demokratizatsiya: The Journal of Post-Soviet Democratization.*

No one is more aware of Kazakhstan's plight than President Nazarbayev, who has been his country's leader since it declared its independence on December 16, 1991, and whose term of office was recently extended to the year 2000. Eric Rudenshiold quotes a Nazarbayev speech to top government officials in 1992 on the need for strong executive rule in Kazakhstan if it is to succeed in its wrenching change from communism to capitalism. "Tough executive, vertical power is needed," he told them, "not for usurping power . . . (but) to implement a radical economic transformation." This transformation will be helped by increasing U.S. aid, which President Clinton said will rise from the $91 million appropriated in 1993 to $311 million in 1995, plus another $85 million to help underwrite the "safe and secure dismantlement" of 104 long-range SS18 missiles, each tipped with ten nuclear warheads.

Kazakhstan boasts incredible mineral wealth awaiting large-scale exploitation, with oil only the icing on the cake. The country is rich in copper, iron ore, chromium, magnesium, lead, zinc, silver, uranium, natural gas, and coal, and has major reserves of gold, molybdenum, titanium, vanadium, beryllium, tungsten, manganese, rhenium, and gallium, along with a large ferro-alloy industry.

Kazakhstan is developing a major natural gas field at Karachangak on its northern border with the help of foreign investors, while continuing to buy its ongoing natural gas needs from Russia. The country has big coal reserves, with production totaling some 130 million tons a year of both high quality coking coal and low-quality subbituminous coal mainly used to generate electricity. The country does not yet produce enough power to meet demand, so the south buys it from neighboring Kyrgyzstan and Turkmenistan, and the north gets it from adjoining Russia, which has recently cut supplies, triggering severe power shortages.

All this natural underground wealth is augmented by a rich agricultural sector. Kazakhstan ranks third in grain production behind Russia and Ukraine and is the only former Soviet country producing large agricultural surpluses. It specializes in spring wheat but also produces important amounts of cotton, rice, meat, and wool, which it exports to other formerly Soviet nations.

The Chase Manhattan Bank and Kazakhstan have entered into a fifty-fifty joint venture partnership to create the Kazakhstan International Bank, which President Nazarbayev hailed as a major boost for his country's economy. The agreement, he said, will help bring new foreign investment and sophisticated banking practices to Kazakhstan and will give local businesses far greater access to global capital markets. The new bank will be located in Almaty and provide financial and advisory services, including foreign exchange, commodity hedging, project finance, trade finance, and syndicated loans. The only other foreign bank in Kazakhstan is Turkey's state-run Ziraat Bank, which set up a joint venture in Almaty in 1993. "Right now we see great potential in Kazakhstan," says Chase Manhattan Chairman Thomas Labrecque, who entertained President Nazarbayev at the company's New York City headquarters following his visit to Washington.

The Marlboro Cowboy Goes East

Philip Morris International, which leads the world in cigarette production, and whose Marlboro cowboy helped sell 421 billion cigarettes outside the United States in 1993, has been growing explosively in the former Soviet empire, including Kazakhstan. The company is in the midst of spending more than $200 million to buy 49 percent of Kazakhstan's state-owned Almaty Tobacco Kombinat, which employs some 1,700 people, and intends to acquire enough additional shares to gain majority ownership.

Philip Morris has launched a five-year plan to modernize the Almaty plant and increase its production to 20 billion cigarettes a year, which will be supplemented by exports from the company's U.S. plants. Philip Morris also plans to invest another $25 million in a tobacco growing and processing program in Kazakhstan in cooperation with the Universal Leaf Tobacco Company of Richmond, Virginia.

Philip Morris, like so many other U.S. companies, is aggressively expanding overseas because markets at home are either approaching the saturation point or actually declining, as we have seen with McDonald's and the other fast-food giants. Tobacco consumption in the United States has fallen by more than 2 percent a year since the 1980s, and the reduction is expected to continue.

Foreign demand, on the other hand, has been climbing steadily—especially for Marlboro, the world's top-selling cigarette. Philip Morris's tobacco profits continue to far exceed that of its food divisions, whose revenues are higher, and this growth differential shows no sign of letting up. The importance of tobacco sales in Kazakhstan and other overseas markets is expected to advance even more in the years ahead as America's concern about tobacco and health continues to slow cigarette consumption, not to mention the huge and unrelenting tax increases being slapped on cigarettes in an effort to reduce both consumption and the U.S. budget deficit.

Kazakhstan is firmly on the road to democratic capitalism as President Nursultan Nazarbayev made clear during a 1993 interview on, of all things, the CNBC-TV program "MoneyTalk." "Overall," he said, "we've chosen the same path as the rest of the civilized world. For instance, over 8,500 state entities have been privatized by early 1994, and 20 percent of our industrial output is now being produced by the private sector. We've privatized all of our housing, and about half our service sector which we'd like to complete by year's end. 1994 will also see the second stage of privatization, and I hope it too will make a major contribution to our economy. I think our people are prepared for it, and statistics show that 80 percent support it—particularly our young people." Nazarbayev was considerably less sanguine, incidentally, about the outlook for democracy in neighboring Russia. "I don't think democratization has been completed in Russia. Its people were for generations brought up in a spirit of totalitarianism and are not capable of becoming democrats overnight. It's impossible."

GEORGIA:
THE GUN-SLINGING WILD WEST REVISITED

Georgia's capital of Tbilisi brings back memories of fabled Dodge City or Tombstone, where the sound of gunfire was as familiar as rain on the roof. People hesitate to leave home after dark, theaters and concert halls confine their performances to the afternoon, the city's only luxury hotel asks

guests to check their guns at the door, and gun-slinging ban-
dits rob and murder people seemingly at will.

American envoy Fred Woodruff, riding in a jeep driven
by Georgian President Eduard A. Shevardnadze's chief of
security, was shot and killed by a twenty-one-year-old soldier who was later caught and confessed he was after the
jeep's gasoline.

Georgia's 5.5 million people live in a mountainous, West
Virginia–size land inhabited by ancient warlike tribes and
clans surrounded by turmoil. Uneasy Muslim Turkey butts
up against Georgia's southern border, as do the mutually
hostile hair-trigger regimes in Armenia and Azerbaijan, not
to mention Muslim Iran to the south.

The country's first popularly elected president was Zviad
K. Gamsakhurdia, a fire-breathing linguist and Soviet-
condemned political exile who led Georgia's struggle for
independence, became president following a landslide vote
in 1991, was ousted from office six months later in a military putsch because of his dictatorial style and his regime's
human rights violations, and took to the hills of his native
western Georgia, where he assembled a small army.

Gamsakhurdia was replaced by stoic, power-loving
Eduard Shevardnadze, a native Georgian who was Mikhail
Gorbachev's foreign secretary and had won the presidency
in his mid-sixties by an even greater plurality than his predecessor. Shevardnadze had no sooner taken office than
he was caught up in wars with Georgia's two Russian-backed
breakaway eastern provinces of Abkhazia and Ossetia, as
well as with Gamsakhurdia's rebel army, which attacked
the Georgian capital of Tbilisi but was thrown back and forced
to retreat to its stronghold in Mingrelia province in the west.

Shevardnadze flew to the Abkhazian city of Sukhumi,
vowing to remain holed up there until its fate was decided
since the city's loss could mean the breakup of Georgia.
He regained control of his impoverished country in October
1993, but the price he had to pay was to call on Russia for
military help, agree to join the Moscow-dominated Commonwealth of Independent States, and give Russia power over
his country's defense and foreign policy (along with the free

use of its land, sea, and air bases at critical points, including the big Black Sea port of Poti).

Two months after Shevardnadze agreed to let the Russian Army help him govern Georgia, his old enemy Gamsakhurdia was reported to have died from a self-inflicted gunshot wound at age fifty-four after being surrounded by Georgian government troops. So it looks like Shevardnadze may, at long last, have some time to begin thinking about improving his country's beleaguered economy so his people can finally get on with their newfound independence.

What Shevardnadze has to work with is a nation whose warm climate and location on the edge of the Black Sea make it particularly well-suited for tourism and agriculture. Almost half of Georgia's exports consist of agricultural products such as tea, citrus and citrus products, tobacco, mineral water, and its renowned wines, produced in what claims to be the oldest wine-making region in the world. Georgia used to bottle 110 million gallons of wine a year, but by 1993 that figure had plummeted to 10 million gallons. Now a group of wine enthusiasts, including former U.S. secretary of state George Schultz and California's Wente Brothers wine company have joined with a group of Georgian winemakers and launched a joint venture called Chalice Wines to help revive the industry.

Georgia's leading imports are primarily energy (including electricity), meat, wheat, sugar, dairy products, and heavy machinery. Manufacturing is oriented toward the production of light industrial goods, but even here there is heavy dependence on imported raw materials, intermediate goods, and energy even though the country has small quantities of oil, coal, and natural gas.

In the meantime, the Russian Bear is holding Georgia and its president in an ever tighter embrace. Georgia has signed a treaty giving Russia the right to keep three military bases on its soil past 1995 in return for training and supplying its army. And Russia is talking with Georgia about reentering its ruble zone, which would be another giant step toward absorption by Moscow.

International Monetary Fund statistics indicate that soaring inflation and falling growth have been plaguing Georgia and the fourteen other former Soviet republics—with the exception of Turkmenistan, which, although reeling from sharply higher 1993 consumer prices, managed to increase its GDP by nearly 9 percent thanks to substantial natural gas exports. Georgia and Tajikistan suffered the biggest GDP declines in 1993 with national output plummeting by 30 percent in each case. Ukraine, Albania, and Kazakhstan were hit by horrendous consumer price increases in 1993 with inflation running at an annual rate of 5,000 percent in Ukraine, 2,500 percent in Albania, and 2,146 percent in Kazakhstan.

11

The Future Begins to Crystallize

"I see Russia—resource-rich, with an educated populace, no longer hamstrung by collectivist ideology—returning to superpowerhood and, even if democratic, dominating its neighbors."

William Safire, columnist
New York Times

"Stormy weather lies ahead."

Dr. Peter Reddaway, political science professor,
George Washington University

Capitalism's failure to quickly improve material living conditions in the recently communist nations of the former Soviet empire has prompted Hungarian voters to elect former communists—now called socialists—to a majority in their parliament. No sooner were they seated, however, than socialist leader and former foreign minister Gyula Horn vowed to continue Hungary's free market reforms, just as newly elected leftist leaders had already done in Poland and Lithuania.

U.S. Ambassador to Hungary Donald M. Blinken unraveled this anomaly for a *New York Times* reporter by explaining that "even though the road map and driver may change, the ultimate destination—a democratic society, market economy and full integration with the West—remains the same."

Russia's Foreign Minister Andrei Kozyrev echoed this sentiment by noting that "Russia and its East European neighbors are grappling with the same strategic task, that of securing a worthy place in the club of highly developed democratic states."

The drive toward a free market society is almost certain to continue, but with intermittent backsliding already visible, from the renewed flirtation with socialism in Eastern Europe to the demands for superpower respect from impoverished Russia.

The easiest prediction is that the countries of Eastern Europe and the former Soviet Union will continue to strive for admission into the West's economic and military alliances. They have already been given junior membership in the North Atlantic Treaty Organization through its "Partnership for Peace" initiative, and several have been offered the possibility of joining the European Union as soon as they have a track record as stable, market-oriented democracies that respect human rights.

While some Eastern European countries such as Poland and Romania were admitted to the 123-nation, Geneva-based General Agreement on Tariffs and Trade (GATT) while they were still communist, none of the fifteen former Soviet republics has yet joined this group which in its recently completed seven-year Uruguay Round of negotiations agreed to reduce import tariffs worldwide by an average of 40 percent that some believe could generate up to $5 trillion in new global business by 2005.

Russia has formally applied for membership in GATT, which was succeeded by the more powerful World Trade Organization on January 1, 1995. It is expected the other fourteen former Soviet republics will follow suit, although it is likely to take a year or more before they are through answering hundreds of pre-admission questions on everything from their tariff structures to agricultural reforms and industrial subsidies. Only then will they be welcomed into the club, which carries with it important advantages such as preferred trading status with other member states.

No former Soviet empire countries are yet members of the twenty-five–nation Organization of Economic Cooperation and Development (OECD), headquartered in Paris, which monitors and forecasts the industrial world's economic performance. This, however, is about to change. The OECD already considers Hungary, Poland, the Czech Republic, and Slovakia to have met its conditions for membership, and it has just signed an agreement with Russia allowing the nation to use its regional and national economic reports and join some of its key committees.

The emergence of all these former Soviet empire countries from the economic backwater of communism is irreversible, barring a military-backed takeover unleashed by economic collapse followed by civil disorder. The one nation where this appears most likely, and the only one in which it really matters to the rest of the world, is in a suddenly desperate nuclear-armed Russia.

Just such a scenario is chillingly discussed by Yuri N. Afanasyev, a historian and rector of the Russian State University for the Humanities, in the Summer 1994 issue of *Foreign Affairs*. After asserting that Russia's economic and political "reform movement is now nothing but rhetoric," Afanasyev goes on to predict a disastrous return to a planned economy run by the country's military-industrial complex in league with corrupt bureaucrats, milking state-owned industrial and agricultural monopolies into the grave.

It would be foolish to pooh-pooh this nightmare scenario out of hand even though it is a rerun of the madness that brought Russia's economy to its knees less than a decade ago.

What has changed in the intervening decade is the rebirth of free enterprise, the privatization of thousands of companies (many of which are admittedly still being run— and gutted—by those who managed them under communism), the creation of millions of stockholders with a vested interest in the success of newly privatized companies, the emergence of capitalist institutions such as raw materials exchanges and investor-owned banks, the enactment of laws and regulations that private companies need to operate, and the rising tide of investment capital and entrepreneurial know-how streaming in from the West. Every day Russia's private sector gets stronger as it builds up both the economy and the political clout of those profiting from it.

RUSSIA AS
"THE ENVY OF THE WORLD"

In an earlier *Foreign Affairs* article called "The Future of Russian Capitalism," Jude Wanniski, president of Polyconomics, Inc., an economics consulting firm in Morristown, New Jersey, dismissed the idea that the beleaguered Russian economy was beyond salvation. "In fact," he said, "quite the opposite conclusion might be drawn. During the 70 years of the communist experiment, the competitive impulse of Soviet man has not been extinguished at all, but rather has been channeled into the awkward mazes and blind alleys that ultimately led to abandonment of the Marxist-Leninist idea. Now freed of these constraints, it is easy to imagine these competitive impulses racing ahead of our Western form of corporate capitalism, which has grown flabby and slow. It is possible to imagine a future of Russian capitalism that asserts itself early in the 21st century as the envy of the world."

A less rosy but also upbeat portrait of a likely Russian future is outlined in depth in *Russia 2010: And What It Means for the World,* written by Daniel Yergin, an authority on international politics and energy and president of Cambridge Energy Research Associates, and Thane Gustafson, director of Cambridge Energy Research Associates and a professor at Georgetown University.

In *Russia 2010*, the authors outline several scenarios of Russian futures. One dubbed the "Russian Bear" reflects the grim predictions of Yuri Afanasyev, while another called "The Russian Economic Miracle" is given the best chance of actually coming true. In between these scenarios are:

♦ "Muddling Down," which resembles what is actually happening today since it consists of a "society and an economy that are running out of steam. Lawlessness is increasingly a fact of life. Nostalgia for the old order and the politics of resentment and humiliation can become potent political forces."

♦ "Two-Headed Eagle" is an alliance between Russia's "defense industrialists and industrial managers—with the army and police. It aims to restore self-respect, but reimposes the state on the economy."

♦ "Time of Troubles" is a family of scenarios, including the "Long Goodbye," which is a basic weakening of the Russian state with its far east and Siberia moving into "the orbits of Japan and China," while Saint Petersburg and the Russian northwest "orient themselves toward Scandinavia and Germany." Eventually, however, any period of chaos is likely to be followed by a "regathering of the Russian lands."

Yergin and Gustafson say their best-bet "Russian Economic Miracle" scenario resembles the German and Japanese economic revivals, which did not happen overnight but rather "emerged out of very unpromising beginnings and unfolded over a decade, in very difficult, even treacherous conditions." But Russia, unlike Germany and Japan, the authors contend, "does not have a commercial tradition or a preexisting base of private property. It does, however, have a highly educated and technically adept population, enormous pent-up demand for goods and services of every kind, an eager and hungry younger generation, and extensive resources." Finally, Russia's "integration into the world economy and the application of 'enabling technologies'—computers and communications—could accelerate economic change, much more so than generally expected."

TWO SCENARIOS
FROM RUSSIA'S TOP ECONOMIST

During a lengthy lecture at the University of Tulsa on February 26, 1994, Yegor Gaidar, former deputy prime minister of Russia and its best known economist, outlined both negative and positive economic scenarios for Russia during the coming years, insisting that the upbeat one is more likely to emerge. Part of the reason, he said, can be seen in the failure of malcontents to overthrow the Yeltsin government in October 1993 and the Gorbachev/Yeltsin governments in August 1991.

"After the events of the 3rd and 4th of October," Gaidar told his Tulsa audience, "I turned to my wife and said, 'Well, we've survived August 1991, and we've survived October 1993, and I hope we will not have these types of problems again.' Well, now it is evident that we will. But I'm sure, because of my faith in human nature, of my faith in the Russian people, that we will win this very difficult battle."

Gaidar then painted a graphic picture of Russia again descending into the cauldron of totalitarianism. "I don't think it's very probable," he said, "but we can't exclude the scenario where the government yields to all the pressures and grants all the money because it's much easier to give money than to refuse it. This is a very dangerous scenario because it will immediately result in a radical increase in the money supply, a drastic change in the exchange rate, a drastic devaluation of the ruble, the flight from the ruble, then to radical increases in the rate of monetary inflation.

"This will inevitably lead to attempts by the government to freeze the exchange rate, and to impose some administrative ways on the regulation of the hard currency units," Gaidar said, "then to the attempts to freeze prices on basic commodities, then to attempts to rule in the field of price control. Then it will be evident that you cannot anymore buy the hard currency and you have to distribute it by administrative means, that you do not anymore have the possibility of buying the goods you need, and that some additional state decisions like orders or directives are needed to get the resources that are needed.

"Then, of course, it will be evident," Gaidar said, "that you need a huge new state apparat that will elaborate on the state orders about the distribution of the material resources. Then it will be evident there is no more goods in the shops, that you need a new system of controlled consumption, that you're unable to supply enough goods to fulfill your promises about consumption. And then you will see that the ownership of private property is inconsistent with all these policies, and that you will have state control of property, and it will not take you long to understand the system can only work under totalitarian political control which will lead Russia to economic and political disaster."

Gaidar then described a more optimistic scenario for Russia. "My solution," he said, "is that we should first of all support people and efficient industries. It's so much more logical to help the people to be retrained, to help people who are unemployed, to help people who are poor, than to help keep an enormous amount of military production just to provide work for the people who are producing things that are absolutely unnecessary for the national economy. A lot of Russian industries are potentially competitive," he concluded, "but they need a lot of initiative with a knowledgeable management and the energy of private enterprise. It's the only possible choice from my point of view."

A GLIMPSE OF
RUSSIA'S NEW RULING CLASS

A likely scenario with a better than even chance of actually coming true is suggested by Victor Yasmann, a research analyst at the Radio Free Europe/Radio Liberty Research Institute in Munich, Germany, and an associate editor of *Demokratizatsiya*, in which his analysis appeared.

Yasmann draws attention to a nongovernmental group of young Russian businessmen, politicians, and academics he says is "important because its upscale membership will have an impact on the formulation of Russian foreign policy for a considerable time. First, it reflects the views of a new ruling social class in Russia. Second, it presents a 'centrist' line." A highly placed member of the group, says Yasmann, has published a report that he feels accurately reflects its aspirations.

Yasmann says the report begins with an appeal to recognize the following fact: Measured by many indicators, present-day Russia is a medium-sized power comparable to Canada, Brazil, and Argentina in the Americas; France, Britain, and Italy in Europe; and India and Indonesia in Asia. Second, the report postulates that in the foreseeable future Russia most likely will be a moderately authoritarian state with an economy of a state-capitalist type. These characteristics, in many instances, are predetermined by the nature of the new Russian ruling class, which is heavy with the old and new state *nomenklatura*, academocrats, directors of state enterprises and young businessmen; and KGB, army, and Interior Ministry officers.

"For self-motivated reasons," Yasmann concludes, "the new ruling class will be resistant to the complete openness of the Russian economy, but for the same reasons it will be interested in close cooperation with the West as a guarantee of its wellbeing. The report calls such a foreign policy course an 'enlightened post-imperial integration.'"

THE TEMPTATION TO BACKSLIDE

Still another plausible scenario, and not a very pleasant one to contemplate, is that when Boris Yeltsin's presidency ends in 1996 he will be replaced by Vladimir V. Zhirinovsky, 49, whose party received the largest percentage of the vote in the last election, or by the man Zhirinovsky says would make an equally good head of state, Aleksandr Rutskoi. When Russians choose their next president, said Zhirinovsky as he greeted General Rutskoi upon his release from Lefortovo Prison—where Yeltsin had put him months earlier following his unsuccessful coup attempt, the choice will be "between me and Rutskoi."

The Russian economy, which began its serious flirtation with cold turkey market reform a decade ago, reversed field in early 1994 following the poor showing of reformers in the December 12, 1993, Parliamentary elections and the sudden emergence of Zhirinovsky and his curiously named ultranationalist Liberal Democratic Party, which had come out on top making him the single most powerful figure in the Duma.

Zhirinovsky hit the headlines following Russia's 1991 presidential election when he came in third behind Boris Yeltsin and Nikolai Ryzhov, winning 7.8 percent of the ballots or 6 million votes. James Baker, secretary of state in the Bush administration at the time, says Zhirinovsky "can be very, very scary," and that "he's at least a demagogue, and at worst a clear fascist."

Zhirinovsky and his wrecking crew can delay, but not derail, Russia's determination to become a key player in the global economic arena unless they are determined to have their country commit national economic suicide a second time. It could happen. Zhirinovsky is quoted as saying in a North German Radio interview: "If a German looks at Russia the wrong way when I'm in the Kremlin, you Germans will pay for all that we Russians have built up in Germany. We'll create new Hiroshimas and Nagasakis. I will not hesitate to deploy atomic weapons." The same fate apparently awaits Russia's Japanese neighbors to the east if they misbehave. "I would bomb the Japanese," warns Zhirinovsky. "I would sail our large navy around their small island and if they so much as cheeped, I would nuke them."

The MacNeil-Lehrer NewsHour saw Zhirinovsky as a stick of political dynamite several years ago and sent a reporter to Russia to interview him. Among Zhirinovsky's on-camera comments were that he favored the "free immigration of Jews out of Russia to Israel," and he did not think much of America. "I have been to New York," he said. "I have seen no white Americans at all—the blacks are all over the place. You're running a serious risk of the key positions in the political and economic life of the country being eventually seized by the blacks, and Hispanics, and white America may be on the verge of disappearance. You can end up being turned into a second sort of people." Then, as a parting shot, Zhirinovsky promised that if he is elected president of Russia in 1996 he will immediately reincorporate Ukraine, Kazakhstan, and Kyrgyzstan into Mother Russia.

RUSSIA'S UNCERTAIN FUTURE

No one knows what is going to happen to Russia in the years ahead, although it is conventional wisdom that Russia matters and should not be ignored. What we do know with virtual certainty is that Russia will end up as a socialist/capitalist state, while the West roars into the twenty-first century at warp speed, raising the question of just how successful Russia will be economically if she does make it through to the other side of her revolution. Particularly in view of her insistence, even in her vastly weakened condition, that she be treated as a great power—an equal of the rich G-7 countries of Germany, Britain, France, Italy, Japan, Canada, and the United States (with neighboring China coming up fast on the outside).

The world, however, refuses to stand still. And while Russia's embrace of a new sociocapitalist economy can take her just about anywhere she is determined to go, other already economically formidable countries are gaining still more strength as they enter what can only be described as a new world of mind-boggling advanced technology that already has adults' heads spinning, even as their children are ingesting it as if it were mothers' milk (which intellectually it probably is).

This is instantly apparent in the United States, which has moved from the Industrial Age into the converging nexus of computing, communications, and television heralding the new Information Age, whose dimensions are beyond measure and fast becoming even more so. Texas Instruments (TI), for example, recently introduced a new computer chip to help drive this revolution that is packed with 4 million transistors and four digital processors capable of performing 2 billion operations per second. The tiny chip is so powerful that, in the words of TI's Senior Vice President Rich

Templeton, it "opens the doors for new applications that only exist in our imaginations today."

Part of the payoff from such technological wonders is that it has made the American worker the most productive in the world, turning out nearly $50,000 worth of goods and services in 1990, or $10,000 more than the Japanese and $5,000 more than the Germans. The American worker's productivity has also been growing at an annual rate of 2.5 percent for the past three years. Gains on the factory floor have been even more impressive, soaring about 5 percent in the same period.

This has helped America increase its exports by nearly 9 percent a year since 1985, compared to 6.6 percent in Japan and 4.2 percent in Germany, while giving it the resources to continue its high-level investment in productivity-raising technology, with a heavy emphasis on computers that help keep overhead low. Studies show the Japanese would have to slash their white-collar workforce by a pernicious 15 to 20 percent to match America's tightly controlled overhead costs.

What we have been doing, of course, is comparing the United States not with, say, Britain, France, or Canada—whose affluence most countries of the world would give anything to match—but rather with the two economic superpowers of Germany and Japan. In this league Russia is not even a player. And it gets worse.

The Clinton administration has been deliberately focusing America's attention on the new markets exploding in Asia, where the action is and is likely to remain well into the next century. Former U.S. Senator Lloyd Bentsen, who has stepped down from his post as treasury secretary, is ecstatic about the economic outlook in Asia. At a talk to investors in Los Angeles before a kickoff meeting with the key finance ministers of the new Asia Pacific Economic Cooperation group in Honolulu on March 18, 1994, he predicted these countries excluding Japan will spend $1 trillion on infrastructure alone in the next ten years.

Bentsen reminded the moneymen that Asia with its more than 2 billion consumers could be far more powerful economically than the United States and Europe combined within less than two generations. Rich rewards await Western capital in Asia while Russia—which like the United States also borders the Pacific washing the Asian continent—can only marvel at these lip-smacking investment opportunities as it struggles with crushing internal problems destined to restrain its foreign economic growth for as far as the eye can see.

THE COLLAPSE OF TYRANNIES

The reason for Russia's abandonment of communism for capitalism is discussed early on in Francis Fukuyama's acclaimed recent book, *The End of History and the Last Man.* Fukuyama, who is a former deputy director of the U.S. State Department's policy planning staff and currently a resident consultant at the RAND Corporation in Washington, D.C., suggests that two powerful forces—"the logic of modern science" and "the struggle for recognition"—inevitably lead to the collapse of tyrannies such as those that flourished under communism and "drive even culturally disparate societies toward establishing capitalist liberal democracies as the end state of the historical process."

While a nuclear-armed Russia could plunge the world into the "chaos and bloodshed of history," says Fukuyama, the more likely outcome is that it will continue its struggle toward the uplands of capitalism. The experiences of the Soviet Union and other socialist lands, he says, "indicate that while highly centralized economies are sufficient to reach the level of industrialization represented by Europe in the 1950s, they are woefully inadequate in creating what has been termed complex 'post-industrial' economies in which information and technological innovation play a much larger role."

Russia today is what one of its best-known poets calls "a proud beggar with an atomic bomb," struggling to rebuild its tattered economy. The dimensions of the economic transformation confronting Russia, Belarus, Ukraine, Kazakhstan, and the other former Soviet lands are absolutely daunting. Old factories must be shuttered. New state-of-the-art ones must be erected. Armies of workers must be retrained. A modern infrastructure of roads, bridges, communication networks, and the like must be built. A vast and unfamiliar consumer-oriented marketing system must be created. Outlets for their exports to the West and elsewhere must be put in place. And as all this is going on, their central banks must keep pumping out subsidies and loans to keep the old system running, even though it means printing billions of extra rubles, coupons, and so on, further degrading the currency.

A "WAIT-AND-SEE" ATTITUDE TOWARD RUSSIA

American and other foreign companies should definitely not rush into Russia right now, warns Marshall J. Goldman, professor of Russian economics at Wellesley College, associate director of Harvard's Russian Research Center, and author of the new book *Lost Opportunity: Why Economic Reforms in Russia Have Not Worked.* Instead, says Goldman, foreigners should wait until Russia's leaders demonstrate that they can control the criminal gangs terrorizing business, abolish outrageously onerous and arbitrary taxes, and establish the legal and commercial rules needed to build profitable enterprises.

In the meantime, the United States, Japan, Germany, and the other advanced nations are blanketing the planet with state-of-the-art factories, research laboratories, retail outlets, and office complexes valued at more than $1 trillion and counting. They're also joining forces to build extremely expensive facilities to push back the frontiers of science, as America's Advanced Micro Devices Inc. and Japan's Fujitsu Ltd. are doing with their recently announced $750 million manufacturing plant to produce flash computer memory chips that will not lose their contents if the system's power source goes down.

The incredible sums of money needed to produce today's advanced-technology systems is almost entirely consumed by the cost of capital, research and development, and marketing. Human labor, which the ex-Soviet Empire has in abundance, represents a hardly noticeable 3 percent in the output of semiconductors and 5 percent in color television sets, and a mere 10 to 15 percent in far more labor-intensive automobiles.

Massive capital costs will likely keep the countries of Eastern Europe and the former Soviet Union out of the lucrative market for high-tech manufactured goods for some time to come even as their economies and living standards visibly improve. One example is the highly-efficient Western system of "just-in-time" delivery of components to the factory floor that cuts inventory costs to the bone, but is unlikely to be implemented in the former Soviet bloc anytime soon. The reason is that this hair-trigger system cannot function without absolutely dependable vendors, power supplies, and transportation networks able to deliver finished goods to customers when needed.

Russia and its neighbors are bound to benefit from the fact that they will be able to copy such efficiency-enhancing manufacturing strategies already at work in the West, while the advanced countries are investing billions on new breakthroughs to maintain their rapid growth. This helps explain why it took Britain fifty-eight years and America forty-seven years to double their real national incomes, while copycat South Korea was able to do it beginning in 1966 in eleven years, and China more recently in less than ten.

Since a country's economy is a lot more than Fax machines and VCRs, and since world trade is expected to grow at an impressive pace in the years ahead, the less wealthy countries have a lot to look forward to—including rapidly increasing orders from the West for low-profit items with heavy labor content. In Germany, for example, the Continental tire company recently bought control of a Czech tire maker and moved the production of its standard tires there, an auto parts manufacturer shifted headlight production to Malaysia, and a clothing company moved 30 percent of its work to Hungary.

But perhaps the most encouraging news of all is a new World Bank report predicting that real gross domestic product growth in the countries of Eastern Europe and the former Soviet Union will surge from an annual average of 1 percent from 1974 to 1993, to 2.7 percent from 1993 to 2003. Equally interesting is a study by the Cologne, Germany, market research firm Empirica, which examined 404 European production sites and concluded that by 2020 the most promising will be located in Bratislava, Slovakia; Western Bohemia, Czech Republic; Gyor-Sopron, Hungary; and Poznan, Poland.

Russia's economic outlook is also being brightened by the October 1994 decision of foreign banks to give it a five-year grace period during which it need not pay principal or interest on $26 billion in loans, freeing these funds to help build its economy.

This building process got another much-needed shot in the arm several weeks later on November 5, 1994, when President Yeltsin named his government's leading free-market reformer Anatoly Chubais, thirty-nine, to the post of first deputy prime minister, responsible for the country's main economic ministries. Chubais is highly regarded in the West for successfully pushing through Russia's privatization program against hardcore conservative opposition.

The point is that the United States and the other rich nations are transforming their economies into a global, interdependent, smoothly functioning network which is increasingly subcontracting basic work to less advanced countries to the benefit of all.

While *The Economist* views the economic prospects for Russia as "fragile," its abundance of valuable raw materials from oil to timber, its prowess in science, its traditional love of learning, and now the raw energy of free enterprise being put to work in the midst of a growing world economy hold demonstrable promise for the country's future along with that of its neighbors.

Former president Richard Nixon, who completed his tenth visit to Moscow right before his death in early 1994, said in an Op-Ed piece in the *New York Times*: "Those who suggest that because of its vast problems Russia should no longer be treated as a world power ignore an unpleasant but undeniable truth. Russia is the only nation in the world that can destroy the United States. Therefore Russia remains our highest foreign policy priority."

No one can deny Russia's still-impressive nuclear capability, although it is no longer the superpower it was for several decades during the Cold War years, when it was the heart of the old Soviet empire.

Russian leaders keep plaintively insisting, as Foreign Minister Andrei Kozyrev did just the other day, that "Russia remains a superpower." But as former U.S. ambassador to the Soviet Union George F. Kennan said during a Council on Foreign Relations party on February 15, 1994, honoring his ninetieth birthday: "We are now in a new age. It is an age which, for all its confusions and dangers, is marked by one major blessing: for the first time in centuries, there are no great power rivalries that threaten immediately the peace of the world."

This means, as Japan attests, that only nations with mighty economies, rather than massive arsenals, can qualify as superpowers today—which leaves Russia very much an also-ran even though it is still widely considered to represent the leading threat to world peace. A new survey of more than 1,000 people in the United States, Japan, Germany, and Britain revealed a continuing deep-seated distrust of Russia and its overtures to join the freedom-loving nations of the West.

Still, Russia has the intellectual, physical, and now the growing entrepreneurial energy needed to lift the country off its knees and turn it into a major economic contender. Perhaps Russia will become worthy of at least joining the major powers of Western Europe as an equal partner sometime in the future.

A recent survey in Russia's popular weekly newspaper *Argumenty I Fakty* revealed that some 50 million Russians—close to one-third of the country's population—currently earn salaries of up to 500,000 rubles a month or about $250, putting them squarely in Russia's middle class. An additional 9 million people representing 5 percent of the population are in the upper-middle class with monthly incomes of more than 500,000 rubles, while 2.5 million or 3.5 percent of Russia's citizens qualify as ruble millionaires with incomes of from $1,000 to $1,500 a month.

Thousands of these more affluent Russians are beginning to get their feet wet in the country's nascent, marginally regulated stock market, dominated by shares in fifty or so of its largest companies.

A few of these firms are even moving to list themselves on the U.S. over-the-counter "pink sheet" market, where small American companies are traditionally traded at often bargain-basement prices. Lukoil, the big energy supplier; Rostelecom, the large telephone company; and United Energy Systems, the country's major utility, are among those which appear headed toward OTC listing, with others to follow should these trailblazers prove popular with American investors. One reason they might is that they're dirt cheap compared with U.S. companies, for reasons ranging from the political and economic risks facing Russian companies to their low market capitalizations compared with U.S. companies with similar sales and earnings.

Free enterprise is energetically moving east following years of blood-stained communism. The capitalist countries should do everything they can to ease this vast part of the world into their club.

HOW TO LEARN MORE ABOUT DOING BUSINESS
WITH THE COUNTRIES DISCUSSED IN THIS BOOK

For detailed information about the Czech Republic, Slovak Republic, Poland, Hungary, Bulgaria, Romania, Slovenia, the former Yugoslavia, Lithuania, Estonia, Latvia, or Albania, contact the:

Central and Eastern European
Business Information Center
United States Department of Commerce
14th Street and Constitution Avenue (Room 7412)
Washington, D.C. 20230
202-482-2645

For detailed information on the Russian Federation, Ukraine, Georgia, Kazakhstan, Turkmenistan, Belarus, Kyrgyzstan, Uzbekistan, Tajikistan, Moldova, Armenia, or Azerbaijan, contact the:

Business Information Service
for the Newly Independent States
United States Department of Commerce
14th Street and Constitution Avenue (Room 7413)
Washington, D.C. 20230
202-482-4655

Sources

Note: Sources are listed in the order in which they appear in the chapter.

The Triumph of Capitalism

Eisner, Robert. Review of *21 Century Capitalism* by Robert Heilbroner. *New York Times* Sunday magazine, September 19, 1993, 18.

International Finance Corporation. *Annual Report*. 1993.

Chapter 1: Capitalism Returns to the Former Soviet Empire

Hungarian-American Enterprise Fund. *Third Annual Report for the Fiscal Year Ended September 30, 1992.*

Genco, Pietro, Siria Taurelli, and Claudio Viezzoli. *Private Investment in Central and Eastern Europe: Survey Results*. Working Paper No. 7. European Bank for Reconstruction and Development, July 1993.

European Bank for Reconstruction and Development. *Annual Report*. 1992.

Henderson, Carter. *Winners: The Successful Strategies Entrepreneurs Use to Build New Businesses*. New York: Holt, Rinehart & Winston, 1985.

"U.S. Aid to Russia Is Quite a Windfall—for U.S. Consultants." *Wall Street Journal*, February 24, 1994, 1.

Riordan, Daniel, deputy vice president of investment development, Overseas Private Investment Corporation. Interview with the author.

"East Europe Loans Backed." *New York Times*, January 14, 1995, 35.

Kohl, Helmut, chancellor, Federal Republic of Germany. Statement distributed by the German Information Center. New York, 1993.

Regional Cooperation: Countries of Central and Eastern Europe including the Former Soviet Union. European Bank for Reconstruction and Development, March 1993.

Chapter 2: The Czech Economy Springs Back to Life

"A Shock for German Steel." *Business Week*, November 14, 1994.

"Car Production Rises at Skoda." *New York Times*, January 21, 1994.

Spokesperson. Lauder Investments, Inc. New York.

Spokesperson. Kmart Corporation. Troy, Michigan.

Locke, Martin. Summary Report. Citizens Democracy Corps Consultant. Washington, D.C.

Kennedy, Robert. Summary Report. Citizens Democracy Corps Consultant. Washington, D.C.

Ryan, Tom. Summary Report. Citizens Democracy Corps Consultant. Washington, D.C.

Chapter 3: Slovakia Learns the Price of Independence

Preston, Ken. Summary Report. Citizens Democracy Corps Consultant. Washington, D.C.

Lavin, Carl. Summary Report. Citizens Democracy Corps Consultant. Washington, D.C.

Petty, John R. Chair, Czech and Slovak American Enterprise Fund. Interview with the author.

Petty, John R. Testimony before the U.S. Senate Foreign Relations Committee's Subcommittee on International Economic Policy, Trade, Oceans, and Environment. May 27, 1993.

Czech and Slovak American Enterprise Fund. *Annual Report.* 1993.

Chapter 4: Prosperity Comes to Poland

"CBOT to Help Create Exchange in Warsaw." *Wall Street Journal,* November 11, 1994, C7.

Kissinger, Henry. Speech to the World Economic Development Congress.

Brzezinski, Zbigniew. Interview. *MacNeil-Lehrer NewsHour,* September 20, 1993.

"Poland to Build Toll Roads." *Wall Street Journal,* October 28, 1994, A12.

"Conoco to Invest $300 Million in Poland." *New York Times,* December 22, 1994, C3.

Wilson, Gavin. "The Privatization of Swarzedz Furniture Company (SFM): Lessons from Poland's First Underwritten Public Offering." *The Columbia Journal of World Business* (Spring 1993).

Winger, Richard. Summary Report. Citizens Democracy Corps Consultant. Washington, D.C.

Piker, Robert. Summary Report. Citizens Democracy Corps Consultant. Washington, D.C.

Kilponen, William. Summary Report. Citizens Democracy Corps Consultant. Washington, D.C.

Birkelund, John, and Robert Faris. "Letter from Management." In Polish-American Enterprise Fund, *Annual Report.* 1992.

Polish-American Enterprise Fund. *Annual Report.* 1993.

"Kellogg Seeks to Reset Latvia's Breakfast Table." *New York Times,* May 19, 1994, 1.

"Orchestrating Freedom." *World Monitor,* December 1991, 16–20.

"Lithuania Asks to Join NATO, Angering Russia." *New York Times,* January 6, 1994, 1.

"Yeltsin Now Says He Plans to Keep Troops in Estonia." *New York Times,* July 11, 1994, 1.

Chapter 5: The Richest Country in Eastern Europe

Hungarian Ministry of International Economic Relations. *Hungarian Business Herald.* August 1993.

Vital Speeches of the Day. April 15, 1992, 405–9.

Smith, Don. Summary Report. Citizens Democracy Corps Consultant. Washington, D.C.

Evans, Hugh. Summary Report. Citizens Democracy Corps Consultant. Washington, D.C.

Hungarian-American Enterprise Fund. *Annual Report for the Fiscal Year Ended September 30, 1993.*

Hungarian-American Enterprise Fund. *Annual Report for the Fiscal Year Ended September 30, 1992.*

"Editorial Commentary." *Barron's,* December 20, 1993, 10.

Chapter 6: Ennui Haunts Romania, Albania, and Bulgaria

"Statement by the Right Honorable John Major." *Blueprint,* newsletter of the European Bank for Reconstruction and Development. July 1993.

"Black Sea Bubble." *The Economist,* December 18, 1993, 49–50.

"Romania." *Blueprint,* newsletter of the European Bank for Reconstruction and Development. July 1993, 29.

International Monetary Fund. *Albania: From Isolation toward Reform.* Occasional Paper No. 98. Washington, D.C.: International Monetary Fund, 1992.

Blue Guide to Albania. London: A & C Black, 1994.

"Bulgaria." *Blueprint,* newsletter of the European Bank for Reconstruction and Development. July 1993, 27.

"The Balkans: Dominoes," *The Economist,* October 29, 1994, 58.

Manning, Kent. Summary Report. Citizens Democracy Corps Consultant. Washington, D.C.

Drummond, Charles. Summary Report. Citizens Democracy Corps Consultant. Washington, D.C.

Johnson, Karen. Summary Report. Citizens Democracy Corps Consultant. Washington, D.C.

Mitchell, James. Summary Report. Citizens Democracy Corps Consultant. Washington, D.C. Also correspondence with author.

Bulgarian American Enterprise Fund. *Annual Report.* 1993.

Morgan Stanley European Emerging Markets Fund, Inc. Prospectus issued March 2 and related material prepared by Morgan Stanley Asset Management. New York.

Chapter 7: The Blossoming of Free Enterprise in Russia

Russian Space History, Sale 6516, Property of the Industries, Cosmonauts, and Engineers of the Russian Space Program. Sotheby's auction catalog.

"Russia and Eastern Europe: Will the West Let Them Fail?" *Foreign Affairs* 72, no. 1 (special issue, 1993): 44–57.

Evening News from Moscow. Moscow State Television Report. December 31, 1993.

"United States Discreetly Shops for Russian Weapons Systems." *New York Times*, December 24, 1994.

"Joint Venture to License Russian Technologies." Press release. East/West Technology Partners, Ltd.

"From Russia with Brainpower." *Business Week*, January 17, 1994, 69.

Russian-American Enterprise Fund. "Fact Sheet." 1993.

The Fund for Large Enterprises in Russia. Material supplied to the author by the fund.

"The Closet Capitalists of Russia and Ukraine." *Business Week*, August 3, 1992, 16.

"Hunting for Homo Sovieticus: Situational versus Attitudinal Factors in Economic Behavior." *Brookings Papers on Economic Activity* (1992). Washington, D.C.: Brookings Institution.

"Privatizing Russia—A Success Story." *New York Times*, June 30, 1994, A23.

International Finance Corporation. *Nizhny Novgorod: First Privatization in Russia*. October 1992. Washington, D.C.

International Finance Corporation. *Model Privatization of Trucking in Russia: First Use of Privatization Vouchers*. January 1993. Washington, D.C.

Webster, Leila, and Joshua Charap. *A Survey of Private Manufacturers in St. Petersburg*. Working Paper No. 5. European Bank for Reconstruction and Development.

Genco, Pietro, Siria Taurelli, and Claudio Viezzoli. *Private Investment in Central and Eastern Europe: Survey Results*. Working Paper No. 7. European Bank for Reconstruction and Development, July 1993.

"Joint Ventures in Russia: Put the Locals in Charge." *Harvard Business Review* (January/February 1993): 44–54.

Berstell, Gerald. Summary Report. Citizens Democracy Corps Consultant. Washington, D.C.

Chapter 8: Communism's Terrible Legacy

"Crisis of Bread and Land Affects Russian Farming." *New York Times*, September 19, 1994, 1.

Kapstein, Ethan B. "America's Arms-Trade Monopoly: Lagging Sales Will Starve Lesser Suppliers." *Foreign Affairs* 73, no. 3 (May/June 1994).

Schweizer, Peter. "Who Broke the Evil Empire." *National Review*, May 30, 1994.

"Listen—Take 20 MIGs and I'll Throw in Some AKs." *Business Week*, June 13, 1994, 54.

Schoenfield, Gabriel. "Troops or Consequences." *Post-Soviet Prospects* (September 1993). Washington, D.C.: Center for Strategic and International Studies.

Sterling, Claire. "The Growing Power of Russia's Mob." *The New Republic* (adapted from Sterling's book, cited below), April 11, 1994, 19–22.

Sterling, Claire. *Thieves' World.* New York: Simon and Schuster, 1994.

"Graft and Gangsterism in Russia Blight the Entrepreneurial Spirit." *New York Times*, January 30, 1994, 1 and 6.

"New Moscow Mob Terror: Car Bombs." *New York Times*, June 10, 1994, A6.

"Wheat Prices Take a Fall after Comments by Yeltsin." *New York Times*, March 10, 1994, D15.

"Russia's Mafia: More Crime than Punishment." *The Economist*, July 9, 1994, 19–21.

"Yeltsin's Anti-crime Decree Sets off a Storm of Outrage." *New York Times*, June 19, 1994, 7.

"Privatizing Russia's Farms: Sowing the Seeds." *The Economist*, June 18, 1994, 59–60.

"How the Soviet Union Poisoned Its Own Wells." *Business Week*, August 3, 1993, 8.

CBS Evening News. Report on Russia's medical system. January 13, 1994.

Bobylev, Sergei. "Russia's Impending Ecological Disaster." *Demokratizatsiya: The Journal of Post-Soviet Democratization* 1, no. 3 (1993).

Feshbach, Murray, and Alfred Friendly, Jr. *ECOCIDE in the U.S.S.R.* New York: Basic Books, 1992.

"Russia Gets First Installment on Aid to Clean Environment." *New York Times,* November 9, 1994.

Hickel, Walter J. "Siberia's Oil Keeps Spilling." *New York Times*, November 14, 1994, A11.

Halverson, Thomas. "Ticking Time Bombs: East Bloc Reactors." *Bulletin of the Atomic Scientists* (July/August 1993): 43–48.

Zhirinovsky, Vladimir. Interview. *MacNeil-Lehrer NewsHour.* 1991.

United Jewish Appeal, Advertisement. *Wall Street Journal,* February 14, 1994.

"Russia Unlearned." *The Economist,* July 30, 1994, 42.

"Educational Upheaval in Former Soviet Bloc." *New York Times*, December 8, 1992, B7.

Fomin, Anatoly. Speech to the Ninth Asia Pacific Petroleum Conference, Singapore. September 1993.

Bonse-Geuking, Wilhelm. Speech to the Ninth Asia Pacific Petroleum Conference, Singapore. September 1993.

Konoplyanik, A., Valeri S. Plotnikov, and Lucian Pugliaresi. *Oil & Gas Journal*, special report on Russia's energy crisis, August 2, 1993.

Chapter 9: Russia Struggles toward Solvency

Talbott, Strobe. Testimony before the U.S. Senate Appropriations Committee's Subcommittee on Foreign Operations. January 24, 1994.

Woolsey, R. James. Testimony before the U.S. Senate Select Committee on Intelligence. January 25, 1994.

Bonner, Elena. "On Gorbachev." "Writings on the East: Selected Essays on Eastern Europe." *The New York Review of Books*, May 17, 1990, 53–64

Aganbegyan, Abel. *Inside Perestroika: The Future of the Soviet Economy.*

Fischer, Stanley. "Stabilization and Economic Reform in Russia."

Brookings Papers on Economic Activity 1 (1992): 77–126. Washington, D.C.: Brookings Institution.

"Foreign Capitalists Brush Risks Aside to Invest in Russia." *New York Times*, October 11, 1994, 1.

Laster, David S., and Robert N. McCauley. "Making Sense of the Profits of Foreign Firms in the United States." *Federal Reserve Bank of New York Quarterly Review* (Summer-Fall 1994): 44.

Chapter 10: Turmoil in the "Near Abroad"

Cohen, Stephen. Testimony before the U.S. Senate Appropriations Committee's Subcommittee on Foreign Operations. January 24, 1994.

"A Survey of Ukraine." *The Economist*, May 7, 1994, 1–18.

"A Brief Introduction." Ukraine Fund. Kiev and Boston.

"Business and Strategic Plan for Stolichny." Prepared by Fred Krieger, Citizens Democracy Corps Consultant, and reviewed by Stolichny Director Irina Marinina.

"Steve Minsky Selling Apples in the Ukraine." *Wharton Alumni Magazine.* University of Pennsylvania. (Summer 1993): 26.

Press release. Alliant Techsystems, Inc. July 28, 1993. Washington, D.C.

Vincoli, Jeffrey W. "Safety and Health—Soviet Style." *Professional Safety* (April 1992): 17–19.

Aviation Week and Space Technology, February 7, 1994, 51.

Spokesperson. RJR Nabisco. Interview by author.

Rudenshiold, Eric. "The Bitter Fruits of 'Democracy' in Kazakhstan." *Demokratizatsiya: The Journal of Post-Soviet Democratization* 1, no. 3 (1993): 13–20.

Press release. Chase Manhattan Bank. February 17, 1994. New York.

Nazarbayev, Nursultan. Interview. *MoneyTalk*, February 3, 1993.

Chapter 11: The Future Begins to Crystallize

"Survey: The Global Economy." *The Economist*, October 1, 1994, 6.

"Finally, Germany is Paring the Fat." *Business Week*, October 17, 1994, 64–66.

"Survey: The Global Economy." *The Economist*, October 1, 1994, 1.

"Giving Russia Some Time." *New York Times*, October 9, 1994, 3.

"Ex-communists Post Big Gains in Hungary's National Elections." *New York Times*, May 9, 1994.

Afanasyev, Yuri N. "Russian Reform is Dead." *Foreign Affairs* 73, no. 2 (March-April 1994): 21–26.

Wanniski, Jude. "The Future of Russian Capitalism." *Foreign Affairs* 71 (Spring 1992): 17–25.

Yergin, Daniel, and Thane Gustafson. *Russia 2010: And What It Means for the World*. New York: Random House, 1993.

"Difficult Choices: Scenarios for Russia's Future." Press release. University of Tulsa, Tulsa, Oklahoma.

Yasmann, Victor. "Five Different Perceptions on the Future of Russian Foreign Policy." *Demokratizatsiya: The Journal of Post-Soviet Democratization* 1, no. 4 (1993).

Zhirinovsky, Vladimir. Interview. *MacNeil-Lehrer NewsHour*. January 13, 1992.

Fukuyama, Francis. *The End of History and the Last Man*. New York: The Free Press, 1992.

"Fantastic Journeys in Virtual Labs." *Business Week*, September 19, 1994, 76–88.

Hahn, Harley, and Rick Stout. *The Internet Complete Reference*. Berkeley, Calif.: Osborne McGraw-Hill, 1994.

"A World Gone Wired." *Time*, August 22, 1994, 24.

"Babes in Byteland." *Time*, August 22, 1994, 56–58.

Index

About the Author

CARTER HENDERSON is the coauthor of several books including the recent *White House Doctor* (with T. Burton Smith, M.D., Madison Books), *20 Million Careless Capitalists* (with Albert C. Lasher, Doubleday), *The Energy Suppliers* (National Council of Churches), and *Winners: The Successful Strategies Entrepreneurs Use to Build New Businesses* (Holt, Rinehart and Winston).

Henderson graduated from the University of Pennsylvania's Wharton School in 1952 and immediately joined the *Wall Street Journal* as a reporter covering banking, electric utility, and telephone industries. He went on to become the *Journal*'s London Bureau Chief and a front-page editor. Henderson's articles have appeared in *Nation's Business, Bankers Magazine, Current History, Bulletin of the Atomic Scientists,* and *The Futurist,* among others. In 1959, he joined IBM as head of stockholder information, public affairs, and speechwriting, and was given a leave of absence to run the Interracial Council for Business Opportunity launched by the American Jewish Congress and New York Urban League.

Since leaving IBM, Henderson has lectured on business throughout the world from the U.S. Army War College and Harvard Business School to Romania's International Law and Relations Institute and the London School of Economics.

He was codirector of the Princeton Center for Alternative Futures. In 1991, he was named to the Steering Committee of the Citizens Democracy Corps established by the president to encourage entrepreneurship in Central Europe and the former Soviet Union. In 1993, he became a lecturer at the International Leadership Institute's Executive Program for Central European Professional Leaders. Henderson currently resides in Ponte Vedra Beach, Florida.